Robert Wa
than 30 years, rising from the grassroots of country journalism in Western Australia to a senior writer with the *Sydney Morning Herald*. His career has ranged from politics to crime, always focusing on the people behind the major story of the day. He is the author of *Rose: The unauthorised biography of Rose Hancock Porteous* (2002) and *The Lost Boy* (2004).

THE KILLING OF CAROLINE BYRNE

THE KILLING OF CAROLINE BYRNE

A journey to justice

ROBERT WAINWRIGHT

ALLEN&UNWIN

First published in 2009

Allen & Unwin
83 Alexander Street
Crows Nest NSW 2065
Australia
Phone: (61 2) 8425 0100
Fax: (61 2) 9906 2218
Email: info@allenandunwin.com
Web: www.allenandunwin.com

The Cataloguing-in-Publication entry is available from the National Library of Australia

ISBN 978 1 74114 851 0

Set in 10.5/13.2 pt Minion Pro by Bookhouse, Sydney
Printed in Australia by McPherson's Printing Group

10 9 8 7 6 5 4 3 2 1

To Don and Steve Creedy
One a great mentor,
the other a great mate

CONTENTS

1	The scream	*1*
2	The shopgirl	*4*
3	A mother's hug	*9*
4	A cry for help	*15*
5	Lycra and lust	*22*
6	A job with Rene	*30*
7	Burning desires	*37*
8	Tim tam man	*43*
9	'He wouldn't hurt a hair on my head'	*52*
10	A false opening	*59*
11	Model behaviour	*66*
12	'Sometimes I think he wants to kill me'	*71*
13	Depression and acne cream	*79*
14	She won't be in tomorrow	*83*
15	'It looks like legs and a body'	*89*
16	A long way out	*97*
17	The lies begin	*106*
18	Her spirit led me	*118*
19	Whitewash	*128*
20	A father's quest begins	*137*
21	I didn't kill her	*143*
22	A new beginning	*153*
23	The coroner	*163*

24	Richo's my alibi	*170*
25	An open finding	*178*
26	'Do you think I did it?'	*185*
27	Irondale	*195*
28	Kiss-kill	*199*
29	An excellent chap	*204*
30	Richo's diary	*209*
31	A gut feeling	*213*
32	Cunning rat	*217*
33	New priorities	*223*
34	Bam-bam-bam	*228*
35	The wrong spot	*233*
36	Megeve	*239*
37	Gary Redding	*245*
38	Spear throw	*250*
39	Cross purpose	*255*
40	'They've got him'	*262*
41	A reasonable prospect	*266*
42	Court No. 3	*278*
43	A policeman's lot	*287*
44	Horse head	*294*
45	A tongue dripping with lies	*302*
46	Dear Bretty	*310*
47	'It matched Gary'	*315*
48	Satisfied in every way	*322*
49	Average testimony	*329*
50	Between fact and fiction	*336*
51	50 questions	*342*
52	'We can do this'	*353*

Acknowledgements	*361*

1

THE SCREAM

The sea wind had died away to a whisper. Watsons Bay was still. In his studio below the towering sandstone cliff tops that guard the entrance to Sydney Harbour, John Doherty was painting. He enjoyed working at night with the windows of his upstairs flat open, even in early winter, to the gentle midweek community sounds of this tiny corner of the city.

Doherty found comfort in this worn, jumbled harbour-front neighbourhood where Arthur Phillip's First Fleet landed in 1788. Its chipped edges and faded paintwork inspired much of his work, not unlike the seafront villages of his Irish birthplace in Kilkenny in which he had divided his time for the best part of two decades. It stood in contrast to the shiny modern, almost American, citadel which continued to rise ever higher across the harbour to the west of his waterfront sanctuary.

The 46-year-old had initially painted traditional landscapes but a background in architecture had eventually led him to photorealism; striving to bring the painted image so close to the original that it would be indistinguishable from the real thing. Composition, colour and texture were the key; a harbour wall, a line of upturned boats, a row of doors and shopfronts, even old petrol pumps. 'Past optimism grown forlorn', as one critic would later note. On this night—7 June 1995—his fine eye for detail would be paramount.

Doherty's concentration was suddenly broken by an argument outside, shattering the bliss. Above the occasional sound of a passing car he could hear loud, aggressive voices in the street below. There were two people; one an angry male and the other a distressed woman.

At first the painter let it wash over him, hoping they would move on so he could return to his artistic peace. Instead, the row grew louder, more dangerous. Annoyed yet intrigued, he put down his brush and moved to the window, peering down to Military Road. The night was clear but there was barely a sliver of a moon. Doherty looked at his watch. It was just after 8 pm.

The woman he'd heard was sitting in the gutter on the other side of the road, almost directly beneath a street light. He couldn't see her face because it was buried in her hands as she cried and moaned. He couldn't make out a word because she slurred as if she was drunk, stoned or perhaps both.

The source of her anguish was clear although Doherty could not see him. A man was standing under an awning on the footpath beneath his window shouting across at the woman on the other side of the road. Doherty couldn't quite hear his words, muffled by the canvas, but it was male and the tone was disturbing.

He stood riveted, wondering if he should intervene before deciding against it. They were probably just a boyfriend and girlfriend, arguing after too many drinks at the Watsons Bay Hotel across the park. It happened all the time during the summer months and somewhat less as it got colder. Midweek on a winter night was rare. Doherty turned back and resumed his painting, wishing they would go home to finish their stoush and let the village return to its slumber.

But they were going nowhere. When the argument was still raging ten minutes later Doherty again put down his brush and looked out the window. He could see the man now, striding across the road towards the woman who was still crying, obviously distraught. His initial assessment of the woman was clearly wrong. This was no ordinary argument between a pair of merry drunks. What could have led to this violent confrontation?

He could tell, even from above, that the man was a tall figure, his long limbs dressed in a dark three-quarter-length jacket, his hair short and pale, cropped behind the ears. Doherty couldn't see his face, or that of the woman who was in the same crumpled pose, arguing back.

And there was a second man. Doherty hadn't noticed him before, probably because he'd been sitting on a wall on the other side of the street in the shadows of the awning outside the pizzeria. His features were hidden in the darkness but Doherty could make out dark clothing and what looked like a beanie on his head. He was involved in some way but wasn't saying anything, just pacing across the shopfront. When the man joined the other two, the artist could also see he was much shorter than the first.

Two men against one woman! Was she in danger?

Doherty watched for a while as the woman rose to her feet and the trio walked north towards The Gap. The men stood on each side of the woman as if guarding her. They disappeared from sight, up the pathway towards the old navy buildings now used for a business college.

'Well, they're going,' he thought to himself. 'Thank God, the argument is over. I don't have to listen to it anymore.'

The wind was returning. He could hear the ocean heaving beyond the cliff tops. The Gap was stirring. Nothing he could do, he thought, turning away from the window. Doherty went back to his painting but kept the windows open, just in case.

The argument wasn't over.

The sounds of voices rose and fell on the breeze as it strengthened and grew into light, steady wind. He guessed they were up on the pathway near the lookout. They were definitely the same voices and it was the same argument. Eventually the sound receded into the blackness and his treasured silence returned.

Until her single, sharp scream creased the night air.

2

THE SHOPGIRL

Tony Byrne met Andrea Jeffree on a September evening in 1957 under a suburban streetlight in Ashfield—a blind date. He had waited at the corner of Georges River Road and Milton Street to meet a mate and his latest girlfriend, who was a shop assistant at Grace Brothers in the city and had offered to bring a young workmate to make it a foursome. It was nothing special, just a night at a nearby pub for dinner and drinks. The situation suited Tony. He was not looking for a wife, even a steady girlfriend for that matter, and the offer of a date with a pretty girl was too good to refuse.

Life had too many options and interests for a young man fresh out of a two-year stint in the National Service. He had grown up, the youngest in a family of seven, with the impact of war ringing in his ears. Aged barely nine when World War II ended, the tall, wavy-haired young man with sad eyes that accentuated a shy smile was now part of a nation's post-war recovery and rebuilding process. Life itself was a bit of gamble for the youth, free at least for the moment from the threat of war. It was a time to be carefree, indestructible. There was plenty of time later for safety and responsibility.

But this shopgirl beneath the streetlight was different. She was sixteen, just out of school and beautiful—'magic', he would recall years later. It wasn't just her looks which struck the young nasho but her poise and her clothes—a beautifully cut dress, full makeup and majestic hair, as if a blind date in a pub was a stroll along the red carpet at a movie premiere.

Andrea Jeffree was unlike any of the young women Tony and his mates knocked about with. Tall and blonde, she looked and walked like the movie stars she longed to be, particularly the breathy Marilyn Monroe and the ice-blonde Kim Novak. It was an infatuation that would, ultimately, kill her but on that night in 1957 neither knew what was to come. By the time Tony drove Andrea home to Glebe in his '34 Chevy they were hooked.

The romance blossomed slowly as each found their feet in the world. Although they liked each other, neither was ready to commit as they explored their adult lives, Tony in the NSW Fire Brigade and Andrea in the heady world of publicity. She became a feature of Grace Brothers department-store promotions as rock'n'roll bloomed into the late fifties and early sixties, interviewing singers, comparing fashion parades and even posing draped across car bonnets for promotional photos. But it wasn't enough. At the age of nineteen and desperate for a cleavage like her screen goddesses, Andrea secretly became one of the first women in Australia to have silicone breast implants.

Tony would never know how she paid for the implants or where the operation was done. He was stationed at Newtown and hadn't seen her in a few months when she telephoned one day, upset. He would always remember her words, pleading for help: 'I've done the most terrible thing. I feel like a freak.'

The operation had been botched. Instead of a heaving bosom, Andrea now had lumpy, uneven breasts, permanently rock hard. The search for something better had, instead, scarred her forever. Tony was confused and angry. He wanted to move on, revolted not only by the physical change but more so by the notion that a woman already blessed with so much physical beauty could want even more. Instead, Tony realised he had fallen in love, and he agreed to keep her secret.

Physical and emotional scars had been pushed into the background four years later when Tony and Andrea were finally married. They were blessed with fine weather on 14 November

1964 for the ceremony at St Kevin's Catholic Church at Dee Why, and it continued as they drove up the north coast on their honeymoon, stopping on a whim at motels as a beach or a meal of fresh seafood took their fancy. It seemed to confirm that life was easy for a 28-year-old and his bride, five years his junior. Life held no fears, only promise.

Home and family were their future. First was the home, in Earlwood, and then children—two boys, Peter in 1966 and Robert in 1968. Daughter Caroline arrived in 1970, and the family moved to a bigger house at Castle Hill, in the city's north-west. Their youngest, Deanna, was born in 1973. The family unit seemed perfect—brothers who would be mates for life and sisters who would bond and be protected. They moved again in 1975, this time to a small hobby farm near Camden on the south-west fringes of Sydney.

It was here that Tony Byrne decided to build his family home—Camelot, he called it in an attempt to capture the Kennedy White House mystique—on a two-hectare lot carved from an old dairy farm turned into residential retreats to meet an increasing demand for city folk wanting to escape the confines of the city. There was no town water and his nearest neighbours were half a kilometre in either direction, visible yet unobstrusive.

Out here, the city and its pressures seemed a world away. The boys baulked at first when Tony announced they would be moving away from their friends around Castle Hill, but the protests did not last long, particularly when their father added a swimming pool. Contrary to the concerns of friends and family who worried about them being so far from the city, the home was a family paradise—like pitching a tent in the backyard but still being able to see the lounge room lights if the night's noises got too scary.

Tony had dreamed of a place like this for years, staying on in a job he had grown to despise until he found the right time to leave. It wasn't that he hated the fire brigade, rather it had become merely a means to an end. He'd fallen into the job after his army service back in the fifties and stayed because it was comfortable, the money was pretty good and he loved the mateship. Like everyone else he lived hard as a young man, even taking a second job driving trucks to buy his first house. But starting a family changed everything.

By the time Deanna was born Tony dreaded the evening shifts, having to leave home as the others started dinner as if he'd done something wrong and was being punished. And the job was dangerous. Tony was a ladder man, specialising in wrestling the hose 30 metres in the air while it pumped water at 140 pounds per square inch into the flames of a dockyard or warehouse blaze or through the roof or upstairs window of a house in the inner city where, invariably, the toxic smell of burning mattresses made it impossible to breathe.

Instead, he longed for a life in the country; a small farm in the Hunter perhaps, even out as far as Mudgee. He didn't know why, given there was no rural background in his own upbringing, but it was a yearning and he began spending weekends scanning real estate ads in the *Sydney Morning Herald* or on the road with his young family checking properties. Finally, he had chosen Camden.

Tony was nine years old before he had a chance to get to know his own father properly. Bill Byrne served in both wars, seeing action in France in the Great War and in the second stationed up in North Queensland as a signalman. Between wars he sired seven children and was in his mid-forties when the youngest—Tony—was born in 1936. By the time Bill finally returned from war and grabbed a well-paying job in Customs, Tony was already halfway through his childhood. It was a household where money and bedding were scarce but religion and family were fervent—in that order. Life revolved around his beloved mother, Dorothy, who would call her scattered children home each night for dinner by banging a cow bell on the front verandah of their home in Ashbury. It entrenched Tony's sense that family was everything, and that children needed both parents. Being a good provider was not enough in itself. A father needed to be around for his children.

Camden had the ambience of the Australian bush but the safety and opportunity of the nearby city. Local schools, friends around the corner, the children riding their bikes without fear of being mowed down by city traffic. There were farm animals—chooks and cows, horses to ride. The boys played soccer and squash, swam in the pool and fished or played battle games in Wattle Creek which meandered past the back of the property. The girls played basketball and tennis and went to jazz ballet lessons. They made their own clothes and learned to cook.

When Tony quit the brigade he began driving the school bus then trucks, carting sand and soil. Opportunity followed and he started his own supply business. It flourished as Sydney surged southwards towards Campbelltown, providing fill for the seemingly endless subdivisions which shamelessly pushed the city's sprawl. Then he opened the property to agist horses, eventually pumping the extra income into a property investment portfolio which included managed apartments in the city.

If Tony Byrne had known a better time in his life, he couldn't recognise it, but innocence, of course, never lasts.

3

A MOTHER'S HUG

From the day she was born, on 7 September 1970, at King George V Hospital in Camperdown, it seemed that Caroline Therese Byrne was destined to be a princess.

She was named after the daughters of two famous dynasties—Princess Caroline of Monaco, due to the hankering of her mother for the fairytale story of a beautiful movie star, Princess Caroline's mother Grace Kelly, and Caroline Kennedy, the daughter of John F. Kennedy. Or maybe it was simply that Tony and Andrea finally had a daughter to dote on after two sons.

As a middle child in a family of four she might have faded into the background, squeezed between the dominance of two older brothers and the needs of a baby sister. But it only seemed to enhance her presence. It wasn't that Tony and Andrea loved Caroline more than Peter, Robert or Deanna but that she simply shone; the sort of kid who'd beam instinctively when the camera turned on her.

It was the little things that Tony would remember: the way she would leap enthusiastically into the cabin of his truck if he had a delivery to make, how she would try on her mother's shoes in a pretend fashion parade down the hallway, or the afternoons she'd get home from school and take a tape recorder into the rumpus room to dance.

Caroline was enthusiastic and uncomplicated, tall with cascading blonde hair and as striking as her mother, and yet somehow unaffected by her looks. Although popular with what seemed an endless parade of friends through the house after school and on weekends, she tended to stick to a few close friends as confidants.

The family's rhythm changed dramatically after Tony sold the business in 1983 to run the farm with a few head of cattle and a growing trade in agisting horses. He was only 47 years old but years of working two jobs and careful investment in real estate meant he could 'retire', as he would describe it, as if tending a rural property was not work. He built stables and leased extra land from neighbours at the back. Within a year he and Andrea, who did the book work as she had with the sand and soil business, had up to 30 horses on the property.

But change could not alter the past. Now in her early forties, Andrea once again began to dwell on her man-made deformity. She had been suffering mood swings for years, sometimes disappearing into her room for days at a time, and had been receiving treatment since Deanna was born. Now she could see that life was about to change again. Peter and Robert would soon be leaving home, either to study at university or to begin their careers and lives as young, independent adults. That would leave the girls at home—Caroline, now a gawky teenager entering high school as puberty temporarily turned her beauty into an awkward tangle, and Deanna, who had just turned ten. The big house in the bush was about to empty. She would have more time on her hands; more time to think, to worry and regret.

The demons returned and Andrea Byrne became trapped, desperate to seek medical intervention and yet unwilling to ask for help for fear of exposing her secret. One night in 1985 she took an overdose of sleeping pills. Luckily Tony found her and she was hospitalised. They sent her home the next day.

Tony watched his wife's torment; the mood swings from deep depression when all he could do was quietly comfort and reassure her, and the aftermath when the last thing she wanted to do was discuss the problem. He too felt powerless to save her; caught between an obligation of loyalty and his desperation that she seek professional help and have the implants removed before it was too late. It almost happened when Andrea found a woman GP at Camden, but she pulled back at the last moment, despite an increasing awareness that breast implants were potentially lethal and liable to leak.

In the late seventies and early eighties there had been a smattering of cases in the United States where women had won out-of-court settlements against companies like Dow Corning, whose product lay inside Andrea. Despite her worry, even watching the television coverage of appeals for women to come forward, she could not get over the first hurdle—her own self-loathing—exacerbated, no doubt, by the onset of menopause.

The Byrne children also watched the tragedy as it unfolded but did so in ignorance, wondering why their mother would isolate herself in the bedroom and then emerge as if nothing had happened. Most of all, they wondered why she never hugged them like other mothers did.

Every November since 1956 the city of Campbelltown celebrates its most famous story—Fisher's Ghost—with a community festival. Like most legends, many of the finer details have changed over the years but not the backbone of this dark tale of greed and murder.

In 1826 a wealthy and respectable farmer named John Farley stumbled into a local hotel in a state of shock, claiming to have seen the ghost of a missing local man; a ticket-of-leave convict turned successful property owner named Frederick Fisher, sitting on the rail of a bridge over a creek. Fisher had gone missing four months earlier, a few days after being released from prison having served a small sentence over an unpaid debt. His neighbour, George Worrall, insisted that Fisher had gone back to England but then raised suspicions by trying to sell Fisher's lands and belongings. With no evidence to the contrary, Worrall's story remained untested. But Farley's claim changed everything: he insisted that Fisher's apparition had motioned towards him and pointed to a paddock down the creek before fading away. A search was mounted and blood was found on the fence where the ghost had sat. Aboriginal trackers then pinpointed the remains of Fisher at the bottom of the creek where the ghost had indicated. Worrall was arrested, confessed to the murder and was hanged. Fisher's ghost is said to still be seen on some foggy nights.

The story is merely an excuse and the festival is about the spirit of a community rather than the restless spirit of a murdered man. It is touted as one of the oldest community pageants in Australia, spanning ten days with a street parade, art and craft awards and exhibitions, a fun fair and races. And a beauty pageant called Miss Spirit with a first prize of a two-week trip to Japan.

In 1987, seventeen-year-old Caroline Byrne wanted to enter the competition, representing a local newspaper. Tony didn't mind; she'd already entered a smaller competition—Miss Waterways, or something spruiking a local amusement park—and won.

Caroline was growing up; a little too fast for Tony's liking. She was changing, spending most afternoons after school working in a local optometrist in Camden. She even had a steady boyfriend, Andrew Blanchette—one of twelve brothers and sisters whose father, Barry, was a local copper and owned a place nearby. Andrew was a nice young kid; solid, like his dad. He and Caroline met at a barbecue when she was fifteen or so and immediately fell for one another. They were a physical match; he as strong and handsome as she was tall and beautiful.

The Miss Spirit competition was simply another step towards adulthood for Caroline and from what Tony could see his daughter was taking it all in her stride. It made her happy and, besides, it kept Andrea occupied and distracted from her own misgivings. And when Caroline was crowned Miss Spirit it opened new possibilities.

A neighbour's daughter had been appearing occasionally in the Sydney newspapers as a Page 3 beach girl, the staple diet of tabloid newspapers through the 1980s. Andrea did not hesitate to make the same arrangements for Caroline who suddenly became the most famous girl at Camden High School when she was photographed in a bikini and the picture was published in the

Rupert Murdoch afternoon paper, *The Daily Mirror.* Lanky had become lithe and gawky gorgeous. Classmates—boys—began pasting her photo on their walls. Camden had suddenly become too small.

He had hoped it would never end but even Tony could see the dream was over when Caroline finished high school in 1988. He and Andrea would move back to the city, if only for the kids. Caroline had done well in the HSC, finishing among the top art students in the state, and been accepted into Sydney University. She was interested in psychology but it was clear that she and her mother were keen on exploring Caroline's modelling options. With the boys now well settled in the city and Deanna accepted into Fort Street High School, it made sense to make the move.

There was no financial impediment to moving. Tony ploughed profits from the sale of his sand and soil business into two apartments near Darling Harbour on the western edge of the CBD, in one of which the boys now lived. Tony, Andrea and the girls would move into the second apartment until they could sell the farm and begin looking for a bigger, permanent place.

They found it at the Connaught, an up-market apartment complex in Liverpool Street opposite the memorial at Hyde Park, although Andrea found the transition from rural to inner-city life difficult. The CBD was both exciting and confronting for a middle-aged woman battling bouts of depression and menopause. Even the apartment was a bit daunting with its rooftop swimming pool and views across Hyde Park and the city. It all seemed a bit much, as if it couldn't really be hers. She got some part-time work back at Grace Brothers in the hope it would give her a sense of belonging.

Tony needed work too, not for the money but because without the farm there was nowhere to potter each day. He jumped at the chance to manage the building where he owned the two apartments—the Windsor Plaza in Sussex Street. It was within walking distance of Liverpool Street which meant he could be home for lunch. It also meant he was close to Andrea whenever her moods returned.

Then there was Caroline's modelling career. Success in a regional beauty contest and a Page-3 spread meant little in the city. She needed an agent and exposure. Caroline and Andrea eventually approached a busy agency in the heart of Double Bay—Gordon's Models and Real Faces—whose owner, Gordon Donald, agreed to take her on as a freelance model. There was plenty of work around and Caroline was soon attending at least one job a week, anything from a one-hour photographic booking to a four-day shopping centre parade.

Andrew Blanchette had also left Camden, although only as far as Liverpool on the south-west fringe of the city. He'd followed his father into the police force, attended the academy, and was now a constable. He and Caroline still regarded themselves as a couple and despite the travelling distance Andrew would drive Caroline to castings when he could, watching with some trepidation the transition of a shy country girl entering the competitive world of modelling. It seemed to upset Caroline at first; not the competition so much as the comparisons when she walked into a room or attended an industry function—the analysis by others of what she was wearing, the cut of her hair or what her makeup looked like. It confirmed all the clichés and irritated Andrew who wondered if it was worth the angst. Caroline was the antithesis of this cattiness and her university course was clearly secondary to this new world. He wasn't convinced there was a future for Caroline there, even though her mother continued to push her. At least Caroline refused to concede to the ridiculous dietary demands. Her only concession was to join a gym. She chose World of Fitness in Castlereagh Street, a short walk from home.

4

A CRY FOR HELP

On the afternoon of 30 March 1991, Andrea Byrne checked into a Kings Cross motel under the assumed name of Anne Kelly. She must have looked out of place—carrying no luggage save her handbag, and paying cash for a single night's accommodation. But whatever the staff may have wondered about an attractive middle-aged woman booking alone into a city motel on Easter Saturday, they could not have guessed her true, dire intent. Despite a happy marriage, four healthy and well-adjusted children and no money worries, Andrea Byrne wanted to die—alone and by her own hand.

The contents of what most would consider a wonderful life and comfortable future lay less than two kilometres away in her plush home. On the vanity unit inside the main bedroom ensuite Andrea had neatly laid out all her keys in a row—unit, security, car, etc. Her Westpac Bank savings account passbook and access card were placed alongside, atop a clean sheet of white paper with her PIN code neatly printed—permission for the finder to assume control of her worldly assets. She did not bother to write a note. The message was clear enough that she did not intend to return. Later that night she lay down to sleep with a cocktail of prescription drugs doused in alcohol.

Andrea Byrne was not afraid of life but chose to abandon it, a few weeks shy of her 50th birthday, rather than continue to face the possibility—the inevitability, in her deeply depressed mind—of an agonising and humiliating death caused by a rash decision made in the name of vanity more than three decades before. Now her husband would be left with a secret he had been forced to bear their entire marriage.

Such was the anonymity and precision of Andrea Byrne's actions that her body would lay at the Glebe Morgue for more than a week before she was identified and her family allowed to grieve.

Tony had begged police to help find his wife, certain she had done herself harm, but was told that no-one fitting her description had been found. Instead, he was forced to make his own inquiries about where she might have been. It was clear the authorities were not interested, assuming they were dealing with a marital dispute that would resolve itself and was therefore a waste of time. Finally, after hopes had been raised that she may simply have needed time alone and would reappear, Tony happened to telephone the motel where his wife had checked in. The receptionist was shocked by the call: 'Oh, yes, we had a woman of that description here last week,' she stammered. 'You might want to check with police.'

She was dead, ignored by a law enforcement system that did not appear to care once it discovered she had no identifying documents. Tony did not have the strength to demand an explanation afterwards, figuring all he would get might be a shrug of the shoulders. He was angry but what could he do about it? He knew it was coming. She'd talked about killing herself for years although more after they moved to the city and her fears about growing old intensified.

She had quit her job and abandoned plans to study when she had realised she didn't need the money and had satisfied the urge to be seen as a productive city housewife, but it meant she'd had little to do except dwell on her perceived imperfections.

She had disappeared one night three months before; taking $1200 in cash, she caught a cab to a motel in Glebe where she drank a bottle of whisky and took about 75 sleeping pills. Staff sent her home the next morning where she slept off the effect of the drugs and the booze. It didn't kill her but deep down Tony had known it was a matter of time.

Two things had seemed to set her off that day. Peter was about to go travelling in India and Andrea had spotted him having a coffee with another woman in the foyer of the apartment complex. There was nothing in it, but it was clear it had magnified her own misgivings about herself and her value. She had also kept talking about how difficult it was to get drugs strong enough to kill herself.

'Why do you want to do that?' Tony would ask, knowing it was pointless.

'Because you'd all be better off without me,' she'd typically reply. He had had no doubt it was all to do with ageing.

And now she was gone and he had his children to protect and to help grieve, as well as his own confused feelings. It was a portent of things to come; a measure of the complacency of justice in a city too fast and selfish at times for the individual.

Tony liked to walk to work each morning. It was a five-minute stroll down the hill. He enjoyed the routine—up early, a leisurely breakfast, out the door just before 9 am, back home for lunch around midday—as there was something terribly normal about it which was comforting given that he and his kids were still fretting over the death of Andrea. Thankfully, he had Caroline and Deanna at home so there was company most of the time, even for lunch when one or both of them would usually be around.

Monday 27 April 1992 was no different. He left on time, saying goodbye to Caroline who was still in bed, and spent most of the morning in the office on paperwork. Around 10.30 he took a phone call. It was Caroline. She wanted a chat. It was not unusual that she would call during the day but as they talked Tony knew this was not just a pleasant chat. This was about her mother's suicide.

Eventually the subject came up: 'Life can be cruel, Daddy,' she offered, as if asking for some explanation.

Tony hesitated, then softened his voice. 'It doesn't just happen to us, love. This is a part of life that everybody has to deal with and accept. It just takes time. Time is the best remedy. I'll be home for lunch shortly.'

'Okay Daddy, I'll see you then.' She hung up.

There was nothing alarming about the call. The family had often talked and cried together over the past year. It was part of the grieving process and he wanted his kids to communicate their feelings. Still, it was hard.

At 12.30 pm, as promised, Tony arrived home for lunch. Almost at once he knew that someone was in the bathroom. In the darkened corridor he could see the light at the base of the door.

'Caroline, are you in there?' he asked, knocking gently.

'Yes,' came the muffled reply.

Tony walked towards the kitchen, past the bedroom the sisters shared. He glanced inside and then stopped. There was an empty pill container lying between the two single beds, and a handful of tablets strewn across the carpet.

Tony panicked. He rushed back to the bathroom and tried the door. It was unlocked. Caroline was in the half-full bath, eyes closed. His mind raced. Oh God, first Andrea and now Caroline. Tony pulled the plug and tried to rouse his daughter to no avail. It was clear she had taken the tablets—whatever they were—and was now in trouble. He felt her pulse; it was still strong—that was good. His experience as a fireman kicked in and he gave her mouth-to-mouth resuscitation. She responded; she was breathing. He called the ambulance, telling them the situation was not life threatening.

By 3 pm, when Tony and the other three children arrived at Sydney Hospital, Caroline was sitting up in bed. She had recovered quickly after having her stomach pumped and was embarrassed more than anything else.

It had been a cry for help rather than an attempt on her life, Tony reasoned, taking the pills knowing her father would be home in less than two hours and leaving the bathroom light on and the door unlocked so she could be easily found and rescued. And there was no note.

He thought back to the night of his wife's death. She didn't leave a note either but, unlike Caroline, there was a clear message of goodbye through the keys and bank details she left on the vanity.

He wondered if Caroline was somehow paying him back, angry that he hadn't done more to save his wife from herself. It was a natural reaction, he supposed, but the truth was there was little he could have done. In hindsight there had probably been signs that Andrea was in trouble but they were mixed; depressed for a few days and then normal. And anyway, he couldn't have followed her everywhere.

This was a glitch, nothing more. Caroline had been seen by a doctor who was letting her out the next day. The hospital staff seemed to have no fear that she would try again. Caroline begged to go home: 'I didn't want to do myself any harm. I don't know why I did it; I was just feeling down over Mum. I'm sorry.'

She told Andrew Blanchette the same thing. 'I didn't mean to do it, I didn't mean to do it,' she repeated over and over again as he sat at her bedside, blaming himself because he had been the one who told her the details of her mother's death.

Tony still hadn't been able to bring himself to discuss his wife's problems with anyone. The kids didn't know about Andrea's breast implants and the terrible psychological battle she'd waged against herself all those years. He realised they had no sense of why their mother had killed herself. It was something he would have to rectify.

'If I ever feel like that again I'll come to you and tell you all about it, no matter what's troubling me. I'll talk about it openly with all of you,' Caroline told her family reassuringly.

Tragically, it was a promise she would not keep. There were some secrets that would emerge when it was too late.

* * *

During their courtship in the late 1950s Tony Byrne would drive into the city on a Tuesday night around 9 o'clock to pick up Andrea. After finishing her shift at Grace Brothers she would take a bus into George Street to attend a deportment course for young ladies run by the city's grand dame of good manners, June Dally-Watkins.

Miss Dally, as she preferred to be known by her charges, was already an icon in a city that cherished success; a woman who had somehow risen from the obscurity of a bastard childhood in a tiny NSW town, made her way to Sydney seeking fame and fortune and become Australia's model of the year in 1949. If that wasn't enough, a few years later she was swept off her feet in a fleeting romance with Hollywood star Gregory Peck. They had met in Rome where the divorced father fell for the young Australian, kissed her in moonlight above the Roman Forum and pleaded that she accompany him to Paris. She politely rejected his advances, as a good girl should, and history took care of the rest. Peck went to Paris by himself where he met his second wife while Miss Dally returned to Sydney, found a man who reminded her of the dashing movie star and settled down to become a mother and enduring career woman. Her story seemed incongruous, like some saccharin movie script a young Andrea Jeffree might have adored.

Now, three decades later, Caroline Byrne was going to see June Dally although not for deportment lessons but for a job. Gordon Donald, owner of the modelling company, thought she'd make a good deportment teacher—something to complement her modelling work—and recommended her to Miss Dally. Caroline was a likable young woman; always well-groomed, punctual and friendly. She got a lot of repeat business because of her positive attitude but she was still only averaging four or five jobs a month. He wanted to help out if he could and ensure she stayed in the industry.

Caroline had thrown herself into modelling as if to cope with the truth of her mother's death. Tony had finally unveiled his wife's secret. He'd expected a shattering reaction, particularly from Caroline and Deanna, but both girls appeared relieved more than anything. Caroline even smiled, as if a weight had been lifted, and hugged her father: 'I always wondered why she would sort of pull away from me and not let me hold her close.'

But events had taken their toll in other areas, like the relationship with Andrew Blanchette. It was probably inevitable, she thought. They had met as teenagers and had grown up as friends more than lovers. Besides, the further Caroline enmeshed herself in the modelling scene—Glamarama, they called it—the more the couple drifted apart.

Andrew saw it coming. After Caroline's overdose he was granted a transfer into the city on compassionate grounds to be closer to her but the move had the opposite effect. He was stationed at Newtown, in the city's inner west, and suddenly his own options expanded: new friends, new activities, new possibilities. Rather than draw him closer to his childhood sweetheart it took them further apart, forging new lives and friendships separately.

The situation came to a head, as he would recall, on 12 December 1992. The previous day he had telephoned but she'd fobbed him off with the pretence of being sick. On this morning she'd called back: 'Andrew, we need to talk,' she said simply.

They met later that day.

'Look, it's been a really traumatic year,' she began. 'I've had to make some changes.'

Andrew waited, silently, for the punchline he knew was coming: 'I'm involved in a life and a society that is taking me away.'

He had to agree. It was over.

5

LYCRA AND LUST

They were late. Caroline Byrne and her closest high school friend, Narelle Cook, crept into the mirror-lined room of the cavern-like gym in Castlereagh Street and tried to slip unnoticed into the back of the midweek aerobics class.

But the instructor was watching. 'Here's Caroline. Thanks for coming, Caroline,' he announced, shouting through the microphone strapped to his head to be heard above the blaring music. Caroline giggled nervously, slightly embarrassed but thrilled at being noticed by the tall, lantern-jawed man strutting at the front of the packed room. So that's why Caroline has brought me here, thought Narelle, to check out the instructor. She would later mark the day—17 November 1992—in her diary, for all the wrong reasons as it turned out.

Gordon Wood did not take his attention off the leggy blonde for the next 45 minutes: 'That's it, Caroline, lift those legs. Faster, faster. Work harder, Caroline.' No-one else in the class seemed to matter.

He thought she was cute, as he would later tell close friends, but she was giving off mixed signals. She was young and naïve, had only had one boyfriend in her adult life and was clearly confused about her existing relationship.

Narelle was less than impressed, slightly uncomfortable at the sight of this guy prancing around in a leotard and his interest in her friend. He was flirting in the middle of an aerobics class, and Caroline was lapping it up.

It was true. They met at the beginning of the year, when she joined the gym and Gordon did her fitness appraisal. Now it was developing into something much more carnal, fuelled by Caroline's sense that her relationship with Andrew Blanchette was coming to an end. Within a few weeks she would formally end the seven-year relationship.

She allowed herself to flirt back; a glance, a smile, a hello, hoping he would take the next step and ask her out. It hadn't happened yet but she felt it was about to. That's why she brought first Narelle and then her sister Deanna on another occasion. She wanted approval.

But Narelle wasn't about to give it. She could see the attraction but it irked her, probably because she was loyal to Andrew. It was clear their relationship was struggling; typical of the childhood sweetheart thing, she supposed. It was either marriage or bust, and by the way her friend was flirting with this instructor, it looked like the latter.

Narelle worried that Caroline was vulnerable, looking for someone on the rebound to make herself feel better about the inevitable break-up. This guy obviously had the right touch; able to say the right things at the right time to make her feel important, beautiful.

Caroline had always been noticed throughout their childhood around Camden. Always pretty and smiling, she had a simple, uncluttered beauty that radiated and embraced rather than made her appear unapproachable.

She and Narelle had known each other since Year 2; they'd ridden the bus together, bikes together, taken holidays together. In high school they played basketball together and laughed through school musicals together. Even after school when they'd both moved into the city they saw each other twice a week. Caroline had been a bridesmaid at Narelle's wedding in February.

But their lives were not totally intertwined. Things had begun to change in Year 10 when Caroline got that modelling assignment and her photo ended up in the newspaper. It wasn't that they moved apart, but Caroline was suddenly willowy rather than skinny and she started to pay particular attention to her appearance, as if she realised that her face and body would be her future. And now, at 22, it was happening.

Within a few weeks, not only were Caroline and Gordon dating, but Gordon wanted her to move in with him in his flat near the Cross. He seemed nice enough but that was not sufficient reason to start up a house together. How did this happen so quickly and with a guy eight years older than her? It didn't make any sense for someone who was usually so careful.

Narelle had reason to be concerned. Caroline was also trying drugs for the first and only time, sharing a tablet of the sexual stimulant ecstasy with Gordon. At a New Year's Eve party a few days after Caroline moved into the Victoria Road flat, Gordon offered to buy drugs for one of Caroline's closest friends, Natalie McCamley.

'It's safer to get it off someone who knows what they're doing rather than buying it off some stranger,' Gordon told Natalie. 'I know people who do drugs. I can get it for you.' She declined.

Narelle wasn't the only one with misgivings about the relationship. Angelo Georgiou, joint owner and manager of World of Fitness, was worried about the impact on other staff. Gordon and one of his star instructors, Laurie Ingleton, had been in a relationship when the Caroline thing started. They'd been living together for months but it was over and Gordon was trying to get Caroline to move in. It spelled danger for Angelo. This sort of stuff tended to have repercussions inside the staffroom.

Locker-room chatter wasn't healthy for a booming business with 4000 members and 40 instructors. He didn't want to get rid of Gordon, even though the bloke was a pain in the arse. Although he was a show pony in a lycra circus ring, he was a good instructor and the women loved him.

In fact, Gordon had just demanded a pay rise; collared Angelo at the front counter and demanded a conversation. It was typical of the bloke, always wanting to talk about money. They'd sat in a nearby coffee shop to chat. He knew what Gordon wanted. The lesser instructors earned $30 a class and the best $40. Gordon was somewhere in the middle doing up to ten classes a week. An extra $5 a class seemed a small price to pay for peace.

The dealing over, the men began to talk more generally as they finished their coffees. As usual, the conversation turned to Gordon's favourite themes—himself, ambition and money.

'What do you dream about, Angelo?' Gordon asked.

Angelo shrugged: 'Being a slave to this place I suppose. I can't see anything else.'

Gordon dismissed the notion with a wave. 'You've got to think ahead. I'm going to make millions.'

Like other workmates, Angelo was intrigued by Gordon's persona. In a world where the body beautiful was everything he stood out even among his contemporaries—a complex character, always well dressed, slightly effeminate in his demeanour, probably enhanced by his soft English accent.

Caroline stood out in the busy gym because of her looks and her sweet, almost shy personality. Angelo was surprised that she was so down-to-earth and self-conscious about her beauty. That's why the relationship didn't seem right. Gordon and Caroline didn't seem to fit as a couple. He was self-obsessed to the point of arrogance and she was delightful, at times seemingly afraid of her own stunning looks. Some felt Gordon was only interested in Caroline because she made him look good; an accessory for his image. It summed up a man who needed to be noticed.

Then there was his sexuality. Although he constantly sought the attention of females, Gordon's strutting and preening raised questions. Popular opinion was that he was gay or at least bisexual.

Even Caroline had doubts. 'Do you think he's gay?' she asked her sister Deanna as they stood watching Wood take a class one day.

* * *

Deep down, Laurie Ingleton knew her relationship with Gordon Wood would be fleeting. The fact that she suspected he was cheating or at least flirting with another woman made the decision even easier. She and Gordon had even thrown a break-up party at the tiny flat they had shared for almost five months in Victoria Road, Darlinghurst, just to make light of what had been a mistake to take a friendship into a romance.

It was an easy mistake to make. They'd met at the gym; two young people in a body-beautiful world where minds and personalities were a distant consideration. Of course that changed, as it does with all relationships, when the initial physical attraction wore off. They moved in together but it only confirmed the main issue—that he was just the wrong sort of bloke. In fact that was the problem. She wanted him to be a bloke instead of being so expressive and needy, a SNAG before his time who, if anything, was too open with his feelings.

Maybe it was the loss of his father, Michael, soon after the family emigrated from the United Kingdom in the mid-1980s or the fact that he had grown up in a household of women, with mother Brenda and sisters Jacqui and Michelle. Whatever the reason, it got too much, smothering at times. Gordon was polite, charming and thoughtful but he was more of a girlfriend in his manner than a boyfriend, always talking about emotions rather than being the traditional strong male.

Laurie was ready to move on. She had enjoyed the time with Gordon—who called her 'Little L', with some affection—but the lie was hard to get over. She wondered what else he might have lied about.

She didn't really know that much about him other than he was an economics graduate from Sydney University and had dreams of being an actor. He even had an agent when she met him at the gym—or said he did—but she never saw any real evidence of an acting career. The dream, if it was real, seemed to have ended.

It was real enough and it had ended in frustration. Gordon had been involved in the University of Sydney's Law Revue acting fraternity and had even applied to be enrolled at NIDA. He worked casual jobs in a theatre restaurant in Goulburn Street and another out at Homebush where he was a waiter and singer.

After graduating in 1986 Gordon got a job at the Sydney Opera House ticket office in Surry Hills and pursued his theatrical dreams in places like the Marion Street Theatre at Killara and got an assistant's role with the producer Baz Luhrmann in a production of *La Boheme*. He even had two small onscreen roles: as a paramedic in a 1991 episode of the television drama *Police Rescue* and as a police trooper named Suggs Dicks in the 1989 Australian sci-fi fantasy movie *Sons of Steel*.

His mother disapproved and was glad when he finally abandoned the folly after five years or so when he found he could make better money as a gymnasium trainer.

University friends and acquaintances would recall a Walter Mitty-type character (a description that would be repeated later by stockbroker Rene Rivkin), full of imagined possibilities to make, invest or star in movies. It was never quite believable. He also had a tendency to rub people up the wrong way with a know-it-all attitude, not helped by his British lilt and imposing physical stature which made him appear superior.

Others saw him differently. His close circle of friends saw a sensitive man who wore his emotions on his sleeve. Given his good looks, he was always popular with women and had several long-term relationships. He was always devastated when they ended, as if it was a slight on him rather than the reality of being young and exploring life.

Gordon took Laurie to meet his family a few times, at Cherrybrook on Sydney's north-west fringe. It was obvious that Gordon was very close to his mother. They were peas-in-a-pod physically and doted on one another. Brenda Wood insisted her son's confidence was a shield against shyness; a polite young man, perhaps overly tactile but respectful and comfortable around women.

They never discussed Gordon's father, Michael, who'd been a salesman of some sort at an ink manufacturing and printing company. He contracted cancer in 1986—the same year Gordon started university—and succumbed quite quickly. It had clearly affected Gordon although he never spoke about it to Laurie.

Perhaps it was because the relationship was always going to be fleeting. What Gordon had not told her, but made quite clear to his mother, was that Laurie was a passing romance. Caroline Byrne was the woman he really wanted. 'He was smitten,' Brenda would later say. 'He went out with Laurie because he couldn't see Caroline. She had a boyfriend.' He was even writing to one of his mates about his feelings, not daring to mention her name in case Laurie found out.

Brett Cochrane had met Gordon at a self-development class run by the American new-age education program called the Landmark Forum. Gordon liked his eccentric ways, how he would dress like an Indian, complete with turban and blackened face, and walk around the Cross talking in a strange accent. Brett, or Basquali as he later called himself, would make his name in photography, not so much for the standard of it as the subject matter. In 1993, after Laurie and Gordon had split, the rugby league player Andrew Ettinghausen successfully sued Australian Consolidated Press for publishing a photo of Ettinghausen, with his genitals exposed, in a post-match shower with fellow Australians Ben Elias and Laurie Daley on the 1990 Kangaroo tour of England and France.

Brett's response outside the court was typical. 'It's worth more than a Brett Whiteley,' he said of his photograph. 'I'm shocked. I feel like fainting. I'm speechless…I can't believe it because the photograph is not pornographic, it's not offensive. It's very tasteful. I mean, my grandmother likes it and my grandmother lives in South Wentworthville and she's a conservative grandmother.'

It was why he and Gordon liked each other. They were looking for something different, a break perhaps which set them apart from the other young men who sought fame and fortune in Australia's biggest city. The Forum classes they attended and their infatuation with another self-help guru, Anthony Robbins, were pointers to the character of young men who pushed their personalities as assets in a quest to succeed. Life was about opportunities and meeting the right people.

Besides, 'Bretty' doted on 'Gordy'; he even persuaded the vain fitness instructor to pose nude for him. Gordon was proud of the pictures, the way the water cascaded down his rippled torso. He would show people, women particularly, when one of them found its way into a copy of *Black and White* magazine. There were other photos on the same day which weren't published because he had an erection, as if posing in front of another man had turned him on.

Laurie had her own photos of Gordon, taken on their holiday at Noosa. They had the appearance of a happy, loving couple with a future together. They were not true. It was over and Gordon Wood was moving on. It was a decision that would change all their lives.

6

A JOB WITH RENE

At 4.27 am on 24 September 1993, a diminutive Spanish politician in a Monte Carlo ballroom fumbled with an envelope, paused as if he couldn't quite believe its contents and then sent Sydney into spasms of joy. Juan Antonio Samaranch's accented pronunciation of Syd-e-ney as the host of the 2000 Olympics seemed only to accentuate the achievement and acknowledgement that the city had arrived on the world stage—a metropolis of significance, not just for its natural beauty but a confidence in its ability to deliver on a promise.

Around the same time, Caroline Byrne had made her own dramatic decision about a promise, but for the opposite reasons. She wanted to put an end to her relationship with Gordon Wood.

In January she had moved into Gordon's tiny flat above a laundry in Victoria Road, Darlinghurst. Barely nine months on she was convinced Gordon was not the right man. He may have been handsome and charismatic but there was little else attractive about him, and certainly no long-term future.

On her 23rd birthday—7 September—she went to lunch with Narelle Cook. The conversation at what should have been a happy occasion was dominated by Caroline's misgivings and decision to leave her boyfriend. She was having doubts, particularly as Gordon was pressuring her to get married and she simply wasn't ready. Narelle later noted it succinctly in her diary:

Caroline broke up with Gordon. Wasn't sure about the relationship and needed time to think.

Caroline was more specific with her father. 'He doesn't work apart from doing a few gym classes. He just lies in bed until lunchtime every day,' she complained, explaining why she wanted to move back into the Connaught apartment.

Tony was not surprised by her decision. He had nothing against Gordon Wood and had not stood in the way of his daughter moving in with a man she'd only just met. She was 22 and was entitled to make her own choices.

Their flat was appalling; tiny and noisy and located above a laundry, with almost no furniture, including a dining table on milk crates. Neither of them had a car. In fact Gordon took to using a car owned by one of his personal training customers in lieu of payment for their weekly sessions.

A few days after she moved back Gordon showed up at Windsor Plaza. He wanted to win back Caroline and needed a job to impress her. Tony felt sorry for the young man. Normally supremely confident, it was clear Gordon's anguish was genuine. Tony promised him the next vacancy.

The offer was short-lived. His daughter didn't want to see Gordon, let alone her father giving him a job. Tony backed off. It seemed to be an end to the matter, particularly when a new boyfriend was introduced to him just a few weeks later.

Like Gordon Wood before him, Adam Baczynski met Caroline Byrne at a gym although it was the City Gym in Crown Street, East Sydney, which Caroline and Gordon also frequented because it was the place to be seen. The divorced baker and part-time model from Warsaw was used to women falling over themselves, and even though he was in his early forties he had still caught the eye of the much younger Caroline.

He asked her out for coffee at first, aware that she had a live-in boyfriend but also aware there were growing problems in the relationship. Caroline told him she had worries about Gordon Wood's sexuality. She never detailed what made her suspicious but she'd been concerned enough to demand HIV tests soon after they'd moved in together. Adam was quick to take advantage. 'Listen, Caroline, you are such a wonderful girl. Don't worry about someone who is confused about his sexuality. You can find someone else.'

Their affair began the day she left Gordon—it was instant and passionate, as if she was throwing herself into a relationship to distance herself from him as quickly as possible. She was different from many of the others who frequented the club; somehow untouched by the hedonistic lifestyle, not interested in drugs or late nights. She had a sunny personality and yet could also be reserved, far from innocent and yet somehow fragile. Adam knew the relationship might be brief but quickly fell in love and showered her with attention, flowers and even a stretch limousine, although he could tell she was torn and friends told him she was still seeing the boyfriend.

When she told him one day over coffee that she was arranging another HIV test, Adam knew he had lost the battle. Gordon Wood had convinced her to go back to him. He wondered what had changed.

So did Tony Byrne on the day in November when he walked into his apartment for lunch to find Gordon Wood with his daughter. They were clearly back together. Caroline, excited, jumped up to explain. 'Daddy, Gordon's got a job with Rene Rivkin.'

She said it as if she expected her father to know the name. Tony did. 'What sort of job, Gordon?'

'I'm his personal assistant.'

With that, the couple left to seal their reunion with a spin around the city in one of Rivkin's BMWs.

Rene Rivkin would most likely have been awake in the dark hours before dawn when Samaranch made his stuttering announcement in Monte Carlo, but he would not have been among the throng gathered beneath the arches of the Harbour Bridge, nor one of the millions in front of television sets across the country. Sport, in any form, was not among his interests, even though at its highest levels it reeked of his two favourite interests—money and influence.

He was often awake around 3 am, mostly busy trading on overseas markets, sometimes troubled by his own thoughts or woken by the pager which sat beside his bed. The public might see a jovial, at times belligerent businessman smoking an eternal cigar above a double chin badly in need of a shave and twirling a set of gold worry beads, but he had as many moods as cars and a personality as complex as his twisted finances.

Now almost 50, Rivkin may not have been the king of Sydney's financial world but he was certainly its eccentric jester, its lucky charm and feted media darling—a man who had made his name share-brokering for the likes of Kerry Packer and Sir Peter Abeles during the heady days of the 1980s boom before going into semi-retirement in the wake of the 1987 market crash, followed by a nervous breakdown and an operation to remove a benign brain tumour.

Now, as the market emerged from its slump he was once again at the head of the queue of aggressive traders, with his own money and the funds of those who believed him to be infallible. His new company in the heart of Double Bay was on the verge of an explosion in market activity of what would become the Dot.Com boom of the late 1990s.

Just how and why Rivkin came to meet and then hire Gordon Wood as his chauffeur was perplexing. At first glance they appeared an odd couple—an overweight, middle-aged multi-millionaire father of five and a chiselled, thirty-something athlete without prospect or a cent to his name. Both men would give different versions of their meetings although both stories had the same genesis—Joe's Café in Victoria Road, Kings Cross.

Joe Elcham was the Joe, a flamboyant businessman himself who would later fail a probity test conducted by the Casino Control Authority. It was shortly after he'd opened the ultra-chic place in 1991 that Elcham noticed Rene Rivkin sitting in traffic outside in his Bentley.

'I tapped on the glass,' he recounted to a journalist several years later. Rivkin lowered his window a few centimetres, unsure of why this bearded Lebanese man wanted him. Elcham beamed: 'Hi, Rene. I'm a big fan of yours. I've got this little café across the road and I'd love you to come in one day and have a coffee.' And that was that. The next day Rivkin showed up. 'Okay, show me this great coffee.'

It wasn't the coffee that Rivkin kept coming back for but the company. He had been lost, still lamenting his downfall both physically and financially, and struggling against a depressive illness. Bored with life and waiting for death, he would later say. The chance meeting with Joe Elcham meant he was suddenly surrounded by a new crowd of friends—a flock of good-looking aggressive young men who lavished on him attention and respect. He was soon a regular, often coming in twice a day; occupying an outside table where he held court with his new friends. It didn't matter that every one of them wanted something from him. In fact, it was reinvigorating; a reminder of his painful days at Sydney Boys High where he was a fat kid in the playground who resorted to buying hot chips to win attention from classmates who would otherwise ignore him. The crowd at Joe's was no different and neither was Rivkin's modus operandi. The café was his school yard and the clientele his classmates. This time, however, the chips he dolled out were plated with gold—the loan of an expensive car, antique watches bought from an eccentric trader in an airman's suit, financial offerings in the guise of business loans, sun-filled holidays to the Whitsundays. There were strings attached, of course, but fealty was an easy price to pay for the select coterie of young men, all of whom aspired to money and influence. Greed was still good in Sydney town.

Into this shallow world wandered Gordon Wood. The café was his local along the groovy strip atop the glossy gateway to the city's rich eastern suburbs and alongside the seediness of the Cross's drug culture. But Gordon did not fit comfortably. Not only was he a late-comer and a loner, but he was a bit older than most of the others and his soft English accent and distinctive South African lilt set him apart.

Still, he was cut from the same cloth. He later recalled how obvious it was that the businessman was impressed by his physique, so he would deliberately hang around the café in his gym gear, attempting to appeal to whatever Rivkin might be hankering for. He was right in a sense because Rivkin had noticed the pale man with the 'cultured accent' who seemed to be waiting for him to arrive. It was amusing, like having a puppet on a string, but nothing more, he'd say. Gordon was certainly different to men like George Freris and Gary Redding who were leaders of the largely denim-clad and tattoo-marked pack at Joe's.

Freris had become indispensable to Rivkin, nominally his chauffeur but in effect much more—a physically imposing right-hand man. Gordon was jealous. He wanted George's job, or anything else that came along for that matter; a piece of the action he could see was being garnered by others.

In an unpublished biography years later, written with journalist Ros Reines, Rivkin would recount a strange evening which both horrified him and endeared him to a man he regarded as a Walt Mitty-type character, strangely the same description given by university contemporaries. Even Rivkin found it hard to explain his tolerance of Gordon Wood.

> 'As a sign of his enthusiasm and in a crazed effort to try to win my favour he dragged George and I along to a meeting that he said would provide an excellent business opportunity for me,' he recounted.
>
> 'This meeting took place in a large, upstairs apartment and, as soon as we got there I looked around and realised we'd been suckered. There were bookshelves everywhere filled with appalling motivational tracts written by Americans with strange names and shiny white smiles. The titles included *Ten Steps to Unlimited Wealth and Total Happiness*—that sort of rubbish. There were lots of others in the meeting. Most of them had that tails-at-half-mast optimism, that wet dogs display when they're locked outside in the rain and they hope that someone will let them in.

> 'This was exactly what Gordon's meeting was all about. For two hours we sat there subjected to speeches by the head of the group, the head of the region—even the head of the state. We also endured a surreal demonstration of comparative detergents where, mesmerisingly, the Amway product removed brown boot polish from a white handkerchief better than anything else. We then learnt that seemingly after no time at all, you could have a veritable army of distributors under you—even scattered across the globe, bringing you home the bacon.
>
> 'Since I am basically a polite person I stuck it out to the end but how Gordon even thought I'd be interested in becoming an Amway distributor, demonstrating pots and pans along with cleaning products in peoples' homes is beyond me. Perhaps he thought that he could impress the Amway bosses by proving that he could get someone as well known as me to the meeting? I don't know. But when it was all over, I said to him: "Look Gordon, thanks very much, mate but why Amway? You must be joking!" He wasn't, however. He thought that the whole thing was a winner and tried to convince me to go on with it, arguing that EVERYONE can do with a bit of extra income. "Gordon, I've got news for you, I don't want the extra income. I'm very happy with the income I've got. I'm not going to sell Amway"—at which point—dejectedly, he relented. I suppose that I should have realised then that he was a dope, but I always give people the benefit of the doubt—which sometimes lands me in hot water—as it did on this occasion.'

Despite his misgivings, Rivkin gave Gordon a job a few months later, towards the end of November 1993.

> 'In light of the Amway debacle, you're probably wondering why,' he wrote. 'In hindsight, I certainly am but I guess it was because he had been so keen and had been campaigning for the job since I first met him.'

7

BURNING DESIRES

It was December 1993 and Caroline and Gordon were back as a couple, albeit tenuously and still living apart. Caroline remained unconvinced about resuming their live-in relationship, even after both had been cleared by HIV tests, although Gordon was once again becoming a regular visitor to the Connaught apartment. He was also busy casting around for a bigger place himself now that he had a full-time job. He never mentioned exactly how much Rivkin was paying him to drive his fleet of cars and tend to his needs but offered plenty of talk about promises and potential.

Tony didn't care really. All that mattered was that Caroline was bright and bubbly for the first time in ages. Maybe the devastation of Andrea's death and his daughter's brush with death were finally behind them, he thought as he prepared Christmas lunch.

The kids always joined him but this year Gordon was coming as well. Tony didn't mind, even though he wondered about Gordon's own family. Gordon wasn't all that forthcoming with details about his life, other than that his family had emigrated from the UK via South Africa when he was in high school. His mother, Brenda, still lived out at the family place in Cherrybrook. A little bit like Camden, he supposed, although he'd never been out there.

Tony loved the family get-togethers. Peter, 27, was now working with him managing a clutch of city properties and the other three had gone to university. Amazingly, given her hiccup the previous year, Caroline, 23, had finished her degree in psychology at Sydney University and was settled, at least for the moment, doing her modelling and working at June Dally's. Robert, 25, was doing his masters in town planning at Sydney University and Deanna, 20, was at the same campus studying languages. He wished Andrea could have got the help she needed and was here with him. Life could be lonely without a partner in this stage of life.

A single photograph taken that afternoon would always suggest a happy family event even though the lunch would prove a significant point in a looming tragedy. Gordon took the shot of the Byrne family laughing and joking around the still-laden table. It captured the lack of formality around the table where T-shirts and singlets denoted a hot summer's day. Peter is playing up to the camera, slightly obscuring his brother Robert on one side of the table. Deanna and Caroline, slightly less animated but enjoying the moment nonetheless, sit on the other side. Between them sits Tony, looking almost quizzically at his camera in the hands of Gordon. The plates are empty but the champagne glasses are still half full. The photo would sit in Tony's lounge room in the years to come, not as a reminder of Christmas joy so much as a reminder of the events which followed.

Not long after the photo was taken, Gordon's pager went off. It was just after 2.30 pm. He looked at the message and excused himself, asking if he could use the phone which sat on a side table next to the couch, just out of earshot of those around the table. Tony could see him through the door, standing hand on hip as he listened. He appeared to be taking orders.

'That was Rene Rivkin,' Gordon announced as he returned to the table. 'His printing factory burned down last night. He's on his way back from Singapore. He'll be arriving at the airport at about 7 pm and I need to pick him up.'

Although he didn't mention it by name, Tony knew Gordon was referring to a company called Offset Alpine. He'd mentioned it several times before in general conversation; nothing specific beyond bragging about what he knew of Rivkin's business activities.

Gordon left around 6 pm to go to the airport. He was back two hours later, having delivered his boss home. It had been a leisurely day and the interruption hardly seemed to matter. They were used to Gordon having to run off and tend to Rivkin's demands. After all, that was his job.

The problem was that Gordon wasn't telling the truth.

New South Wales burned through the summer of 1993–94. The bushfires flared on Boxing Day and raged for weeks. Television flashed the mayhem around the world—800 fires, three lives lost, 206 homes destroyed, and 20 000 volunteers risking their lives. The future Olympic city was ringed by fire, or so it seemed from afar. And yet a single blaze wreaked more havoc than the others combined, at least in financial terms: Rene Rivkin's printing press company, Offset Alpine.

The official reports into the fire would state the fire brigade was alerted by a thermal alarm at 11.04 pm on Christmas Eve. Five minutes after the first brigade units arrived at 50 Derby Street, Silverwater, the building was well alight. A pall of dark smoke billowed into the night sky, the severe heat stopping an electric clock inside the factory as it climbed into the second floor and through the roof. By the time seventeen units from fourteen stations brought the fire under control more than two hours later, most of the roof had caved in and the factory was in cinders.

There had been a party that afternoon at the factory. It was a tradition for the 150 or so staff at the plant which normally ran 22 hours a day. On a baking hot Christmas Eve they knocked off at midday and lit a couple of barbecues in the loading dock at the north-western end of the building. The beer and cheap wine flowed freely for the next four hours as the printers stood around the hot concrete bay and wondered about the future under the new owner, Rene Rivkin. He was a different character entirely to the previous owner, Kerry Packer, who had sold out for just under

$16 million. It seemed a good price, as Packer deals always appeared; particularly given the age of the presses, although Rivkin had been busy talking up the deal which had been made through his publicly listed investment company, Stroika.

The workers speculated about Rivkin's apparent dismissal of problems. He only wanted to hear goods news not bad, according to stories filtering out of the boardroom.

The party wound up just after 4 pm and the site was secured 30 minutes later by a supervisor, one of four men who had keys to the property. Three cleaners remained for another two hours. Then they too left, shutting off the lights and air-conditioning as they went. The place went up in smoke four hours later.

Investigators concluded that the fire must have started inside, and on the other side of the 50-year-old building to where the workers had their party, because the damage was most intense on the north-eastern wall between printing presses number two and three. What caused it was too difficult to say, not helped by the fact that workers regularly used alcohol to dampen the presses. Bins full of rags, pallets full of magazines, solvents, ink and enormous rolls of printing press paper simply fuelled the blaze.

The reason for the conjecture and suspicion, which would last for years, was the 'industrial special risks'—a new-for-old insurance policy which became effective on 30 November, barely three weeks before the fire. Unless it could be shown that the fire was deliberate, the policy triggered a massive $53 million insurance payout on assets worth just $3 million. That would make it one of the largest insured property losses in Sydney's history—more, as it turned out, than the sum total of the bushfire claims.

Angelo Georgiou wasn't surprised to see Gordon Wood at his gym one morning in February 1994. He came in often, sometimes for a workout and always to big-note himself. This time he had a business proposition that would make them both a lot of money.

Angelo was dubious but agreed to have a coffee and at least listen to the idea. Barely had they sat down and ordered at a café around the corner in Park Street than Gordon launched into his sales pitch. It was a share deal, he explained, involving a printing company owned by Rivkin which had burned down. The share price was going to go up and anyone buying now would make a killing. Gordon was desperate to get in on what he appeared to know. He needed a benefactor.

'Look, I need $500 000 to make this happen. If you can get me the money I'll turn it into $1 million in six months. Leave it to me.'

Gordon began scribbling on a piece of paper to show how the deal would work. It looked complex and illicit to Angelo who had always been suspicious of the share market and preferred an investment he could see and touch, like a business or bricks and mortar.

Gordon kept at him: 'This is guaranteed profit. There are government people involved. These people don't put their money down without knowing what they are doing. That's how the system works. That's how they make money. I'm doing you a favour.'

It smelled like a rort. How else could he say he knew that the shares were going up? 'You're talking to the wrong person. I don't have that kind of money,' Angelo declared, offering to talk to his business partner but knowing it would amount to nothing. When he told Gordon as much a few days later his former employee was angry.

It was not the only time Gordon would mention the issue. He convinced his mother, Brenda, to spend $10 000 buying 7000 shares at $1.30 each—an investment which would eventually double when she sold them almost two years later—but the profits were a long way short of his desires.

And he was not the only one. The company's share registry would show a rush of speculation about the company and whether the insurance claim on the Christmas Eve would be met. It seemed that everyone knew Rivkin's luck was in. If Gordon was worried about perceptions he didn't show it, even offering advice to Caroline's friends as well as his own. A university mate, Peter

Cameron, would buy 5000 shares on Gordon's advice and sell them at a profit.

According to Tony Byrne, Gordon would take it a step further one night in March when Caroline and Gordon were over for dinner. They arrived around 7 pm with Thai takeaway. Caroline went to the kitchen and began dishing the food onto plates while the two men stayed in the dining room a few metres away.

In his hand Gordon held a share price indicator about half the size of a mobile phone. He looked at it and said quietly, 'Offset Alpine is at $1.37. I've recently bought shares in Offset Alpine. They are going up in price. The insurance company is going to pay up.' He looked up and added, 'The fire was a set-up.'

Tony glanced up towards the kitchen where Caroline had finished divvying the food. She returned her father's questioning gaze but said nothing. She had heard what her boyfriend had just suggested—the Offset Alpine fire was arson.

8

TIM TAM MAN

Rene Rivkin's employment of and friendship with George Freris was entrenched long before Gordon Wood came on the scene, which made Gordon's growing jealousy of the muscled, tattooed former boxer all the more risky. Not only did Gordon's behaviour perplex and unsettle his boss but it made him unpopular inside the group at Joe's Café.

Either he was too wrapped up in his own ambitions or he didn't understand Rivkin, who regarded his relationship with Freris as a Pygmalion exercise—he as Professor Henry Higgins and Freris as Eliza Doolittle—through which he could turn a raw recruit with a shady background into a man of substance and dependability. It fitted his sense of worth—or lack of it—having fallen out with much of the mainstream financial world and intent on recreating his powerbase through this world of young men. He created a role for Freris to manage his cars and drive him around town.

In a perverse way it was empowering for Rivkin to appear physically helpless, unwilling to drive his fleet of cars let alone understand their mechanics. Freris' role would evolve and include flying Rivkin's helicopter and captaining his motor yacht—the 'resident can-do man'. Besides, Freris was a willing and capable foot soldier; a natural leader who watched over Rivkin's growing new street interests—real estate developments, nightclubs and even a tattoo parlour called Skins and Needles which he financed for Freris and his mate Gary 'Pommy' Redding just up the road from the café. Above all, Freris was intrinsically loyal.

Gordon Wood was another matter. Having established a formal role in the Rivkin clique Gordon wanted to expand his niche at the expense of Freris. He began complaining to Caroline about the inequity of gifts and attention that his boss was giving his rival—a Harley-Davidson motorbike, a home unit and holidays. And she passed the complaints on to her father.

'Rene has set George up in a business and is showering him with gifts,' she repeated one night when she went alone to visit Tony. 'It's all for sex, of course. George is Rene's toy-boy. Gordon is jealous.'

Tony didn't really pay much attention although he was concerned that Caroline seemed to have been sucked into what amounted to gossip, which was very unlike her. The conversations were littered with references to what George was getting and the expectation that one day it would be Gordon's turn to be looked after.

The reality of Gordon's job was a far cry from the stories he told others. He was, in effect, a manservant for an unpredictable boss. Rivkin would behave as if he ruled the world one day, throwing around money to strangers and inviting them to his table, and the next retire to his darkened room to sulk.

Gordon Wood bore much of the brunt of the mood swings. He was on call 24 hours a day, armed with a mobile phone and a pager, and endured a routine which could quickly become monotonous. He was required to wait for Rivkin in the morning at Joe's Café, along with other members of the group, or hangers-on as Rivkin's wife, Gayle, referred to them all. Rivkin would arrive when it suited him and expect to be waited and feted, often for hours. If Rivkin wanted to make a telephone call, his chauffeur would dial the number, wait for the person to answer and announce, 'The big fellow wants to talk to you', before handing the phone to his boss. It was a theatre in which Wood was a willing actor.

More often than not Rivkin lunched luxuriously, usually at one of a dozen restaurants in the eastern suburbs and particularly around Stanley Street in East Sydney. The lunches might last a couple of hours, depending on his dining partner, after which he would invariably be taken, or occasionally stroll, around the corner to a two-bedroom apartment across the road from the City Gym for a sleep. It became known as The Sanctuary. When he awoke, some time around 5 pm, Rivkin would demand the presence of his boys who, once assembled, would resume the general adulation until, promptly at 7 pm, he went home for dinner with his wife and five children. Gordon would take him most nights before knocking off for the day.

Rivkin was aware of his chauffeur's jealousies. Some of it was reported back to him by one of his sons, Damien, who'd reacted badly when Gordon told him that he wished George would crash his plane and die. Rivkin had been confronted by Gordon's strange behaviour himself, sometimes crying, or bitching about others behind their backs.

Rivkin, who had his own problems dealing with conflict and often used others to deal with problems he couldn't face, hated the whingeing. And he cringed each time Gordon sent him a message on his pager, signing off with lines like: *From the son you don't need but hope you want. Love Gordza.*

Rivkin was not the only recipient of Gordon's adoration. His frequent notes to Caroline were just as sickly sweet:

> Now you've heard of the packet of Tim Tams that never runs out, well, I am giving you the dessert that never runs out—& it is sweet & pure & full of goodness. That dessert is my passionate, undying & deepest love for you. You can tuck into this dessert whenever you want, as often as you like, & what is more, eat as much as you like & never fear—it is endless, unlimited & will be there as long as we both shall live.

Despite all the planning for Rene Rivkin's 50th birthday on 6 June 1994, no-one remembered the cake until the afternoon of the party. It was a last-minute arrival at the marquee set up on the Sydney Harbour foreshore between the Botanic Gardens and Mrs Macquarie's Chair—a tiered black and gold concoction from a Paddington made-to-order cake designer, big enough for 250 slices and featuring three items to reflect Rivkin's life and current state of mind—a miniature cavalcade of Harley-Davidsons, a string of silvered almond worry beads strung on gold thread and a Rolls-Royce emblem.

Its entrance was not as grand as the birthday boy's and paled in comparison to the motorcade of Joe's Café bikies who rode their throbbing machines through the tent at one point just to emphasise Rivkin's departure from the mainstream. Above all, it was a night of copious opulence. Rivkin lounged like Jabba the Hut, smoking his umpteenth Monte Christo cigar of the day, declaring raucously that he was not in jail and never would be, and receiving guests as they presented their extravagant gifts. He would tick them off with a journalist a few weeks later.

'I got a 2000-year-old piece of pottery from one of these people. I got a gold watch from another one. I got three sets of gold cufflinks. I got some beautiful books. I got four or five caricatures of me by various cartoonists. I got a beautiful 1910 Lalique decanter which I love...'

He had every reason to be content about his future. Within days of the $400 000 bash, Offset Alpine announced to the stock exchange that its insurance claim had been accepted in full. Progress payments of $18 million had already been received and a final cheque of $34.85 million would soon be arriving.

Among the guests were Gordon Wood and Caroline Byrne. A photograph of them dancing, a tuxedoed Gordon smiling at his consort, would capture a couple apparently very much in love. They were also looking to buy their own love nest, preferably at someone else's expense.

Tony Byrne was keenly aware that his daughter and her boyfriend were house hunting, mainly because they wanted his financial help. It was also clear that they, and Gordon in particular, were not in a financial position to take on such a huge commitment, at least not unless Rene Rivkin came good with the promises of the bonuses that Gordon kept mentioning. Tony had no idea to what the bonuses were linked but Gordon constantly referred to it when they came to dinner. He kept talking about the *big deal*, but was never more specific about it other than suggesting it would be within a year. It was always followed by an expectation that Tony would then be able to lend them money to buy a house.

He was keen to help the young couple but was cautious and protective. As far as he knew they kept their finances apart, each with their own bank account. Caroline paid for the food and Gordon paid the rent. It all seemed a bit flimsy considering they wanted to buy a property together. And Rivkin apparently felt the same way, according to Caroline, who told Tony one day that the businessman had turned down a request by Gordon to help finance the Darlinghurst property, on the market for $300 000, because he didn't think Gordon could service the loan repayments.

The issue dominated family conversations until one night in September when the three of them were having dinner at the Connaught. Deanna was there that night, still happy at home and with her own bedroom now that Caroline was gone.

The conversation, as usual, turned to the house hunting. They'd found an art deco apartment in Macleay Street, Potts Point, on the market for $270 000. Gordon had said Rene Rivkin had declared he was prepared to give the young couple $100 000 towards the home, but only if Tony agreed to finance the rest.

Caroline wasn't as sure as Gordon. The look on her face contradicted Gordon's confidence and worried Tony. If he participated he would raise money from the family trust he'd set up to protect his children's interests. Tony was proud of the arrangement because it offered them financial security for the rest of their lives—money carefully salted away into investment funds and property in such a way that any of them could access the money if they needed to. There were several properties, like the Connaught unit, two more in the Windsor Plaza and a fourth at Cronulla. In all, APR and CD Pty Ltd (Anthony, Peter, Robert, Caroline and Deanna) was worth over $2 million and Tony wasn't about to take a big risk on a man he still did not really know.

'Look, I'm happy to help, Gordon, but only on the following conditions. I want my solicitor to handle the conveyancing and that my name is the only one on the mortgage, as the mortgagee.'

Gordon relaxed. 'Okay, I'll talk to Rene.'

Two days later Gordon phoned Tony despite the fact he was power-walking through the Domain behind Parliament House. The reason quickly became clear: Rivkin had agreed to the terms.

'The $100 000 is a gift and Rene is not worried about which solicitor handles the conveyancing because he won't be on the mortgage.'

Tony breathed a sigh of relief. He'd hoped there would be a solution. 'Okay Gordon, if that's right then the money's yours.'

Gordon was excited. 'Look, I'll be earning huge bonuses within the next twelve months. Rene is going to pay me when he sells the printing company. I'll be earning so much money I'll be able to pay you back and have enough left to invest in other property.'

Gordon had lied. The $100 000 contribution by Rivkin was not a gift but a loan. Not only did Rivkin also expect to be on the mortgage papers but he was also under the impression that Tony Byrne would front up with the $27 000 deposit to secure the apartment. What he didn't realise was that his chauffeur was playing him off against his girlfriend's father in a crude game of bluff designed to win him the keys to a $270 000 home without paying a cent.

Andrew Smyrnis, Tony's solicitor, was on the phone—and worried. The contracts for the flat in Macleay Street had just landed on his desk but the details were wrong. The draft agreement drawn up by Rivkin's solicitor secured Tony's $180 000 contribution to the mortgage, as he wanted, but the mortgagee was the businessman. It was supposed to be the other way around.

Tony couldn't believe it. He'd already agreed to go back on one of his conditions, and allowed Rivkin's solicitors to handle the conveyancing, but this was too much. In truth, he hadn't ever expected Caroline and Gordon to repay the money, which was part of Caroline's share of the family trust, but he wanted it protected via the mortgage document which gave it some value if they foreclosed or the property was sold. This was the last straw.

Smyrnis was firm in his advice. 'Look Tony, enough is enough. I have to advise you that you should not go into this arrangement with Rene Rivkin on this basis. It's too dangerous.'

Tony agreed. 'Okay. Can you send a copy over and I'll have a look. If what you say is true—and I'm absolutely flabbergasted that this has happened—then I'm not going ahead.'

He hung up, confused and angry. The whole thing was a nightmare. He felt duped and, what was worse, put in a situation where he was disappointing his daughter. But there was no choice. He telephoned Caroline. He wanted to tell her himself.

Caroline listened quietly to the news. She seemed unmoved after Tony had finished his tirade against Rivkin. 'Daddy, don't get involved, don't touch it,' she said emphatically.

Tony was relieved. He knew Caroline would understand. 'Thanks. Can you pass on my decision to Gordon?'

Gordon's reaction was swift and vitriolic. The next afternoon he turned up at Tony's, ready to confront his would-be benefactor. Tony had half expected this would happen but he was not prepared for the verbal assault that would follow.

Gordon did not mince words. 'You can't do this; you can't pull out of the agreement, you can't!'

Tony was unfazed, lowering his voice to contrast with the anger confronting him. 'You go and tell your boss to stick by his agreement.'

Rather than quell Gordon's mood, it seemed to fuel his outrage. Tony had never seen Caroline's boyfriend like this. 'You can't pull out now,' he demanded again.

Tony would not back down. 'You go back to your boss and tell him I don't care if my solicitor doesn't handle the conveyancing, but my name is to be the only one on the mortgage.'

Tony had had enough. It was rare for him to get angry but he felt his voice rising. 'That $100 000 was to be a gift from Rene. Go and tell him, Gordon; the money is still there but I am the only one to be on the mortgage. Go on, go and tell Rivkin that I'll stand by my agreement if he will stand by his. Go on, go and tell him.'

Tony stopped and took a deep breath. He had never been treated in such a manner. Gordon mumbled something he couldn't understand, turned and left the apartment, slamming the door behind him.

Deanna was in the bedroom and heard the confrontation. When Gordon left she came out to find her father standing in the middle of the lounge room. It was the moment Tony realised he had been deceived and that Gordon Wood could not be trusted. And he wasn't going to be cowed by the likes of Rene Rivkin, not for an amount of money which was a drop in the ocean compared to the businessman's financial capabilities. The deal was off, and there was now no going back.

Then, suddenly, there was a solution. Rivkin agreed to put up the money. He'd been persuaded during one of his regular lunches with ALP heavyweight and former federal minister Graham Richardson although Gordon, as usual, injected himself into the process.

'I had lunch with Rene Rivkin and Graham Richardson today and Graham and I have talked Rene into buying the unit,' Gordon told Tony.

'Well, that's good, Gordon.'

'Yeah, Graham and I said why lose your deposit. Go ahead and buy it; me and Caroline can live in it and look after it, and when the prices go up Rene can sell it and he won't lose anything.'

'Oh, that's great, Gordon, fine.'

Caroline and Gordon would move into the home unit as owners, although it would be fully encumbered to Rivkin. After all the fuss, Gordon and Caroline were still renting even though their names were on the documents as having bought the place. The main thing for Tony was that Caroline's money was safe.

9

'HE WOULDN'T HURT A HAIR ON MY HEAD'

Angst was creeping into Tony's feelings about Gordon Wood. It was like some silent tug of war, as if he was trying to take Caroline away from him and the family. Gordon phoned her constantly during the day, obsessed, it seemed to those who watched. But was it love or was it all about money? Tony had his doubts. The row over the apartment had overshadowed and tarnished what would otherwise have been great excitement. In late October 1994 Caroline had jetted off to the Philippines as the Australian representative in the Miss Asia Pacific Quest.

She'd gone by herself, which amazed Tony, given that it was her first overseas trip. But the celebrations on her return—after she made the semi-finals—were soured by Gordon who sat glumly through a dinner at an Indian restaurant in Newtown, apparently still annoyed that his apartment scheme had fallen flat. It contrasted sharply with another of his love letters to Caroline, written on 9 November—four days after she finished the competition:

> You are my purpose in life. I am on this planet to love you. This is the meaning of love. I now believe it is a crime to use the word LOVE in any way that doesn't relate to you. Not only are you my princess and my goddess, but in my eyes

> you are Miss World, Miss Universe, Miss All-Time Greatest and Most Beautiful Woman.

When Caroline returned home a few days later, another of Gordon's penned letters of love lay waiting:

> You are my only love in my whole life—I have never experienced this before I met you & I will never experience it again. I want for nothing. I love you my princess, my chicky-babe. I am yours forever with passion & deep, deep unbridled love.
>
> My love, my love forever.
>
> Gordy X

Tony hoped they could all settle back into some sort of harmony. The apartment was finally bought and they moved in December just before Gordon was due to fly out on some sort of trip to the United States with Rivkin and his family. But it all started again when he got back. First, it was the house-warming party. Tony wasn't invited. Rivkin was apparently still miffed at the financial fallout and somehow blamed Tony. Gordon and Caroline didn't want them in the same room. Missing out on the party didn't bother Tony but the reason was galling. It seemed to go on through the summer of 1995, mostly in conversations alone with Caroline. She seemed to be mouthing Gordon's rather than her own observations but they stung nonetheless, coming from his daughter.

'Gordon has come home from work very angry. Rene is most upset about the outcome of the home unit transaction. Rene believes you have doublecrossed him and misled him.'

On another occasion she said, 'Rene is very depressed and does not want to see Gordon. He is depressed because of me.'

Still another: 'Rene is still very depressed and he is trying to drive a wedge between Gordon and me. Rene believes I know too much about his business and private life, especially his relationship with George. Gordon is really worried.'

And another: 'Even if we got married Rene will not come to the wedding. It has snowballed into an obsession. His mind is tormented and it's all because of me.'

Tony and Caroline had a routine on the days she worked at June Dally's. She would drive her car from Potts Point, pick up Tony outside the Connaught and drive to her office in Clarence Street. Tony would then drive the car back to Sussex Street and park it in the basement of the building he managed. At the end of the day Caroline would walk the three blocks back to Sussex Street, pick up the car and drive home. It seemed complicated but they both enjoyed the company.

Caroline was worried one morning in March as they drove past the cinema complex in George Street. 'Gordon has come home from work absolutely devastated. Rene has told him that he will not be able to give him the home unit, any bonuses or anything else.'

Tony couldn't hide his growing disquiet. 'Caroline, I don't know about this Gordon Wood. I'm very concerned about your safety and welfare.'

Caroline turned to him as they stopped at the Park Street intersection. 'You don't have to worry about me, Daddy. Gordon loves me. He wouldn't hurt a hair on my head.'

Tony looked at his daughter. It would be a moment he'd always remember and one he found difficult. She obviously believed Gordon loved her. He hoped it was true. He still didn't know much about someone who was talking about marrying Caroline and his instinct said there was something untrustworthy about him. The apartment fiasco only confirmed it. What's more, there was something strange going on between Gordon and his boss, and it was affecting his daughter.

He raised it with Gordon a few nights later when they came to dinner. 'Gordon, what's all this about Rene Rivkin. What's wrong with the man? I haven't done anything to him, he hasn't lost anything. I mean, he's got the property.'

Gordon looked at him blankly. 'It's not the money he's depressed about, it's his ego. You've destroyed his ego.'

The answer did nothing to allay Tony's fears. Gordon was worried too. Everything he had somehow came back to Rivkin: his job, the new apartment, even the car—a little second-hand Suzuki Vitara soft-top Rivkin had apparently bought him. Gordon considered transferring the ownership to his mother.

Tony didn't pretend to understand Rivkin's world but it seemed he was a madman or at least terribly disturbed; capable of enormous generosity one minute and frightening mood swings the next. If the worst happened and Rivkin withdrew his money, then Tony would find them another house and fund it himself. He would even get Gordon a job at the Windsor Plaza, if necessary.

Then, just as Tony was considering buying a one-bedroom apartment in Woolloomooloo, Gordon appeared to be back in Rivkin's favour. The only explanation came from Caroline who told him one day that Gordon had a plan to 'get around Rene'. He presumed she meant that Gordon had devised a way to humour his boss out of the black funk which had descended.

Whatever Gordon did, it appeared to work because as March rolled into April the stories changed from fear of loss to tales of a flourish of gifts—a $1500 television set, money for furnishings in the new apartment, even talk of renovations like a walk-in wardrobe.

Caroline was in the car one day with Gordon while he was driving Rivkin. From the back seat the millionaire suddenly declared, 'Gordon, if you've got an economics degree I'll give you $1000.'

'I've got an economics degree,' Gordon replied before they both laughed.

The largesse made no sense to Tony. And now there was a new worry. Caroline was on the phone telling him she was being pressured into marriage.

'I'm telling Gordon that I love him and there's no-one else but I just don't want to marry yet.'

Tony tried to placate his daughter. 'Caroline, you should be able to explain to Gordon that there's nobody else, you love him, he's got you and it's as if you're already married.'

Caroline wouldn't be comforted. 'He doesn't even want me to work. He just wants me to stay home, cook and he wants to support me 100 per cent.'

'How do you feel about that?'

'I'm very happy with my life the way it is. Maybe in three or four years' time I'd consider a change, but I'm way too young to think about that now. I'm only 24 and I don't want to give up work yet.'

'Surely Gordon can understand that. He's 31 and you're 24. The two of you are already married. You just don't wear a ring on your finger.'

'Rene and Gordon are going to Europe.' Caroline's pronouncement on 27 April did not surprise Tony, given Rivkin's frequent international travel, but his interest was piqued.

'Why Europe?' he asked.

Caroline shrugged. 'It's something to do with the printing factory.'

Offset Alpine again. Tony persisted. 'Where exactly are they going?'

'Zurich and London. Rene owns a small flat in London. They're going to be away for one or two weeks.'

The news didn't bother Tony; in fact he welcomed it, given his growing doubts about Gordon Wood. It seemed that as Gordon's relationship with Rene Rivkin improved, so his relationship with the Byrne family diminished. He avoided family gatherings, particularly dinners for Peter and Deanna who were headed to Asia—Peter following a girl to China in a forlorn chase for love and Deanna to Japan where she had taken a job teaching English in Tokyo.

It was galling to Tony and he feared that increasingly Caroline was being forced to choose between her family and Gordon's ambitions for money. He no longer called himself a chauffeur, rather a financial adviser which seemed ludicrous given who Rivkin was and Gordon's own lack of money and financial background.

Gordon's departure on 7 May was a blessing in many ways, coinciding with news that Caroline had been asked at work if she wanted to travel to Tamworth and Armidale on assignment. Doing a trade show wasn't new but being sent out of the metropolitan area on a three-day trip was a clear sign that she had a long-term future at June Dally's.

It was no surprise when a week or so after returning she was offered a permanent position working from Tuesdays to Saturdays. It appeared to be the perfect scenario although Caroline was torn about the prospect of giving up modelling.

In years to come, 3 May 1995 would come to be seen as the day that the world of Rene Rivkin began to publicly unravel. Not suddenly but inevitably. A few days before he and Gordon Wood made their way to Zurich, the Australian Securities Commission sought orders in the Federal Court to freeze trading in shares held in what it described as a 'black box'—a block of nine million shares controlled by two Swiss companies, Bank Leumi Le-Israel and EBC Zurich, which amounted to almost 40 per cent of the Offset Alpine group.

The companies were refusing to reveal the beneficial owners of the shares worth $18 million, citing Swiss federal banking laws. In turn, the ASC was trying to stop any sales until they could enforce their demand. Under Australian law, anyone with such a substantial interest in a company must make a declaration to the stock market. With Offset shares at around $2, the Swiss banks were sitting on a paper profit of up to $15 million. But who were the lucky owners? ASC investigators clearly believed Rivkin was one of them.

Although ASC would win the order, it would take seven years to reveal that the ASC was right: the ultimate beneficiaries were Rivkin and two close friends and business associates, Graham Richardson and former Qantas director Trevor Kennedy. The accounts in which the shares were held formed part of a string of secret bank accounts that were used to move millions of dollars in and out of the Australian stock market.

Rivkin's trip to Zurich was no coincidence. He spent five days ensuring the two companies would not release any information to Australian investigators and then flew with Gordon Wood on 12 May to London where he kept an apartment in Mayfair. It was not clear if he had any business in London other than a couple of weeks' grace before he would have to return and face the ASC investigators—a gauntlet upon which his entire fortune depended.

Tony and Caroline had no knowledge of this. Although the story of Rivkin's problems ran prominently in the financial press, it was too complicated to be picked up by general media and Gordon did not elaborate when he telephoned his girlfriend after arriving in London to tell her the trip had been extended by a couple of weeks. Tony and Caroline's brother Robert were over for dinner that night when the phone rang promptly at 6 pm.

Tony could openly hear the conversation and the distressed tone in his daughter's voice, not only because Gordon was staying longer but because he was whispering. She looked worried as she returned to the table.

Tony couldn't help himself. 'Why was Gordon whispering?'

Caroline tried to brush it off. 'It's only a one-bedroom flat and Gordon is sleeping on the couch. He didn't want to disturb Rene.'

Tony was incredulous. 'You mean that Rene Rivkin, with all his money, has a one-bedroom flat?'

He immediately dropped the subject. It was obvious that Caroline was embarrassed and did not believe Gordon's explanation. Sometime later, when it was too late, he would discover that his daughter was indeed suspicious. She wondered if her boyfriend was in a homosexual relationship with his boss.

Rivkin would later confirm that she had suspicions—as baseless as he claimed they were—and he told police he happened to be watching Gordon Wood talking to Caroline on the phone from his spacious, two-bedroom London unit.

'He came back and said, "She's very strange. She's just asked me if we are sleeping in the same bed or separate bedrooms." I just scratched my head.'

10

A FALSE OPENING

In September 1895, at the height of his fame and powers and the depths of his financial misfortune, the American novelist Mark Twain arrived in Sydney aboard the steamer *Warrimoo* as part of a long lecture tour of five continents. In his account of the brief visit—*Following the Equator*—published two years later, the writer told of dropping anchor in Watsons Bay:

> And in the morning went oh-ing and ah-ing in admiration up through the crooks and turns of the spacious and beautiful harbour—a harbour which is the darling of Sydney and the wonder of the world.

He also described his entry into the harbour the night before; the marvel of what he thought were porpoises, but rather dolphins 'collected in a wild and magnificent jumble under the bows' and the 'sword of light' from the lighthouse on Sydney Heads which pierced the darkness as they neared the entrance to the harbour.

In doing so, he recounted the tragic story of the clipper *Duncan Dunbar* which had run aground 38 years before as it also tried to enter the harbour, killing all but one of its 122 passengers and crew. It remains the state's worst peacetime sea disaster.

The mistake by the captain, a Master Green, was to attempt to navigate through Sydney Heads at night and in high seas. He misjudged the entrance, instead heading for what Twain described as a 'false opening' immediately to the south—a place later named The Gap.

> There was no saving the ship. The great seas swept her in and crushed her to splinters and rubbish upon the rock tushes at the base of the precipice... The tale is told to every stranger that passes the spot, and it will continue to be told to all that come, for generations...

The Gap claimed its first suicide victim just six years after the *Dunbar.* A publican's wife named Anne Harrison took her life in 1863, apparently distressed over the accidental death at the same place of her nephew although it seemed there must be more to the story. It quickly became the city's place of personal oblivion, and by the 1940s so many were leaping off like lemmings that a dedicated rescue team was formed. Even though hundreds would die here just a handful would be formally recorded as having committed suicide, the remaining cases concluded as open findings.

A century after Mark Twain's visit, in the early afternoon of a pleasant March day in 1995, Caroline Byrne sat having lunch overlooking the final resting place of the *Dunbar.* She was with a friend, a young trainee model named Michelle Whelan whom she had befriended at June Dally's. The younger girls often found a friend in Caroline. Her manner was easy and approachable and even though she was still only 24, she seemed worldly to a teenager.

Michelle was only fifteen when she started a three-month weekend modelling and beauty workshop. Caroline was her deportment teacher and they had stayed in contact since the course finished. This was the third time they had been to The Gap.

Despite its dark backdrop this was also a place of raw beauty, from the descent by road into Watsons Bay where the harbour appears as a canvas—a mass of languid white sails, the arrogant wake of power boats and the churning ferries all framed by the jungle green canopy of the northern shoreline. Sydney Heads stand like gargantuan twins, daring rather than inviting anyone to enter from the Tasman Sea whose rolling mass spreads to the horizon.

Gap Park was established in the nineteenth century when the tramline was extended to accommodate the tourists who flocked to the area. Restaurants, cinemas and hotels followed and enterprising businessmen set up permanent cameras and telescopes on the cliff top. Every Boxing Day families lined the cliffs to cheer the Sydney–Hobart yacht fleet on its way down the coast.

The Gap itself is a geological weakness—a 400-metre-long sweep of sandstone crumbled and collapsed by time, wind and water. At the southern end lies a geological formation known as Jacob's Ladder; a two-metre-wide cleft in the cliff face, probably caused by volcanic activity. It was below this point that the anchor of the *Dunbar* was recovered and set in stone next to the pathway as a permanent memorial to those who lost their lives. The path then led north to the Gap Bluff, an area controlled by the navy for a century or more and used for an artillery school and radar station before being reclaimed as a public park. Most of the buildings remain, used as a business college and hidden by trees just beyond the walkway and shoulder-high wooden fence which keeps sightseers a safe distance from the cliff edge until they reach a lookout in the middle of the curve, where a sturdier steel construction permits a wider, safer view of the ocean below. A stone stairway then leads up to the top of The Gap and beyond to the headland which forms the southern post of the gateway into Sydney Harbour.

It was Caroline's suggestion that she and Michelle meet there—a favourite picnic spot of her and her boyfriend's, she said. But when Michelle tried to question her about Gordon and what he was like, Caroline changed the subject and turned the conversation to modelling.

On this day it was Michelle's turn to be troubled. Caroline had picked her up from her home in Ashfield and driven to Watsons Bay where they climbed the stone steps to a circular concrete slab within sight of the *Dunbar*'s rusted anchor. They sat silently for a while, Michelle consumed by problems at home and the devastation of having broken up with her boyfriend.

Without warning, Michelle stood and walked to the waist-high wooden fence which guarded the edge of the cliff. She looked down, transfixed by the white water 30 metres beneath her feet, smashing onto the flat, grooved rocks, like some giant platform carved in square slabs by a millennium of pounding waves.

Caroline's voice broke through her thoughts: 'Michelle, come away from there. I want you to come back to me.'

She looked back. Caroline was standing now, beckoning her away from the fence. She obeyed the older woman.

Caroline's words seemed distant but compelling. 'If you're thinking what I think you are then it's not the answer.'

Michelle tried to sound surprised. 'What, suicide?'

'Yes, exactly,' Caroline persisted.

Michelle didn't reply, confirming Caroline's fears. What would drive a fifteen-year-old girl to even contemplate casting herself from a cliff top?

'You know there's always someone you can talk to. I get depressed and upset at times but suicide wouldn't cross my mind.'

Michelle burst into tears.

'What's wrong? Come on, I know something's wrong. Talk to me.'

Michelle relented. Details of the break-up and her problems tumbled out. To a teenager, it seemed like the end of the world.

Caroline listened and put her arm around Michelle. 'Take it from me, take it from my experience: be careful who you love.'

Michelle looked at her friend. There was a trust, a bond, and not only because Caroline had her own boyfriend problems. They both knew the anger and confusion of a parent who'd committed suicide—Caroline's mother and Michelle's father.

As they walked back to the car Caroline confirmed her assessment. 'Suicide has never crossed my mind and never will. Think of all the people you would leave behind and what would happen to them. It would be easy for you but not for them. Suicide is not the answer.'

It was the second last day of May when Caroline took up the full-time job at June Dally's. She still drove to work in the mornings with her father. The conversations were buoyant, mainly about Gordon's imminent return and Caroline adjusting to full-time work. The only dark spot appeared to be a chance meeting with Andrew Blanchette the month before. They'd had an argument in the street which had upset Caroline, although she'd never explained to Tony what the confrontation was about. He had dismissed it as an indication of the strong feelings he knew Andrew still held for his daughter; brotherly, protective feelings rather than the teenage infatuation they'd shared. They had apparently made up a few weeks later.

But beneath his daughter's mostly cheerful countenance there were major problems brewing. Caroline was having misgivings about the job and Gordon wasn't happy, or so she told Natalie McCamley over a coffee one afternoon. Apparently she'd phoned him while he was still overseas with Rene Rivkin and was a bit shocked by his negative response.

Caroline had also been speaking to Andrew, mostly by phone but occasionally over coffee and once even dinner. The conversations usually ended badly, mainly because Andrew couldn't hide his feelings about Gordon. He was a faggot, Andrew told her one day, to which she ended up slapping him and leaving. It didn't change Andrew's opinion and it was obvious she had her own doubts. Why else would she have made them both take two HIV tests?

It happened again towards the end of April when they met for dinner at the restaurant strip along Stanley Street in East Sydney. The conversation initially ranged across what was happening in their respective lives but eventually came back to Gordon and his relationship with Rene Rivkin. Was it sexual?

Before it degenerated again, Caroline's mobile phone rang. Andrew could hear a loud male voice but not the words. Caroline went white. Her reaction told him it was Gordon Wood.

'I've got to go, I've got to go,' she stammered apologetically.

Andrew tried to calm her down. 'What's wrong? Is that Gordon?'

Caroline was on her feet now, distressed. She didn't answer the question. 'Never mind, never mind. I've got to leave,' she said, walking out, her food half eaten.

One evening about a month later Caroline approached him at the gym where they were both members. Andrew had finished a training session and was riding a stationary bike to cool down. He heard his name being called and looked over to see his former girlfriend standing at the entrance. She needed to talk, she said, beckoning him over.

'No, you come here,' he shouted back indignantly.

She hesitated, then walked across and stood in front of him, placing her hand on top of his on the handle bars of the bike. She stood there looking at Andrew, tears forming in her eyes but saying nothing, just squeezing his hand.

Finally, she spoke: 'Something is troubling me. Can we talk?'

Andrew refused. 'No. Leave me alone.'

She was silent, squeezing his arm as if she didn't want to let him go. Eventually she gave up, released her grip, turned away and left the gym.

Andrew watched her go. He wanted to call her back but couldn't bring himself to do it.

It was the last time Andrew Blanchette would see Caroline alive.

If Caroline was still harbouring doubts about her boyfriend, they were not evident when Gordon arrived home just after 6 am on 27 May. Caroline rang her father from work after dropping Gordon at home to sleep off the jet lag.

'Daddy, Gordon's arrived home this morning. I'm so happy; it's wonderful to have him home.' She sounded relieved to Tony, as if she had been worried that he might not return at all. The next day Gordon took her shopping, lavishing her with $1000 worth of clothes for a job he apparently hadn't wanted her to take.

11

MODEL BEHAVIOUR

The evening of Wednesday 31 May would haunt Tony Byrne as much as any of the nights he'd have to endure in the years that followed. As he sought answers to the events that occurred Tony would think back on this night: how Caroline looked and acted, what they discussed and what might have been said, and if anything would have made a difference to the tragedy which unfolded over the next week.

He'd telephoned Caroline about 6 pm because he was worried about Peter, who hadn't been in contact since he left for China two weeks before. Caroline was at the modelling agency finishing a shoot and would come over afterwards for dinner.

She arrived fifteen minutes later. Tony gazed at his eldest daughter as she put her bag down and walked into the kitchen. She looked amazing, dressed impeccably as always—brown skirt and matching jacket—beautiful, like her mother. She was healthy and had a future.

There was something they needed to discuss: the family trust. The bank wanted Tony to update the signatures because the children, who were each directors, were now adults. Caroline signed in a flourish, without question.

Documents completed, they settled on small talk as Tony rumbled around the kitchen preparing the meal. How was she? Caroline sniffed. 'I'm okay except I've got a head cold and a bit of the flu. It's not too bad now but I had to take Demazin so I could go to work. But I haven't been able to go to the gym, and I'm missing it.'

Caroline turned the attention back on her father. 'Why are you worried about Peter, Daddy?'

'I'm not worried really. It's more that I'd expected he might have contacted me by now.'

Caroline laughed. 'China's not like Japan, Daddy. Peter can't just stop by the side of the road and make a phone call. I'm sure he's all right.'

Tony accepted the gentle chiding. The lack of contact said more about him than Peter. He needed the comfort of always being in touch with his kids.

The conversation drifted to Deanna who was teaching English in Japan and had written to her elder sister the week before, talking about the fun she was having and a new boyfriend. Caroline had just written back, talking about her own plans for the future. She had penned it a few days before Gordon had arrived home, sitting in the tiny flat whose purchase had caused so much angst and yet was the cornerstone of her future. The letter detailed some of the love-life problems of her close friends, like Natalie McCamley and Geraldine Howarth with whom she would confide her own problems outside the modelling agency a few days later when she found Geraldine weeping over boyfriend problems. 'I understand your dilemma,' Caroline told her. 'I'm having relationship troubles myself.' Geraldine looked at her friend. She had clearly been crying and looked frazzled which was unusual. Normally Caroline was so poised. 'Men can be a bit of a trouble, can't they?' she added as she covered her red eyes with a pair of sunglasses and walked away.

She missed Gordon but took advantage of his absence to let her hair down socially. She also gave what would turn out to be an important insight into her working life.

> Work has been fairly consistent. I went to Armidale and Tamworth from May 8–May 11 representing Dally's at career

> markets for country schools. At $250 a day, with all expenses paid, it definitely seemed worthwhile.
>
> Dally's have booked me for all their career markets which means I'll be travelling to all sorts of exciting venues and, yes, definitely appreciating Sydney on return.
>
> Modelling is quiet all-round so I'm very glad for the extra work at Dally's. With winter fashion so much more expensive this money doesn't go far.

The letter never made it to Tokyo. Instead, it was recovered by police from Gordon Wood, opened but still in its envelope. Tony and Deanna would not see it for another fourteen years.

Tony changed the subject again. He had a few niggling concerns for her, he said, like why she had suddenly stopped parking her car, as arranged, in the basement carpark at Windsor Plaza when she went to work at June Dally's.

'That's because Gordon needs the car,' she replied, chopping off the inquiry. 'When he can't give me a lift I get a taxi.'

Tony thought it sounded strange. Why did Gordon need a car when he had Rivkin's fleet of vehicles at his disposal? It sounded like an excuse.

He tried again as they settled down to eat. 'What are you doing over at the agency for a casting? You're working full-time at June Dally's. I thought you'd given up modelling.'

Caroline contemplated the question. It had been bothering her as well. 'I miss the modelling, and the extra money doesn't go astray.'

'But Caroline, you don't have to have two jobs. I'm behind you. I mean, you've just signed a document which gives you plenty of money.'

'You're right, Daddy, what do you think I should do?'

'It's obvious. You enjoy the modelling, and you only have a limited career so make the most of it. Why don't you go back to the casual arrangement at June Dally's which will give you time to do both.'

The conversation was interrupted by Caroline's mobile. It was Gordon. Caroline walked into the lounge room, away from her father and stood with her back turned. Tony couldn't hear the conversation. The call lasted less than a minute.

'Was that Gordon? Is he coming over for dinner?' Tony asked.

Caroline put her phone in her handbag and stood to leave. 'No, he's in a shitty mood. I'll have to go.'

She kissed him on the cheek and walked towards the door. 'Don't worry about Peter; I'm sure he's okay.' With that, she was gone.

There was a reason for Gordon's bad mood. Earlier that day, he and his boss had received notices from the Australian Securities Commission demanding they present themselves on Tuesday 6 June—Rivkin's 51st birthday—for questioning about the ownership of Offset Alpine. It was a notice they'd both expected but even the assurances from Rivkin—who was sure the ASC investigators had chosen his birthday on purpose—that they had nothing to worry about could not lessen the apprehension for his chauffeur. And it was clearly having an impact at home.

The frustration bubbled over one night at the gym. It was a slow night which was probably why Christine McVeigh, a manager and wife of one of the owners, noticed an argument as she tidied up a magazine rack. Gordon Wood, a man she knew by sight as a regular, was standing over his girlfriend who sat on a weight bench crying. It was a one-way conversation; an angry man berating a woman who said nothing. McVeigh couldn't make out what it was about but heard one phrase: 'You're a fucking idiot, Caroline.'

Another man stood alongside Wood. Gary Redding was a man she knew by reputation more than anything else—one of Rene Rivkin's henchmen, and someone to be avoided because of his alleged temper. His girlfriend, a striking young gym instructor named Ariane, also stood by watching, unwilling or unable to get involved.

Ariane, who would dispute McVeigh's account, would later tell police she regretted becoming involved with Redding. After fifteen months she'd had enough of his erratic ways, alternatively charming and fun-loving and then suddenly physically violent. According to some accounts, there was no pattern to what was evidently a bipolar disorder and she became particularly frightened one day when, without warning, he turned on her as they walked down a street and shoved her against a wall. She fled to Victoria.

12

'SOMETIMES I THINK HE WANTS TO KILL ME'

Kylie Watson was another troubled schoolgirl who had discovered a mentor and confidante in Caroline. They met as deportment teacher and student at June Dally's and became friends, exchanging phone calls and the occasional letter when Kylie was back home in Canberra, and going to the gym or shopping together when she was in town. Kylie stayed with Caroline on occasions when Gordon was away with his boss and went to the house warming in January where she met Caroline's agent, later signing a contract that would lead her into beauty pageantry and a brief television career including a role with the TV soap *Home and Away.*

It was late in the afternoon on Friday 2 June when Caroline bumped into Kylie in the laneway outside the June Dally office. Caroline had just got back from a careers day out at Narrabeen on the city's northern beaches and, from the younger woman's perspective, looked like shit—run-down and flat. Caroline shrugged it off as the pair rode the train to Kings Cross and sat down for a coffee at the Fountain Café, just across from Caroline's unit.

As usual Kylie poured out her troubles. It was a constant in their friendship and Caroline never seemed to mind, but today was different. Kylie kept catching her staring off into space as if preoccupied.

'Caroline, are you all right? You seem really flat.'

'I'm all right although I feel like shit. It's this flu and I can't get to the gym. And I didn't realise how tough this promotion would be.'

Kylie was not convinced. There was something amiss but she couldn't put her finger on it. Later that night she phoned her friend at home but got nowhere. Caroline seemed happy enough and was looking forward to the long weekend so Kylie thought no more about it.

A few hours before meeting Kylie, Caroline had phoned her father. She'd decided to take his advice about talking to the agency owner Gordon Donald to see what her modelling options might be. Was she kidding herself that she still had a career? Could she do both or did she have to make a choice?

'Daddy, his advice was exactly the same as yours,' she began, still sounding fluey. 'He told me not to close the door on my modelling career. I'm never going to be a top model—I know that—but he says he's got some good contracts for me doing things like Westfield parades and catalogues and some hand modelling. I can't do that if I'm working full-time.'

Tony was relieved. 'There's your answer Caroline. You know what you have to do.'

Caroline hung up. She wanted to resolve the issue with Carel Clifford, the general manager of June Dally's, before the end of the day if she could. When she telephoned, she discovered Carel had already left to pick up her youngster from preschool.

'I've got assignments next week so it'll have to wait until next Thursday,' she concluded.

Caroline worked the next day, Saturday 3 June. During the day she telephoned a couple of friends, including Narelle Cook, to get some advice. Despite telling her father that she'd made up her mind to go back to working casually at June Dally's it seemed Caroline remained undecided, or perhaps she just needed confirmation from her old school friend.

The conversation was brief and unfulfilling, at least for Narelle. It was like much of their contact nowadays—fleeting and almost always by telephone. The pair, once inseparable, now rarely saw each other since Caroline had got back together with Gordon.

The truth was that Narelle hadn't liked Gordon from the moment Caroline pointed him out in the gym. There was something unnerving about him; a fakeness or insincerity, like the day they met when he declared, 'Hi, I'm Gordon; I feel like I've known you forever.'

She couldn't understand why Caroline was attracted to him. After all, there would be dozens of good-looking men falling over themselves wanting to date her. Why him? Perhaps it was the Rivkin connection and she'd been seduced by the promise of a fabulous lifestyle.

The strained relationship between the school friends had reached a low point when Narelle and her husband, Peter, had joined Caroline and Gordon and another couple in Blackheath for a disastrous weekend away.

Gordon started niggling at Narelle from the moment they arrived at the rented house; over-sugaring her coffee and pouring cooking fat over her breakfast, embarrassing her with sexual overtures and suggesting swapping partners and having orgies. He said it in front of Caroline, in such a way that Narelle couldn't tell if he was joking or trying to get a reaction. Whatever his motive, it effectively ended the weekend and Gordon and Caroline went home early.

As they left, Caroline told her, 'Don't worry, it'll be okay in the end.' But she knew it wouldn't because Gordon seemed intent on wrecking their friendship, as if he was threatened by it and wanted her to himself, free of outside influences. He was overly possessive.

In the months afterwards she and Caroline would talk by phone but only occasionally get together. Narelle could tell that Caroline was shielding things from her; worries or doubts that were once discussed openly were now waved away as not important or simply a no-go area. Gordon was rarely discussed and mostly in glowing terms.

On one of their meetings over coffee Narelle had been talking about the future and the prospect of turning 30 when Caroline interrupted.

'I'll never make it to 30 and I'll never have kids,' Caroline declared.

'What do you mean?' Narelle demanded, shocked by the statement.

'I'll tell you later,' Caroline replied quickly.

Narelle left feeling uneasy, as if Caroline was trapped.

Deanna Byrne was also perturbed but was in even less position than Narelle to help her sister. She had telephoned from Japan to share her excitement about a new job in Tokyo but she was also worried about her older sister, mainly because of a conversation they'd had a few days before she flew out of Sydney.

Deanna had given Caroline her keycard for safe-keeping while she was away. It served a double purpose because Deanna owed her older sister $300 and thought Caroline might want to withdraw the money when she needed it. Caroline wrote the PIN code in her Filofax diary.

They had been driving through Darlinghurst and had stopped at a set of traffic lights outside the line of cafés when Caroline confided that she and Gordon were fighting about their future. Gordon wanted to marry but Caroline was not ready for the commitment. She was too young and they had plenty of time. Deanna agreed. Besides, she had never quite trusted Gordon. There was something about him; he seemed secretive about his past, as if there was something to hide, and he also came across as over-confident and could be manipulative.

When Deanna telephoned on 3 June Caroline sounded as if she had a cold. The sisters chatted for a while but Caroline was tired and wanted to get off the phone. As they said their goodbyes, Caroline mentioned that she had replied to Deanna's letter and it should arrive any day. It never did.

Caroline was concealing fears far more serious than simple doubts about if and when to get married, and Deanna and Narelle were not the only ones with whom she had confided. Caroline had sought out Angelo Georgiou at the World of Fitness gym in April and the conversation put a much darker slant on the state of her relationship with Gordon. Gordon was possessive, jealous and sometimes suggested sexual liaisons—threesomes. She was unsure if Gordon was joking. Was he simply being outrageous for the fun of it or was he serious?

'Gordon has changed,' she told Angelo. 'We're arguing a lot. Sometimes he gets physical. He is moody and then he apologises. I don't like what he is involved in. He is doing all these get-rich-quick deals to make money and he tells me to shut up when I try to talk to him about it. Sometimes I think he wants to kill me.' Angelo was taken aback by the comments.

He checked on her a week or so later when she came in one night around 8.30 pm. The gym was almost deserted and they stood at the reception desk, Angelo leaning casually on the counter and Caroline standing uneasily on the other side, gym bag in hand.

'So are things any better?' he asked, expecting her to brush off her previous anxiety. The answer stunned him.

'Angelo, things are not getting any better. He's under a lot of pressure. Sometimes I fear for my life with Gordon. I have to break this off and leave him. I have to do it cleanly because he gets in a lot of jealous fits.'

Angelo couldn't believe what he was hearing. 'You don't really mean it?'

'I don't know. I just get scared, not just because of the relationship but because I don't like the way he handles his business dealings. Sometimes he gets in these angry moods and it's not getting any better.'

Angelo listened as Caroline fearfully detailed how she was being stalked by Gordon. 'He gets really jealous and possessive.'

Angelo walked around the counter and put his arms around Caroline. 'If you feel that way then you must break it off,' he offered firmly.

'Thanks, Angelo. Thanks.' She walked out, forgetting that she'd come for a workout. It was the last time Angelo saw Caroline Byrne.

Brenda Wood could barely tolerate the woman her son wanted to make his wife. Caroline Byrne may have been young, beautiful and pleasant but as far as Gordon's mother was concerned, she lacked spirit and charisma. Worse still, according to a bitter statement Brenda would later give police, Caroline had no domestic abilities to speak of. She couldn't knit or arrange flowers, let alone cook—she didn't bring so much as a pot or a pan when she moved in with Gordon. He did all the housekeeping while she pranced around. And clothes? All she seemed to have in the wardrobe was black. Perhaps that's why the magazine jobs she got were all second-rate.

But her son saw something in this young woman. He chased the girl hard enough, smitten by her for some reason. It couldn't be the family, Brenda mused. They were the most dysfunctional lot she'd known and the father, Tony, didn't help because he seemed to do everything for them; he smothered them so they had no goals, nothing to strive for. The assessment ignored the fact that three had university degrees.

Not like her son Gordon, who once told her, 'Mum, Caroline had been someone's daughter, someone's boyfriend all her life and hadn't been her own individual.'

Despite her disdain, Brenda accepted what appeared to be the inevitable: that Gordon would marry Caroline Byrne someday. The family back home in Bath expected it sooner rather than later; their letters were filled with the hope of an announcement and an excuse for a trip to Sydney. Gordon had even picked out a spot in McKell Park at Darling Point where he wanted to have the ceremony. He was ready but Caroline was hesitating.

They had discussed it one night over dinner at Cherrybrook, even about having children. 'I want to marry Gordon but not yet. I'm not ready,' Caroline said.

Brenda wanted her son to be happy, so she replied, 'If you're sure then you should marry him.'

On the night of 3 June, Gordon and Caroline came for dinner to see Brenda's new home in Lancaster Street, Marsfield. Gordon's sister Michelle was also there. She'd moved in the day before, after selling the place at Cherrybrook. Brenda had helped finance the purchase by cashing in a parcel of 7000 Offset Alpine shares bought a year or so before on Gordon's advice. He, in turn, had got a tip from his boss. The shares had more than doubled, netting Brenda a tidy $10 000 profit.

Caroline's cold seemed bad. She was rugged up in a red jumper and new coat bought during a shopping spree the couple had been on the previous weekend. She hadn't eaten properly all week and looked and felt terrible. Still, she ate heartily as they chatted politely about her new job with June Dally-Watkins. Brenda could see the young woman was not happy, moaning about having to drive out to Parklea the next week for a two-day trade show.

After dinner Caroline curled up on the couch and dozed while Gordon, under directions, hung pictures. Brenda offered them a bed for the night but Caroline wanted to go home. Brenda was not sorry to see them go.

Tony was content. Peter was home safe. Tony'd picked up his son from the airport on Monday 5 June and now Caroline was on the phone wanting directions to Parklea where she'd been assigned for a two-day trade show on Tuesday and Wednesday, managing a stall at the exhibition. It was one of a number of course offerings aimed at senior high school students and there was a group of girls in their final year at Northmead High School who might be interested in some deportment and modelling classes. Despite her reticence about the job, it was obvious that Caroline enjoyed her work.

'Dally's have booked me into a motel but I'm not going to stay there if it's only an hour's drive. I'd rather be at home than a motel by myself at Blacktown or Kellyville somewhere.'

Tony didn't respond because it seemed like a sensible option. His elder daughter hated being alone at home, never mind in a strange place, and Gordon had just come back from London after a month away.

The conversation drifted back to her decision to go back to casual shifts on weekends, and give modelling another shot. The weekend had only confirmed her decision.

'I've got another four years and then I see my future at June Dally's. I'll tell Carel when I'm back in the office on Thursday.'

Tony repeated his reassurances that she was making the right decision. 'I'm glad it's resolved. As long as you're happy, Caroline, that's the main thing.'

She seemed placated. 'I know that I've done the right thing. Tell Pete I'm going to be busy the next two days. I'll see him on Wednesday night.'

'Okay. I'll see you Wednesday night for dinner here.'

'Okay, Daddy. Bye-bye.'

Tony didn't give it another thought as he put down the phone. It was a normal end to a normal conversation. Apart from a slight case of the flu, which had eased over the weekend, Caroline seemed back on track. She'd made a decision about work and could see her future, short-term and long-term. He had nothing to worry about.

13

DEPRESSION AND ACNE CREAM

The first time Caroline Byrne went to the Oxford Square Medical Centre in mid-1991 it was for a routine pap test. She chose the surgery because of its convenience as much as anything, as it was a few blocks up the road from her father's unit. There were four or five GPs with offices in the small, busy surgery which catered for a mix of nearby residents and city workers.

Caroline's patient record consisted of a yellow cardboard folder, marked neatly by secretarial hand with her name, date of birth and file number. The rest of the card was strewn with hastily scrawled notes by a variety of doctors; a jumble of abbreviations and staccato observations which made it difficult for anyone but the scrawler to understand. Once the card was filled with notes, a sheet of lined white paper would be stapled to the back for further notes; the longer the patient's history, the thicker the document. By June 1995, there were five sheets of white paper on Caroline Byrne's file, detailing irregular but steady visits over four years—tonsillitis, a prescription for the pill, the removal of a cyst, acne medication. There were a couple of HIV tests too—in January and October 1993. Both were negative.

Cindy Pan was the doctor who ordered the January test. It was the first time she had seen the rangy young model and they immediately struck up a rapport. From then on Caroline would see only the young Chinese-Australian GP, whose pleasant smile would later become well known on television and the cover of the bestselling book, *Pandora's Box*.

When Caroline walked into her consulting rooms in the late afternoon on 5 June, Cindy Pan was unsure exactly what Caroline wanted. Caroline had been to see her in May when they talked about another pap test. Now she was back, firstly to replace a lost referral to a dermatologist. The acne medication had caused a mild case of cloasma—subtle pigment changes on her face—which, given her profession, was of some concern. But there was something else, something much more pressing—Caroline believed she was depressed.

The conversation was stilted. Depression wasn't an easy thing to discuss. It was not a black and white issue; there were grades of severity and vastly different reasons for it. But Caroline couldn't—or wouldn't—pinpoint the reason she was feeling down, apart from its onset a month ago and noticing it was worsening in the past week.

Dr Pan knew that Gordon Wood had been away. 'Maybe it's because you were missing Gordon?' she offered tentatively.

Caroline dismissed the notion. 'No, that's not really it.'

'Is it your new job?'

'No. I can't really tell you why.'

There appeared to be a problem that had to be addressed, but how serious was this? As a doctor, Dr Pan needed to know if she was dealing with someone who might self-harm. As she later told police, there was a standard question she asked patients in these circumstances.

'Oh well, you know, you're feeling bad, have you ever felt so bad that you thought life wasn't worth living anymore?'

Caroline looked surprised at the question. 'No, no, nothing like that.'

Dr Pan looked closely at her patient. Seriously depressed people—those who might harm themselves—were more often than not disorganised and dishevelled, as if they didn't care about what they did or how they looked to others. Caroline was neither; she was sitting calmly in a chair—prim, makeup perfect, hair in place, wearing matching blue jeans and woollen vest. She was immaculately groomed and appeared to be perfectly functional, very together. If it wasn't for the subject matter she might even describe Caroline as serene.

Dr Pan decided to follow her instincts, particularly given Caroline's past problems. She'd noted it down on the sheet: *Same thing about three years ago. Saw psychiatrist, was on medication and help.*

'Well, we'll get you to see a psychiatrist.'

Caroline nodded. She needed to talk to someone, maybe get some medication to help her stabilise her moods. It had worked in 1992 after her mother died.

Dr Pan called the office of Macquarie Street psychiatrist Dr Richard Sippe. His secretary had good news. There was a vacancy the next day. 'They can get you in tomorrow. That okay?'

Caroline shook her head. 'Ah no, I've got to go to PLC at Croydon for work tomorrow. I can't miss it. Can they make another time?'

'Look,' Dr Pan persisted. 'If you're depressed you should get that under control first. I can always write a note for work . . .'

Caroline cut her off. 'No, no. It's really important. I have to do it. I'm the only one who can do it.'

The doctor relented. Caroline's insistence about work was another good indication that she was in control, though fragile. Whatever it was that had triggered her depression had not pushed her off the rails. 'Okay, how about the next day. There's an opening at 4.30 on the 7th. That means you can go to work and see Dr Sippe on your way home.'

It was done. Cindy Pan sat down to pen a note to the psychiatrist. It neatly encapsulated their conversation:

> Dear Dr Sippe,
> Many thanks for seeing 24y Caroline Byrne who is feeling very depressed recently for ~ 1/12 but much more for the

> past 1/52. She cannot understand why because nothing has actually happened to set it off that she can think of. She had the same thing ~ 3 years ago and saw a psychiatrist (? who) and had medication which helped her out of it. She has just started a new job doing sales for June Dally-Watkins. And she's not sure how she feels about it. She feels she can't do anything, can't sleep, can't express herself. No thoughts of self harm.
>
> Many thanks,
> Yours sincerely
> C Pan

She folded the note, sealed it in an envelope and handed it to Caroline Byrne who scribbled the time of the appointment on the envelope, thanked her doctor and left.

14

SHE WON'T BE IN TOMORROW

Rene Rivkin's 51st birthday was as memorable as his 50th, but for opposite reasons. In 1994 he had spent the night bragging to friends at his $400 000 party that he was not in jail and never would be. A year later—6 June 1995—Rivkin began the day contemplating just that possibility. Shortly after 10 am Rivkin sat down with his lawyers in a city office building to a face-off with three ASC investigators intent on extracting an admission from the businessman that he was the secret owner of Offset Alpine. The transcript of the interview was later tabled in a Federal Court hearing, giving some insight into Rivkin's confidence that his secret would never escape the walls of secrecy of the Swiss banking world, and his ability to lie.

He began flippantly, describing how he spent the first day in Zurich—'I met my bed'—and made phone calls the next morning to arrange lunch with his bankers and discuss the controversy about the printing company and the nine million shares held between them on behalf of some mystery client.

'I tried to convince them to release and issue the names of their customers or their clients as the best way to solve the whole problem,' he told them. It was a lie. Rivkin had been doing the opposite, trying to protect himself from discovery by the ASC, and prosecution.

Gordon Wood had been interviewed for 50 minutes before his boss but contributed little. He had been with Rivkin on the trip and was asked what he knew or saw. Nothing, he answered. He knew nothing about Swiss shares and saw nothing other than Rene meeting with his bankers for lunch. He was merely an assistant for his boss and had no role in his business affairs. 'I drive for him, I buy cigars for him, I keep him company, I make phone calls for him, I receive phone calls for him, organise his personal matters like insurance, that sort of thing.' And he always turned his back when Rivkin was on the phone.

It was in complete contrast to what he had been telling others about his role with Rivkin's affairs.

The interview then meandered across what appeared to be a trip of leisure rather than business, as if they were waiting for something to happen. He described days of waking late, eating and drinking in Zurich and then again in London.

Caroline was about to break for lunch by the time her boyfriend and his boss were finishing with the ASC. She'd left early, just after dawn, to make sure she got to Parklea on time. She had to set up among the 100 or so exhibitors expected for what was a careers day for upper school students. It was a bit of a travelling show really, from one part of Sydney to another as schools presented options for their students. She eventually settled next to Hany Mohamed, another sales rep running a stall for the Sydney Business and Travel Academy. Caroline had meet Hany, or Hank, as he was known by friends, at the Northern Beaches Careers Market at Narrabeen the previous Friday. He'd given Caroline a lift back to town in the afternoon because his office was in Market Street.

The morning at Parklea had passed quickly and Caroline and a couple of others nearby grabbed a quick lunch together for half an hour. Hank would later recall that Caroline appeared cheerful, chatting to a saleswoman from a rival modelling school before they returned to their stalls. He was still working when Caroline waved goodbye just after 2.30 pm, obviously intending to return the next day because she had left her stall in place.

Caroline had another appointment. She was expected at a 5 pm photographic shoot in Alexandria for a Woolworths Big W catalogue, and needed time to get back and change. It was another reason she'd decided not to stay in the motel room booked in her name.

The appointment had been set up by Gordon Donald as a way of confirming to her that she still had modelling opportunities. Caroline had appeared nervous on the phone when they'd spoken the previous week, as if her news about the full-time job was going to upset him or mean an end to their business relationship. Donald had assured her otherwise, even invited her to a lunch at a Double Bay restaurant where he was celebrating his partner's birthday. He knew June Dally well; they'd dealt with each other for years and always found a way to work around schedules for the girls. It wouldn't be a problem for Caroline either. If she had an offer for more consistent, substantial work, particularly at a place she knew well, then she should take it. Caroline seemed to accept the advice.

Caroline made a stop on the way back from Parklea. A receipt later found tucked into her wallet showed that she had stopped at the BP Food Plus service station on New South Head Road in Rose Bay. The slip of paper recorded that Caroline used her Westpac debit card to make a purchase for $6.25. Inquiries by police found later that she had bought a litre of milk and some groceries. The receipt also recorded the time—3.39 pm—giving Caroline plenty of time to take the goods home, put them in the fridge and get changed to make her appointment.

Carel Clifford often worked late into the evening. It was necessary if she was to keep on top of a diverse business, running modelling and deportment classes for 600 students and 25 teachers as well as managing a sales department to bring new customers through the door. Carel had more at stake than just her job as general manager of June Dally-Watkins Pty Ltd—it was her mother's business.

On Tuesday night, 6 June, Carel got home about 8.30 pm only to realise that there was no milk in the fridge. She would have to go out again. When she got home 20 minutes later there was a message on her answering machine. It was from Gordon Wood, telling her that Caroline Byrne was ill. She had to replay the stilted message several times to get its full gist:

> 'Carel, it's Gordon Wood—Caroline's boyfriend, umm, I'm not sure what the time is; I've just got a phone call from her doctor. She's been over there since she finished work and apparently she's undergoing some tests. She's pretty sick apparently. She hasn't got over this thing and the doctors, all they've told me so far is that she won't be working for a while which is a problem for you guys, umm, so because she's got all the stuff out at wherever this career show is so, umm, if you want to give me a call at home tonight until about 9.30 on 3681010. Failing that, I'll give you a call at work tomorrow to let you know exactly what the status is but, umm, it's not good at the moment so, umm, but I'm told not to worry, so don't worry, and I'll let you know more. Okay. So I'm sorry about that. Bye.'

The message was perplexing for a couple of reasons. Why hadn't Caroline herself called? And why was the message left on her home machine rather than work? It was as if the caller wanted to leave a message to avoid a conversation.

She'd only met Gordon a couple of times. He was constantly leaving phone messages for Caroline which was annoying because of the time it took the girls on the switchboard to deal with them; not once or twice but a series of them, when he must have known Caroline was taking classes.

Carel decided to call back straightaway. If Caroline was sick then she'd have to find some way to replace her at Parklea. Gordon answered. She was sick, he said, so sick in fact that he didn't know when she would be going back to work. Something about this worried Carel. She decided to take notes of the conversation as Gordon talked.

Caroline had driven to the surgery earlier in the day where they'd done a series of tests, he told her, adding that he'd taken a taxi to meet her there and drive her and her car home. They had arrived home at 8.30. Gordon didn't elaborate on what type of specialist she had seen or what she might be suffering from, only that there was a referral to another doctor the next day.

When she asked to speak to Caroline, Gordon insisted she had been given some medication by the doctor and was now sleeping and yet he made no mention of the flu from which she had clearly been suffering all week.

What was wrong with her? Gordon didn't know. What about the company's equipment? The TV and video player were in the boot of the car, Gordon assured her. The rest of the stuff was still out at Parklea where Caroline had left it.

Gordon promised to call Carel at 1 pm the next day to let her know about the tests.

Carel hung up. There wasn't much she could do about it. What struck her most was the way Gordon talked; he made it sound as if she was not coming back.

She thought back on the last few weeks since she offered Caroline a full-time job. It was an easy decision on the company's part because Caroline had already proved herself as Saturday school manager and doing the occasional career market. The students loved her. She was a real role model, punctual, clean-living, extremely loyal and very serious.

From a promotional perspective she was also important. There had been a lot of feedback from the casual work she had done. People tended to gravitate towards the tall, beautiful woman at the stall. Rival operators were jealous, quipping, 'Please don't employ any other people like that because no-one else at any of the stalls gets a look-in.'

Still, there was some hesitation about moving from casual to full-time. It was clear that Caroline still harboured her own ambitions in modelling and Carel warned her not to jump into a full-time job without considering the impact it might have on her other work. There was a certain amount of flexibility, of course, like late starts when she'd been working at a careers market in the evening, which sometimes happened.

She remembered Caroline's response; she was excited at the prospect that her boyfriend was coming home in a few days from an overseas trip: 'I really would like full-time work because I want to get furniture and make the apartment really nice,' she said.

Carel wanted to be sure. 'Look Caroline, why don't you think about it over the weekend. I don't want to put someone on and then find they want to leave.'

Caroline was back on the phone the next day. She didn't need the weekend to think about it, she wanted the job.

Gordon Wood didn't call at 1 pm the next day as promised but Carel was too busy to notice. So was Tony Byrne. It was just after 4 pm on Wednesday 7 June, and neither he nor Peter had heard from Caroline in almost 48 hours. Tony knew his daughter was busy at Parklea, but on reflection he wondered why she hadn't at least tried to call her brother who'd now been home for three days. Peter tried Caroline's home number and got the answering machine. His message was succinct. 'Hi Caz. It's Peter, how are you? I'm up at Dad's. Give me a call as soon as you get in.'

By 5.30 pm when they had still not heard from her Tony rang Caroline's mobile. There was no response. He tried again, twice, between 6.30 and 8 pm, as well as Gordon's mobile but they were both off. Tony also tried the home unit a couple of times but no-one was home. He didn't bother with a message, confused and a bit miffed that Caroline had not called to let him and Peter know she was not coming around. She must be out with Gordon, he thought, as he went to bed at 10 pm.

It would be a fitful night.

15

'IT LOOKS LIKE LEGS AND A BODY'

Norman Wano and Domenico 'Mick' Brunetta were pissed off. The brothers-in-law had driven halfway across Sydney, from Granville to Watsons Bay, to go rock fishing only to find a white Suzuki Vitara soft-top was in their usual spot. Bugger them, whoever they were. Why would anyone be parked in the laneway behind The Gap Tavern at 10.30 pm on a Wednesday when they could have pulled over anywhere on Military Road? Watsons Bay was almost empty, particularly on a cold, black night like this. Instead they had taken the only parking bay beneath a streetlight; the one place where Norm and Mick could set up their rigs for the night's target: the fighting kingfish.

The men parked their station wagon in the next bay and decided to prepare their lines by leaning the giant rods on the bonnet of the Suzuki. By the time they'd finished, it was going on 11 pm, and the fish beckoned. The men clambered up the embankment, pushing past the spindly ground cover and carefully negotiating the sagging wire fence erected to stop the daily parades of tourists from straying from the pathways. They set their lines from the southern end of The Gap, next to the rusted anchor of the clipper *Dunbar*, to counter the north-westerly wind that had started to pick up.

The weather was turning although Norm and Mick, rugged up in coats and hoods, didn't mind. It was a good night to be out. They chatted about nothing in particular. Both were idle at home during the day; Norm, 37, was unemployed and Mick, 41, was on sickness benefits. They were mates as much as related by marriage, and fishing was a useful occupation to fill in the boredom, though it didn't look like there were any fish tonight. The lines hung limp. Norm didn't care. He wasn't particularly interested in the fishing as much as the company and besides, he'd smoked a joint and was feeling pretty relaxed.

Norm reached for the thermos when the night's silence shattered. A harrowing scream cannoned across the water from the other side of the great chasm. On most nights they could see across to the cliffs as they curved up and out towards the heads of Sydney Harbour, but not tonight. He could barely see Mick a few metres away.

'Far out, what was that?' he said, looking up. From where he crouched, head down to pour a cup of tea, the scream had sounded faint; as if it had come from the cliff 150 metres to the north and higher from their position. Mick was standing, tending the rod. He had heard the sound clearly—freakish, he would later tell police. Still, he wasn't sure. It could have been a laugh. Sometimes you could hear some of the yobbos stumbling out of the pubs around this time of night. Some even came up to the cliff top and tried to jump the safety fence, daring each other on the crumbling edge. Pissed and stupid. This was different, though, as if someone was terrified, really scared. The fish—or lack of them—were forgotten for a moment as they listened for some confirmation. Nothing. Just the heaving ocean below and the sea wind fluffing across them.

The men went back to their lines. The night stilled again, and time passed. Thirty, maybe 60 minutes, when a man appeared. Mick heard him first; a bloke's voice in the darkness. He was calling out to a woman: 'Caroline, Caroline,' he was yelling.

Bloody hell. What a weird night. The man's face appeared from the pathway, a worried, agitated expression across his chiselled features.

'Did you see somebody?' he asked. 'Did you see this woman? She was blonde.'

Mick put down the rod. 'Sorry mate. There's no Caroline here. Haven't seen anyone.'

Norman chimed in. 'But we heard a scream a while ago; came from over there.'

The guy freaked. 'Oh no, she's done it, she's done it,' he said before disappearing into the ink.

It was 12.30 am when the phone rang in Tony Byrne's flat. Peter, still adjusting to the time zone, got out of bed to answer it, hoping the sound would not wake his dad in the second bedroom. It was Gordon, leaving a message. He sounded frantic. Peter lifted the receiver.

'Gordon, it's Peter. What's wrong?'

'It's Caroline. She's missing. I've found her car at The Gap.'

The words fell like ice, numbing. Gordon issued instructions: 'I'll be right over to pick you up.'

'Okay, Dad and I will wait downstairs,' Peter stammered, hanging up and stumbling into the bedroom to wake his father.

They rode the elevator down from the 8th floor. Tony could hear Peter telling him, 'Don't worry, everything will be fine. There will be an explanation.'

This wasn't a dream; it was a nightmare, but so real. There was Gordon, walking towards the front door as they reached the foyer. He was wearing light grey trousers and a dark jacket. Tony couldn't make out the colour of the shirt but there was a red pick-up truck at the kerb behind him, shining under the street-light. Hyde Park was a dark smudge beyond.

Gordon opened the passenger door and Tony slid through to the middle of the bench seat. By the time Peter got in next to him, Gordon was already in the driver's seat, the motor running impatiently. He took off, doing a U-turn and screeching left into College Street past the police headquarters and then right into William Street towards Kings Cross.

Tony found his voice. 'Gordon, what's going on? Peter tells me you've found Caroline's car at The Gap.'

Gordon's reply was high-pitched, alarmed: 'Yes, yes, yeah.'

This was no joke. Caroline was in trouble. They sat in silence as the truck sliced through the Darlinghurst nightlife and into Elizabeth Bay.

Tony tried again. 'What's happened? When did you last see her?'

'At lunchtime, at lunchtime when I came home. We were going out to lunch, out to lunch. I finished up getting my own lunch.'

'What do you mean? Caroline was supposed to be at Parklea today.'

'She didn't go to work today.'

'What! Why not?' Tony was confused. Gordon was acting strangely. None of this made sense.

Peter spoke up. 'Gordon, how did you know where to find Caroline?'

'I don't know. I don't know. I just had this feeling.'

Tony couldn't believe what he was hearing. 'What? You just had a feeling! What does that mean, Gordon?'

His reply made Tony's blood run cold. 'I love you. I love you. You're my father. I love you.'

Gordon kept looking either side, hands tapping on the steering wheel as they descended into the shopping strip at Double Bay where Rene Rivkin's office stood prominently. There were few other cars on New South Head Road as it roller-coastered along the foreshore of Sydney's mega-rich—Point Piper, Rose Bay and Vaucluse. They were almost there. Tony's voice hardened. 'Have you and Caroline had some sort of argument or disagreement? Why would my daughter be out at The Gap? It doesn't make sense.'

'No, no, no. Everything was fine, everything was normal. I came home at lunchtime, Caroline was in bed, I got my own lunch and went back to work. That was the last time I saw her.'

They arrived at The Gap. Caroline's car was not visible until Gordon swung sharply past a café. The familiar white Suzuki Vitara with the black top, rego RRO-066, was parked against the gutter, under the streetlight and covered in dew. It had obviously been there for some hours. Caroline was here, somewhere.

Gordon stopped the truck in front of the Suzuki. He walked to the driver's side, produced a single key from his pocket and unlocked the door. He reached down, picked up a brown leather wallet from the floor and thrust it at Peter.

'Here, Pete, here's Caroline's wallet. Take it. Open it up.'

Peter was taken aback but opened it anyway, seeing there was money inside before quickly handing it to his father. Tony flicked through the contents: Caroline's driver's licence, a few notes adding up to $60 or $70, a handful of coins and something else—a note. It was slightly larger than a business card, with a man's name and phone number scrawled on it. In stilted English it read:

> I will love to invite you for dinner
> Morrocans and couscous
> You look very nice and everythings
> I don't know what to say any more.
> My ph 3604481
> My name is Latif

Some man had spotted his daughter, perhaps as she sat in a café or restaurant, and was asking her out. Had she accepted or merely put the card in her wallet to avoid embarrassment? Tony turned it over. On the back Caroline had written the name of a woman, Jacinta, and a telephone number—maybe a reminder to call someone she met at work.

'What's this, what's this doing in Caroline's wallet?' he demanded, turning to Gordon who was watching intently from a couple of metres away. 'Oh, she gets those all the time; some guy wants to take her out,' he shot back without stepping forward to examine the note. It didn't immediately occur to Tony but he later wondered how Gordon could have known what was written on it unless he had already been through the wallet.

He handed the wallet to Gordon who opened it, took the paper currency—twenties, tens and fives—and shoved them in his own shirt pocket. He tossed the wallet back inside the car without checking anything else.

'Let's go and see if we can find Caroline and see what's happened,' he said, leading them up a steep incline of rough steps before plunging into a series of hedges that were head high. The trio stumbled their way through before emerging at the top. A rusted anchor hung from a wall plaque; a safety fence stopped them from getting closer to the cliff top. The sea swelled ominously beneath their feet although they could not see its rise and fall 30 metres below.

Tony noticed a man standing on the cliff side of the safety fence; he was heavily built, dressed in a large, hooded coat. Tony could barely make out the man's face beneath the hood, watching the three as they approached. Another man was sitting, legs dangling over the edge of the cliff, his back to Tony.

Tony asked the first man, 'Have you seen a blonde girl here tonight?'

Mick Brunetta shook his head. 'No, but we did hear a loud, high-pitched female voice a few hours ago.'

'Which direction?' The man pointed north then, noticing Gordon, added, 'I saw you here earlier.'

Gordon nodded. 'I was here about an hour ago.'

Tony, ignoring the observation, persisted. 'What was this sound? Can you describe it?'

Mick knew his answer delivered a terrible message. 'It was a loud, high-pitched laughter or screaming.'

Gordon interrupted. 'Can we borrow your torch?'

Mick handed it over, reluctantly. The bloke wasn't going to find anything with that. It was bloody hopeless; almost flat battery, barely enough for baiting lines let alone searching the cliff top for a missing girl.

Gordon shone the torch on the ground. The light was faint, flickering. Still, they had to try, setting off north along the pathway with Gordon in the lead. Tony tripped on the first set of steps. He couldn't see a thing, and his plaintive calls went unanswered. Gordon was silent until they reached the end of the path.

'There's an old house up ahead. Caroline knows this place, she might be there.'

The notion seemed ridiculous to Tony. Why would his daughter come here, alone, to this miserable cold black place? There was a building ahead, among the trees. They knocked on the doors and windows but it all seemed pointless, going through the motions and doing what Gordon wanted them to do.

They had stopped calling her name now but Tony tried once more as he stood on the cliff at the end of the track leading from the house. The wind blew straight into his face from an ocean he could not see.

'I'm going back to the truck. This is hopeless,' he shouted to Peter above the wind.

'Okay Dad, we'll keep looking,' replied Peter.

They watched Tony disappear back towards the carpark then kept walking north along the path for a short way before giving up. As they turned to head back, Gordon motioned Peter towards the cliff edge. 'Can you see that, Pete, it looks like it could be something.' Peter couldn't see anything in the blackness, not even an outline of the rock face he knew to be there, but Gordon insisted. 'Look again, Pete, it looks like legs and a body.' Peter still couldn't see anything.

Norm and Mick had been watching the faint light, bobbing and sweeping as the men searched. Now it turned back. Maybe they had found the girl. Two of the men reappeared. The older man was not with them. 'Did you find her?' Mick asked, knowing the answer by the look on their faces. 'No,' the taller man replied, returning the torch without further comment.

Tony had been waiting in the truck for fifteen minutes by the time Peter and Gordon returned. He had decided the worst must have happened. Caroline was dead, but how and why?

'I know we've lost Caroline, Pete. She's gone. Even if she is out there, injured, she could not survive this cold. We're wasting our time here, we have to tell the police.'

Gordon had another idea. 'There's one more place we can look. There's a little hole in the rock where you can climb through and sit on the edge. I used to go there and sit and watch the sun come up when I was at university. It was a place I could think. I showed Caroline when we came out here one day.'

He began to climb the stairs, heading this time to the southern end beyond where the fishermen had returned to their lines. Peter followed, until his father called them back. Gordon did not object, the hole in the rock—where he once watched Halley's Comet and where Caroline might be—now forgotten.

16

A LONG WAY OUT

Judy Weaver and Tracey Smit were on the graveyard shift. It was the sort of roster expected of a couple of police constables in their mid-twenties. Mundane work, particularly on a weeknight between 11 pm and 7.30 am; routine patrols mainly, circling darkened neighbourhoods between Woollahra and Bondi where few ventured outside and most good folk were asleep or watching TV behind drawn curtains. Still, they were expected to be vigilant and within easy reach of the station in case something major happened.

Just after 3 am on 8 June something did happen. The constables were called back to the station—there was a missing woman. When they got back, the duty sergeant Allan Gale had already taken the report from three men. The radio room was notified and help was on its way, maybe even a chopper when it got light. In the meantime the constables were to go with the men and start a search at the cliff tops around The Gap. They knew what that probably meant—a suicide, although a young woman was unusual.

The men in the foyer appeared edgy, raw. It was natural, given the circumstances—father, brother and boyfriend all expecting the worst. And things were starting to fall apart between them. The oldest man—the father—was beginning to have serious doubts about the manner of his daughter's disappearance. The taller man—the boyfriend—was defensive about his relationship with her.

While they'd been waiting Tony had again been questioning Gordon. Nothing made sense. 'Why didn't Caroline go to work today?'

'Because she'd been to see the doctors; she's depressed,' Gordon replied. 'She was supposed to go and see a psychiatrist today.'

The answer rocked Tony. It was the first he had heard of any suggestion that something was wrong with his daughter, apart from the flu from which she had told her father she was recovering.

'Depressed? What's she depressed about?'

'I don't know. I don't know what she's depressed about. Here, look at this. She's got a referral to a psychiatrist. Here it is, read it. Here's proof, she's taken her own life.'

Gordon offered the folded sheet he had produced from his pocket. Why hadn't he mentioned this before? Tony eyed the document, an A4 sheet with handwriting, but didn't take it. It would be conceding the point if he did. 'Gordon, I do not believe Caroline has taken her own life.'

At that moment, standing in the cold light of a temporary police station within a few hundred metres of The Gap, Tony Byrne was ready to accuse Gordon Wood of murder. He had enough reason, at least, to express concerns to police officers who automatically assumed they were dealing with a potential suicide. It may have altered the course of the subsequent debacle. Then again, it may not have made any difference.

But Tony kept his suspicions to himself, instead raising the prospect that his daughter may have been kidnapped. 'She could have met somebody else. There was a note in her wallet. I'm suspicious. Who's the guy? There's a number of things that could've happened. She could have been abducted, brought out here and murdered.'

Gordon scoffed at the suggestion. 'Oh rubbish, she wasn't seeing anybody else; that's rubbish. That couldn't have happened.'

Tony went cold. 'Gordon, you can think and say what you wish but I don't believe, for one minute, that Caroline has taken her own life. You were living with her; she was in your care so you handle everything. But in any statement to friends, family or police, I will be saying that I do not believe Caroline took her own life.'

The conversation was interrupted by the police officers walking into the room. Tony turned his attention to Sergeant Gale. 'I want this kept confidential. I don't want the details given to the media.' Sergeant Gale nodded. He understood, but they still had to find Caroline or, as everyone now expected, her body.

They drove back to The Gap, the police truck following behind with four officers. Even though he had a key, Gordon didn't say a word as he watched one of them break into the Vitara by tearing open the vinyl roof. The official police radio running sheet would later note that the discovery of the car was logged at 3.45 am. The police scoured the vehicle but there was nothing to indicate what might have happened or why Caroline was there. It was more pressing to find her, or her body. Tony and Peter stayed by the cars while Gordon led the police, armed with torches, up the embankment to the cliff top.

The search was fruitless. 'We can't see anything up there; it's too dark,' Constable Weaver exclaimed as she carefully descended the steps.

Tony erupted. He'd been dragged up to The Gap in the middle of the night by Gordon who'd tried to convince him that his daughter had killed herself. He'd withheld a note from a psychiatrist, and had clearly searched Caroline's car before they got there and removed her wallet. He'd had enough. 'This is pointless, Gordon, take me home.'

The trip back to the Connaught was silent until Gordon, in the disturbing high-pitched voice, repeated his earlier wail: 'I love you, you're my father, I love you.'

Tony couldn't believe what he was hearing. His daughter was obviously dead, and here was Gordon professing his love for him as a father.

'What has happened for Caroline to go off like this?'

Gordon's voice returned to normal. 'Nothing, nothing, everything was normal, everything was fine; we even had a bath together.'

Nothing more was said until they arrived back in the city when Gordon announced he was heading back out to Watsons Bay. Neither Tony nor Peter replied. There wouldn't be any sleep while they waited for what they expected would be devastating news.

Judy Weaver was cold and dirty. She'd spent half an hour on the cliff top between Jacob's Ladder at the southern end of the sweep to the top of the bluff 500 metres away where the concrete pathway disappears into the national park, even clambering over the safety fence to lie flat on the edge and shine her torch towards the rocks below. The police standard-issue Maglite with its adjustable beam, fully charged in the truck earlier that night, could not penetrate the darkness beyond a vague outline of the rocks. A sea mist made visibility next to impossible.

The size of the search party had grown steadily. Two police cars from nearby Waverley had arrived as well as the ambulance from Bondi which waited, expectantly. Three units from the police rescue squad had also been called and Helicopter Lifesaver 1 was on its way. The lights and noise would wake the neighbourhood.

Among the gathering army of searchers was Sergeant Mark Powderly. At 45 he was a veteran of cliff rescues, having been involved in 50 or so operations along the NSW coast including a dozen or more at The Gap. He knew the terrain but the conditions weren't going to make it easy.

Powderly ran a series of cables from the generator board on the truck down to the carpark below, hooked up a Mitralux light, and carefully positioned himself outside the safety fence and as close to the cliff top as possible. He judged it to be about halfway along the arc so he could search in a sweep in both directions without having to move. The search light was perfect for these sorts of situations, shaped like a bazooka and designed to focus through a series of optical lenses which, when shone at a distant object such as a cliff face, even 300 metres away, would maintain a bright, defined circle of light rather than dissipate like standard torches and the police Maglite.

Powderly had to move the narrow beam slowly, in a tight grid pattern working down the cliff to the base and then up again, gradually making his way around the arc of The Gap, like a house painter rolling paint on a wall. He was looking for any discolouration; something that would stand out against the bleached rock. A body could be anywhere along there. He'd found them at all points in the fourteen years since he joined the squad which was formed in the 1940s because of the number of people, driven by the destitution of war, hurling themselves from the rugged cliff tops.

Powderly carefully negotiated the beam past ledges, overhangs and caves around Jacob's Ladder and found nothing out of the ordinary. It was slow work. Now, as he worked northwards, the cliff face became much sheerer. It was less likely that a body had been caught on the face itself but he had to be careful about the change in colour at the base of the cliff. The prevailing south-westerly swells tended to push most of the water into that pocket which meant the rocks, worn by time and sea into grooved square slabs, had a lot more sea growth and tended to be dark brown or even black in colour.

Powderly was aware of people milling behind him and the noisy arrival of the police helicopter with its sweeping search light that, despite its power, also dissipated into the darkness and sea mist. It tended to light up a large area but it was almost impossible to pick any particular object against the bouncing shadows.

Powderly's search, by contrast, had picked up the white of a plastic bag, sagging and billowing in time with the sea as it washed up on the rocks. But there was little else that attracted his interest.

It was now 4.40 am. He'd been scanning the cliff for half an hour and had almost completed the entire area before he saw what he was looking for. but hoping not to find. He moved the light back over the area again to confirm what he thought he'd seen. The chopper was in the way now, its sweeping searchlight confusing his vision. It was hard enough seeing through the fine mist which was now clearly visible as the darkness slowly began to soften.

'Can you get them to back off a bit?' he called behind him to one of the support officers manning the electrical leads and ensuring they didn't get caught on the rocks and bushes. The radio conversation was brief and the pilot moved away. Powderly took a deep breath and blinked to clear his vision, then moved the light back over the same spot which, even from this distance, seemed a fair way out from the base to be a jumper. Yep, there was something out there. He couldn't make out what it was, so he'd have to move.

Gordon Wood had gone back to the Macleay Street flat after dropping off Tony and Peter. He later told police that he wanted to pick up a spare mobile phone battery, even though his phone had been switched off most of the day. He also wanted to check her wardrobe, insisting he knew her so well that he could tell what she was wearing by the clothes that were missing. While at the flat, he telephoned his mother and sister, Michelle, to tell them of Caroline's disappearance. They were both on their way, his mother driving from Marsfield and his sister from Erskineville.

When he arrived back at Watsons Bay the search was well underway. He stepped over a line of electrical cables to make his way back up the stairway to the pathway where the cops had set up. The two female constables were still there but it was clear that the experts had arrived. All attention was focused on one man with a long torchlight attached to the cables. It appeared that he had found something—Caroline.

Mark Powderly was shifting north, trying to get as close as possible to the point where he had seen what he could only describe as a discolouration. He picked a spot where The Gap starts to swing sharply towards the bluff at the far end, and clambered back over the safety fence. It was precarious, slippery from the mist and narrow. He had to keep hold of the safety fence to stop himself falling. He moved 20 metres or so north and called for the light which was handed to him over the fence. Then he started to sweep again, quickly picking up what he had previously seen.

It seemed to be a small white square—a shoe maybe. And there was something else; something cream and elongated, attached but at a right angle to the square. Powderly moved again, this time back a few metres to get a wider view. His beam was much more effective here. He could see that the discolouration was in fact a leg, protruding from what seemed to be a pair of black pants. The white shoes now stood out plainly. The rest of the body was wedged somehow in a giant crevice at the base of the cliff. As he paused the beam over his depressing discovery, Powderly was startled by a shout behind him.

'There she is; that's what she was wearing.' It was a male voice. Gordon Wood had followed the search and was standing behind the copper with the torch. Other police would report hearing the boyfriend, upset, making comments about knowing where she was even before anything had been found. All most could see, even now, was the outline of something.

Powderly turned off the torch and walked back to where the other police still gathered. The sensible thing was for him to go down alone, secure the body and prepare the lines for her to be hoisted back up the cliff in an hour or so when it got lighter. The others agreed. It was far too dangerous to send a team of people down there and still too dark to achieve anything.

As senior officer at the scene it seemed obvious that Powderly should go. While his team lit up the area as best they could, he abseiled carefully down the face and slowly picked his way across the slippery rocks to the body. At least the tide was out. It was a shocking scene but his training allowed Powderly to put aside what he could see in the shadows. The girl—Caroline—had landed headfirst in a crevice between a formation of three boulders, dominated by a large pyramid-shaped rock. The top half of her body was wedged in the rocks and the legs pointed absurdly towards the sky.

He checked the body. Rigor mortis had set in already, which meant she'd been down here for several hours. He ran his hand along the length of her legs to her hips to see if there was any indication of broken bones. There was nothing, not even a scratch on the black ski pants she was wearing.

He climbed down in between the rocks to see the rest of the body. He knew what he would find but he had to go through the motions anyway. It was important for the investigation that should follow. He was blocked from the south and east. As he climbed around to the north side a surge of water almost swept him from the rocks. It was dangerous down here. Now wet, he crouched down and looked up through a tunnel. He could see the dead woman's left arm and part of her head. Powderly got down on his hands and knees, prepared to crawl up the tunnel when another two sea surges soaked him. He backed out, afraid that if he got trapped there would be no way of communicating with those above peering down into the darkness.

He radioed for a torch; a Maglite would have to do because it was too precarious to send down the bigger light. Even then, standing opposite the body, he had trouble seeing through the mist as he cast around the area for any clues as to how she fell. There weren't any markings; anything like torn clothes or bits of skin, blood or body parts which might indicate that she had bounced into the crevice. It was doubtful anyway, he judged, considering the impact of being wedged so tightly into the crevice. It was as if she'd been slam-dunked in a basketball game.

He looked upwards, back towards the faces 30 metres above him. She was a bloody long way out from the cliff face for a jumper. He did a quick estimate—nine or ten metres, he'd reckon—a lot further than any of the other suicide victims he'd cleaned up over the years. One or two of them had finished maybe five or six metres out but most had been less than two metres, literally stepping off the top, and he couldn't remember anyone doing a swan dive. She must have had a long run-up, particularly into a headwind.

It was a lonely wait down on the rocks. By the time the litter to carry her body arrived he'd been there 45 minutes, dodging waves as they began washing back up the rocks and busying himself by searching the area so he didn't have to concentrate on Caroline's body. A young constable named Lisa Camwell joined him and, after bracing themselves against the rocks, they managed to remove Caroline, place her in a black morgue bag and lash her body to the litter before hauling themselves back up to the top.

Dawn was still half an hour away but the darkness had lifted. He could see the gathering crowd of onlookers. As Powderly unroped himself a tall man with sandy hair walked up to him. 'Thanks very much for going down there and getting her,' he said before moving away again. It was Gordon Wood.

He didn't think twice about the comment. It had been a frenetic few hours and these incidents were never easy, no matter how many times it happened. But despite his experience, or perhaps because of it, neither Powderly nor any of the other senior police officers at the scene that morning thought to do two important things—take a photograph of Caroline's body as she lay in the rocks, and call in the homicide squad.

17

THE LIES BEGIN

It was a despairing wait. Dropped back at the apartment by Gordon just after 3.30 am, it was too early for Tony to telephone the rest of the family and share the burden. And what would he tell them anyway? He didn't know if Caroline was alive or dead. Sleep was impossible so he and Peter sat silently in the lounge room, trying but failing to fully grasp what had just occurred.

It was 5 am when the phone finally rang. Peter answered. It was Gordon. Tony watched his son's reaction to the call, anxious to get some indication that his eldest daughter was safe. There was none. Peter listened and said something unintelligible before handing the phone to his father. Gordon's message was blunt.

'They've recovered Caroline's body.'

Tony stiffened. In a moment of tragedy he only felt anger. 'Well Gordon, like I told you earlier, Caroline was living with you so you can handle everything.'

He hung up and turned to Peter. He didn't feel like solace. He wanted answers. 'What did he tell you, Peter?'

His son had slumped into a chair. 'That the police had found Caroline's body and he'd been right about where she was when he thought he'd seen legs and a body.'

The answer took Tony by surprise. 'When was this? Was it after I went back to the car?'

Peter nodded. 'Yeah. We stayed up there and he told me he could see legs and a body on the rocks below.'

'Could you see anything?'

'No. It was black, and I've got good eyesight.'

Tony was confused. Another question. How could Gordon have claimed to see Caroline's body in the darkness and without any light, when it had taken police several hours to find her body? It didn't make any sense, none of it did. And his daughter was dead.

But this wasn't the time to unravel the events of the past few hours. There were people to inform. He picked up the phone to call Robert and Deanna and tell them the family had just suffered another shocking death.

Rene Rivkin studied the man at the table opposite him. Gordon Wood was dishevelled and nervous, although none of the small crowd at the Lamrock Café seemed to notice. It was still early morning. The traffic along Campbell Parade outside was thin but still made enough noise to muffle their conversation. Bondi Beach lay beyond, sprinkled with joggers.

Gordon was sobbing. That in itself wasn't unusual; he seemed to burst into tears at the slightest problem, but this was different. His girlfriend was dead and he was in trouble.

Rivkin noticed Gordon's message on his pager when he woke just after 3 am. *Ring urgently*, it read. It had been sent an hour earlier but he'd slept through the buzzing. The pager sat beside his bed but if he was tired it would be ignored until the next morning or until he woke during the night, which happened often.

Rivkin had tried to reach his chauffeur but Gordon's phone was off. He wondered what the problem could be before drifting back to sleep until 5.30. There were two more messages. He tried again; this time Gordon answered.

'She's dead,' was all he said when he realised who was on the phone.

Rivkin was taken aback. 'Who's dead, Gordon?'

'Caroline.' He was crying.

'What? Who killed her?' His reaction had been instinctive. If a young person died suddenly it was the first thing you would think.

Gordon ignored the question. 'Can we meet? I need to talk to you. What about the Lamrock?'

Now they sat there; Rivkin uncomfortable, not knowing what to do, and Gordon relating tearfully the events of the past few hours. It was a strange story. He didn't think he was sitting opposite a murderer, but there was something which didn't fit. Gordon insisted he wasn't with Caroline at the time but Rivkin suspected otherwise.

He considered the scenario: that they were on the cliff top arguing over something, Caroline threatens to jump but Gordon doesn't take the threat seriously. When she does he breaks down, as anyone would, but instead of telling police what happened, fearing he will be accused of murder he concocts some loony story, full of holes, to hide the truth.

He didn't put the theory to Gordon. As much as the guy infuriated him with his strange theatrics and jealousies, he liked him. Maybe it was his fragility or just the fact that Gordon needed him.

Gordon interrupted his thoughts. 'I'm not going to tell anyone she committed suicide. I've decided I'm going to say that she was killed in a car crash.'

Rivkin couldn't believe what he was hearing. Another lie. 'Why, what's the point?' he asked.

'Her father wants it that way; he doesn't want the stigma. I think it's because his wife also killed herself with a drug overdose a few years ago.'

'Look, Gordon. I understand what you're trying to do but the story won't stand up. You'll just end up looking like a fool, or something worse. What about the funeral?'

Gordon stared at him. 'There won't be one.'

'What do you mean? Everyone who dies has a funeral.'

Gordon was adamant. 'Tony doesn't want a funeral.'

Rivkin finished his cup of tea. It was time to leave. Gordon could do as he liked but this was getting weirder by the minute, and it was difficult not to be suspicious. Whatever the circumstances or cause, this girl deserved a decent funeral.

It wasn't the most pleasant way to start his shift but then death is so often the ugly lot of a police officer. Andrew Blanchette stood impatiently inside the Glebe Morgue. It was just after 8.30 am, still dark and cold outside as city workers made their way into the office along Parramatta Road. The front office—the admissions room where the bodies were taken when they arrived—was also chilly. There was no heating here. It added to the discomfort of being in such a place.

He was here only so his offsider could deliver a brief to the coroner's office in the same building. As he waited his mobile phone rang. It was another colleague, Stephen Duvall, who he'd known before they joined the force. But this was not a social call and Duvall struggled to talk. 'Andrew, you need to take a seat mate,' he stammered. 'Caroline's dead. She's been hit by a car.'

The words felt like hammer blows thudding into his head. He struggled to respond. 'I'm at the morgue, I'm at the morgue now. I don't believe it. I'll call you back.'

He hung up and grabbed the admissions book on the counter, a bland diary which allocated a page to each body brought in. The details were as cold as the bodies—name, personal details (if available), cause of death, description of injuries etc. He began flicking through the entries. There it was. He stopped, unable to believe the words on the page in front of him: *Jane Doe, possibly Caroline Byrne. Jumped off The Gap; believed to be suicide.* It went on to note there was no personal property found on the body and to detail the clothes she was wearing: *white jogging shoes, one pair of black tights, one white t-shirt, one blue sweatshirt and one blue denim jacket.*

Andrew gagged and almost collapsed. It couldn't be right, or at least not the Caroline Byrne he knew. After all, it was such a common name.

And suicide? It was too hard to comprehend. He approached a morgue attendant and asked him to check the body. He couldn't do it himself.

'I have to be certain, I have to be certain,' he kept repeating. There would be telltale marks on her body; the incision on her right knee where a cyst had been removed when she was a kid. A mole on the left-hand side of her shoulder and the scar from an infected mosquito bite she got on her left buttock when her parents went camping down at Sussex Inlet one year.

They could identify her in a moment but the attendant looked at him as if he was mad. Andrew gave up and staggered out of the morgue. He couldn't bring himself to see Caroline's body. The thought made him sick. He telephoned Tony Byrne in a panic, unable to say much before hanging up and driving in a daze towards the City Gym to see Stephen Duvall. None of this made sense. Caroline wanted to live, not die.

Later, as they stood on the footpath outside the gym, a white soft-topped Suzuki Vitara 4WD drove past, and slowed. Gordon Wood, dressed in a suede jacket, was at the wheel. He stopped and got out.

'Caroline's dead. She was hit by a car in the Cross last night,' Wood blurted.

Andrew's grief was replaced by instant rage. 'That's absolute bullshit. Why would you tell me that? She was found at The Gap.'

Wood was shocked. 'I've got to go. I've got to go,' he stammered, accelerating away, leaving Andrew clenching and unclenching his fists, amazed he had the control not to strangle the man he believed, from that moment, had thrown Caroline from The Gap hours before.

The phone hadn't stopped ringing in Tony's apartment. It was now 9 am and he was talking to a Constable Craig Woods down at Rose Bay Police Station who wanted to know about dental work so they could identify Caroline. Tony didn't even want to think about what that meant in terms of her injuries. It was far too horrible to contemplate. As he hung up the security buzzer in the kitchen went off. Gordon was downstairs and wanted to come up. He could hear Robert, who'd arrived with his sister, let him in.

Tony had mixed feelings about seeing Gordon. His behaviour had worried him and he had so many questions. They burst out almost as Gordon walked in, peppering him like angry shotgun pellets. Realising he was under siege, Gordon stood across the other side of the lounge room as if to create space between himself and the distressed father.

'What time did you get Peter's telephone message that he left for Caroline?' Tony demanded.

'When I got home at 6 pm.'

'Why didn't you ring me then?'

Gordon did not answer immediately. He did not look at Tony but at the ground. 'I was going to as soon as I watched the news, but I fell asleep.'

'Where did you think Caroline was?'

Gordon stopped again. He was not responding instinctively but deliberately, coolly. Neither was there a hint of emotion in his voice. 'I thought she was with you.'

Tony tried again. Why wasn't this man crying? Where was the hysteria of the night before?

'When you fell asleep you thought Caroline was with me. Where did you think she was when you woke up? Why didn't you ring then?'

Gordon was now staring towards the sliding doors and the view to Hyde Park beyond. He would not look at Tony. 'I knew something was wrong. I borrowed a friend's vehicle and drove past your place to see if I could see Caroline's car. When it wasn't there I went straight out to The Gap and found her car.'

Tony paused. His answer didn't make sense. If Caroline had been at his apartment last night she would have parked beneath the building, not on the street, particularly as the car had recently been broken into and the radio/cassette player stolen. And there was another aspect which bothered him.

'But Gordon, how did you know? How did you find Caroline's car?'

Gordon spread his hands. 'I don't know. I just had this feeling.'

The answer struck Tony as inane. This was getting worse, raising more questions when he should be grieving. He switched tack. 'Gordon, if there was anything wrong with Caroline why didn't you ring me?'

Gordon was pacing now, agitated at the questions and still unable to face the man he had proclaimed to be his father on the cliff tops a few hours before. 'There was no need to ring you. There was nothing wrong. Everything was fine, everything was normal.'

Tony persisted. How could he proclaim nothing was wrong when he had been so quick to declare that she'd committed suicide? 'Was there anything wrong with Caroline on Tuesday night?'

'No, no. Everything was fine, everything was normal. She rang me from Bellevue Hill and told me she was at a friend's house and would be home in ten minutes.' Gordon looked at Tony for the first time. 'Maybe she was out there that night.'

He moved towards Tony and sat on the armrest at the end of the couch with some confidence, as if he'd found an answer. Tony was unmoved.

'Gordon, tell me what on earth happened yesterday.'

Gordon sighed, exasperated by the continuing barrage. 'When I got up and left for work Caroline was still in bed. I came home about lunchtime and she was still in bed. I went out to the kitchen and made myself a sandwich. I then went back into the bedroom and Caroline was still half asleep. I spoke to her and she said "Okay, goodbye Gordy" and I then went back to work. When I came home from work at 6 pm she wasn't there.' He sat back, satisfied at his reconstruction.

It led Tony right back to his first question. 'Well where did you think she was?'

Gordon Wood frowned, clearly riled that his answers weren't being accepted. His voice rose to almost shouting. 'I thought she was with you, or with friends. She often does that.'

The phone rang, breaking the tension. It was the coroner's office. The voice on the other end of the line was emotionless, matter of fact; a call he'd make every day. 'Regarding your daughter. I've found some keys in her denim jacket. Do you want to come and pick them up or hold them here for you?'

Tony asked him to hold on. He repeated the message to Gordon who said nothing but got off the arm of the chair and walked to the window. Tony spoke to the caller, 'Look, just hold them there and someone will come and pick them up. Thanks.'

He hung up and looked at Gordon who was still staring out of the window, apparently deep in thought. Before Tony could say anything Gordon turned and, without looking at him, walked past Tony and out the door. 'I've got to go and get those keys,' he said, and was gone.

Brenda Wood had gone to bed around 10 pm the night before, tired after organising a farewell function for her boss. She was woken sometime between 2 and 4 am by a phone call from her son.

'She's dead.' Gordon was crying.

'Who's dead?' Brenda replied, struggling to make sense of the call.

'It's Caroline. It looks like she jumped off The Gap.'

The next few hours were a blur as she and her daughter, Michelle, first made their way to Watsons Bay to console Gordon while watching police recover Caroline Byrne's body. Thankfully, it was too dark to see anything below the cliff line beyond the vague outline of a body. Eventually, the trio went back to Rose Bay Police Station so Gordon could make a statement. While waiting, Gordon suddenly produced Caroline's handbag and began going through it. He retrieved a letter which Brenda scanned with her son. It was a referral to a psychologist from a GP.

The statement took about 30 minutes. When the police were satisfied the three left. Brenda followed Gordon, who for some reason was driving the red ute normally driven by George Freris, back to the city and he dropped off the car before she drove him and Michelle to the morgue. The silence inside the car was broken by a phone call on Gordon's mobile. He identified the caller as Tony Byrne. Brenda couldn't hear what he was saying but Gordon's reply seemed strange.

'But if I don't say Caroline committed suicide what am I going to tell them?' The question hung in the air as the conversation continued for a few minutes before Gordon hung up and announced: 'That was Tony. He doesn't want to tell anyone that Caroline committed suicide so we're going to say she was hit by a car.'

'Why do you have to say something like that?' she asked.

'That's what Tony wants to say.'

Michelle was equally perturbed. 'How can you say she was in an accident when the car isn't damaged?'

'Okay, we'll say she was run over then,' Gordon replied.

Michelle was sitting behind her brother and would later insist she recognised Tony's voice, having met him on at least a dozen occasions. In fact, Tony called her brother several times that morning, she would testify years later.

Telephone records would tell a different story however. Tony Byrne did not call Gordon several times that morning. In fact, he didn't telephone him at all. The conversation was concocted by Gordon Wood.

Brenda and Michelle waited outside the morgue while Gordon went in to identify the body. A woman attendant allowed him to go and sit with Caroline's body in another room. He returned a few minutes later and sat down between his mother and sister.

'Mum, I could see her hands but not her face because it was too badly damaged. I didn't want her hands, I wanted all of her,' he said.

After leaving the morgue Brenda and Michelle went to Gordon and Caroline's unit. Gordon had some things to take care of, including meeting with Rene Rivkin. The first thing they noticed was the white cockroach powder everywhere and the contents of the kitchen cabinets piled on the dining table. There was also a piece of paper on the floor inside the front door. It read simply: *C, if you get back before me, call me. G.*

They discussed changing the sheets on the bed but abandoned the idea. Exhausted, they sat down to wait for Gordon to return. The note was thrown into the bin.

Gordon had some unfinished business at the morgue. The efforts to see Caroline's body had been frustrating. As he told his mother, it wasn't enough just to touch her hand. He had initially approached two ambulance officers about to drive the body away from the scene who would tell police that Gordon walked up and asked them to wait. 'I want to say goodbye,' he had told them, asking that the men unzip the body bag.

'It would be better if you did that at the morgue, in a more private situation,' one of the officers had said. Wood had walked away without another word.

Morgue attendant Kenneth Nichols was by himself behind the counter in the early afternoon when a tall man walked in and identified himself as Caroline's boyfriend.

'What can I do for you?' Nichols asked.

The man looked at him. 'Do you mind if I look at her tits?'

Nichols later described his shock in a statement to police.

> I didn't know what to say. I have never had anyone ask me something as strange as this in my fifteen years in the funeral industry. I kept looking at him to see if he was dinkum, and he was. The request totally confused me. He was supposed to be the boyfriend of the deceased and I would've thought he would be in some sort of grief but he showed absolutely no emotion whatsoever. The only way I can describe the way he asked me the question was like a person, a stranger, asks me the time on the street.

Nichols said he had explained that a police officer or social worker had to be present during an examination. The man looked upset and raised his voice as he turned to leave. 'Well, don't worry about it, then.' Police would later claim the man was Gordon Wood. Gordon would insist it was Andrew Blanchette.

The day was going slowly. Tony could feel every minute drag as he tired, physically and emotionally. His family was around him but it was cold comfort. In truth, he would rather have been alone with his grief. To make matters worse, Gordon Wood was back and wanted to come up. It was now 3 pm and Tony had been awake since the early hours of the morning. Now he had to find the strength to face a man he was rapidly growing to despise. He greeted Gordon in the lounge room. This time both of them stood, as if holding their ground.

Gordon broke the silence. 'They've found receipts in Caroline's wallet which show she was out there that day; the Tuesday and the Wednesday.'

Tony knew what was coming. 'Gordon, you seem to be telling me Caroline has taken her own life; that she's killed herself and yet you also say that nothing was wrong. They can't both be right. I ask you again, if there was something wrong with Caroline then why didn't you call me?'

Gordon stared at him. 'It was her job; her job was getting her down.'

Tony couldn't believe the suggestion. 'Are you telling me that Caroline's killed herself over her job?'

'Yeah, she was depressed over her work.'

Tony thought back over his contact with Caroline the previous few days. 'Well Gordon, I spoke to her three times on Monday and Caroline indicated to me that she loved both her jobs but was missing modelling, and that it had all been resolved.'

The answer seemed to unsettle Gordon. He turned his back on Tony and walked slowly to the middle of the room. When he replied, his voice had dropped away, almost to a whisper. 'Caroline had not fully accepted and got over her mother's death.'

Gordon waited for the words to sink in, then reached into his pocket and pulled out a plastic pill bottle. Tipping half a dozen into his hand, he offered them to Tony.

'I'd better go. These are Mogadon sleeping tablets. They won't hurt you. My doctor gave them to me to help me sleep. Maybe they'll help.'

Tony didn't know how to respond but Gordon hadn't waited for a reply. He was gone, leaving Tony once again with more questions than answers. This time Gordon was trying to tell him that Caroline killed herself because she was depressed over her work, something he knew to be false. In the next breath, he was suggesting that the cause of her depression was Andrea's death, something he also knew was simply wrong. Gordon was covering up something.

18

HER SPIRIT LED ME

Sleep had been all but impossible for Tony. If he had drifted off it was only for a few minutes and he was neither aware nor refreshed from a moment of peace. Although the worst was yet to come, the first 24 hours had passed in a pit of blackness softened only by the shock of what had occurred. First his wife and now his eldest daughter. Andrea by her own, desperate hand and Caroline by the angry or careless hand of another. Accident or murder—for he could not contemplate the third alternative—the result was the same; his daughter was dead and his life would never be the same.

Then there was Gordon Wood. Tony was confused and angry about the behaviour of Caroline's boyfriend. There appeared to be little or no emotion, just a defensive arrogance. And he was back mid-morning to pick up Peter. They were going to talk to Dr Cindy Pan to decipher what might have happened. It was Gordon's idea, intent as he was to pursue the abhorrent notion that his girlfriend had killed herself and that the clues might lie in what she discussed with her GP the day before.

They were back an hour later without any answers. As she would later tell the coroner, Dr Pan did not believe Caroline was in such a desperate state of mind that she would kill herself. Even so, Gordon had something to tell Tony.

'I've been able to piece together Caroline's movements of yesterday afternoon,' he declared almost triumphantly.

Tony didn't respond so he continued, 'She would have got out of bed not long after I left her about 2.30 or so to go back to work. Then she would have got dressed, got the car and left. She's filled the car at a service station in Paddington and her ATM was used again at Vaucluse—like leaving a trail—and then she's gone to Watsons Bay for a while before taking her life.'

Tony didn't know what to say. Caroline had been dead barely a day and yet Gordon, far from distraught, was preoccupied with proving it was suicide. Tony had not seen him shed a single tear and yet he was even knitting together a story about the sequence of events. If he followed Gordon's train of thought, it meant Caroline was dead by early evening the day before, around the time Gordon had supposedly got home and watched TV instead of finding his missing girlfriend or calling the family.

Gordon could sense Tony's discomfort. He looked at his watch. 'Look, I've got to get back to work. Rene's keeping me very busy at the moment so I haven't got time to think about Caroline's death.'

He left as Peter walked into the room.

'Where's Gordon going?' Peter asked.

'Back to work. I don't know how he can do it. What happened at the doctor's surgery?'

Peter sat down. 'You won't believe what Gordon said on the way there.'

'What do you mean?' Tony replied.

'I told him we were still puzzled about how he knew that Caroline was at Watsons Bay; this feeling he mentioned.'

'What did he say?'

'He said—and these were his exact words—"Peter, it was Caroline's spirit that led me to The Gap. It was Caroline's spirit that led me to find her there".' He paused, watching the incredulous look on his father's face.

'Peter, you're not serious. What do you mean "her spirit"?'

'No, Dad, that's exactly what he told me.'

In other circumstances Tony Byrne might have been angry at what he had just heard but he was barely coping with the impact of Caroline's death and the need to make funeral arrangements. It would leave him floundering and yet here was Gordon Wood—the man who supposedly loved and wanted to marry his daughter—insisting that she was so desperately unhappy with her life with him, she had committed suicide but they were so connected spiritually that she led him to the place where she ended her life. Not only was this offensive, it defied logic.

Carel Clifford had been worried about Caroline. The boyfriend had not called, as promised, on Wednesday afternoon and there was no message on her answering machine. Surely the results of whatever tests she was doing were not that bad. Carel needed to know when Caroline was coming back so she could juggle the roster. By 11 am on Thursday, 8 June, she decided enough was enough and rang Caroline's home. Gordon Wood answered.

'How's Caroline?' Carel asked. There was an edge to her voice, warning him she would not be given the run-around.

'She won't be coming back.'

The answer caught her by surprise. 'Ever?'

Gordon was silent, as if confirming her question.

'Why?' she persisted.

'She was run over last night.'

Carel took a sharp breath. 'That's terrible; how is she?'

'If you believe in heaven and hell she is in heaven now.'

Carel screamed, almost dropping the phone. She couldn't speak, but Gordon hadn't finished. 'Don't tell anyone. Let them find out slowly,' he said before hanging up.

Gordon Wood had not heeded the advice of his boss, Rene Rivkin. In the coming days he would repeat the lie about Caroline's death to dozens of her friends as word spread. And the details kept changing, as if he was making the story palatable or believable to different people in different places. The inconsistencies would be laid bare in statements collected by police or in the witness box when the coroner finally acceded to Tony Byrne's insistence and held a hearing into the death more than two years later.

Gordon had different versions for Caroline's two best friends the day after she died. He told Narelle Cook in a telephone call that Caroline was hit by a car in Double Bay but a few hours later told Natalie McCamley that the accident happened in Bondi. Natalie had called her uncle, a senior officer at the Bondi police, only to be told there had not been such an accident in the last two days, although a woman's body had been found at the base of The Gap.

Caroline's modelling agent, Gordon Donald, thought Gordon Wood looked tired and distraught when he walked into his Double Bay office and relayed the news that his girlfriend had been hit by a car somewhere in Rose Bay as she went to visit friends in Bellevue Hill. Like the others, the shock of the news dampened any questions for details.

But her friends and workmates began calling the agency with their own versions of what happened and where it occurred. The story became muddied and Donald began to question what he had been told. Then Gordon telephoned Donald and confessed. He was embarrassed by the fact that she had committed suicide and just wanted to tell a story so he didn't have to face people who knew and loved her with the truth. And her family did not want people to know of the suicide, he insisted.

Tania Zaetta couldn't believe what she was being told. She considered herself close to Caroline even though they'd only known each other since earlier in the year when Tania moved to Sydney from Melbourne to pursue a modelling and television career. They even lived next door to one another and there was a running joke about being able to see into each other's lounge rooms. She'd had lunch with Caroline and another model pal Tali Blumenfeld on 5 June at a café in Double Bay. The conversation had been normal enough; relationships and work mainly, even arranging to meet on Tuesday night at Tania's to watch the US sitcom *Melrose Place*, as the trio often did. A girl's night. There was nothing untoward in Caroline's behaviour, other than having mixed feelings about taking the full-time job being offered by June Dally-Watkins. But the opportunity for a managerial position at her age was too good to refuse. She also mentioned that she and Gordon were 'having a moment', as she put it. In hindsight, it bothered Tania that Caroline did not telephone to cancel the *Melrose* night, as she was normally so organised and polite. It was very unlike her.

Caroline's cancellation of a modelling job was also perplexing. She had been due at a modelling assignment for Big W in a Waterloo studio which was delayed by one day, moved from the Tuesday to the Wednesday. The running sheet didn't give a reason but her name had been scrubbed and replaced with Tania's. There was a handwritten note scrawled at the bottom: *Caroline having difficulties. Can't make job at 4 pm. Can do 5 pm onwards.*

It didn't make sense for two reasons: few of the girls could afford to cancel a job that paid $150 an hour. It was their bread and butter to pose in pyjamas for a catalogue. And it wasn't like Caroline Byrne who was the most reliable of all the girls.

June Dally-Watkins had fielded calls for several days about Caroline's death. There were several versions of where and how she'd died but none of the police stations in the eastern suburbs could confirm that a young woman had been hit by a car or had died in a car accident on the night of 7 June. It was her youngest daughter Lisa, a television reporter with Channel 10, who found out the truth. She rang the morgue and asked if the body of a beautiful blonde girl, hit by a car, had been brought in. Yes, they did have a woman by that description although she hadn't been hit by a car but had been found at the bottom of The Gap.

Confused, June decided to speak to Gordon. She'd only met him a few times, a nodding acquaintance when he arrived on a rare occasion to pick up Caroline, and yet she felt obliged to warn him that she knew the truth, as others soon would, and it might be best if he started telling people what really happened.

Gordon's response shocked her. At first he acknowledged telling a lie but only because he was embarrassed and wanted to save Caroline's good name. She'd been depressed because she hated her job, he told her boss. Finally the stress had made her snap and she had taken her own life by jumping off The Gap. He was certain of it.

June challenged him. Caroline had only been in the job for one week and had happily told a friend over lunch about her future plans. She'd also left on her desk a report about her first week. 'She wrote that she was happy,' June told him.

Gordon was silent on the other end of the phone. 'Oh that, it was nothing,' he finally said. 'It didn't mean a thing because she told me she was lying.'

June would record the conversation a few weeks later in a diary of events she kept in the office, to keep pace with the changing events.

She tried Gordon again two days later but his mood had hardened further.

After repeating her hatred for the job, he claimed Caroline had been fighting a mental disease since birth. He had her supplementary medication to prove it. She had attempted suicide several times and the only time she was happy was when she was with him. If it hadn't happened now then maybe it would have happened after they'd got married and had a baby. And then the baby would have died too.

It was the last time June would speak to Gordon Wood. She didn't know what to do or think but his behaviour was scary. Could he have had something to do with Caroline's death?

Among the files on her treasured employee, June had found a copy of the entry form Caroline had filled out for the Miss Asia Pacific Quest nine months earlier. It seemed inconsequential at the time but had now taken on new meaning. The information, carefully printed into the prescribed boxes, was a snapshot of the person she would never see again. Her statistics, 5'10", 35 bust, 24 waist, 35 hips, told of her physical beauty and her favourites—colour (blue), food (vegetarian and seafood), sport (skiing), actor (Hugh Grant), actress (Meg Ryan), singer (Mariah Carey), song (*La Bohéme* duet 'O Soave Fanciulla'), author (Shakespeare) and film (*The Piano*)—told of a young woman with conventional if unadventurous tastes that might have developed given time and experience.

Under 'life's ambition' she had written: *To continue to have a positive impact with my teaching whilst fulfilling my personal ambition to be a wonderful wife and mother.*

On a second page, in a neat hand, she had written what she regarded as necessary supplementary information about her life and attitudes:

> I find it tremendously fulfilling being able to combine my interest in psychology . . . with my teaching at June Dally-Watkins and having such a positive effect on the students I teach. I am a very dedicated and strong believer in the benefits of exercise and nutrition for good health. I enjoy teaching this in my classes too. I have always been very self-motivated and disciplined (thanks to my parents' influence) so I exercise at least once per day and watch my food intake—not so much quantity but the quality. I am lucky to have grown up in a very close and loving family and having experienced the benefit of this. I am keen to have my own family—very high on my list of ambitions. Congruent to this I am very lucky to have met the most wonderful and loving man (who treats me like a goddess) with whom I can have this family and spend the rest of my life.

It was clear Caroline was besotted with Gordon Wood, and he with her. June wondered if that might have changed.

The next week would pass in a haze for Tony and his children. Deanna flew back from Japan on 10 June and went around to Caroline's flat the next day with Natalie McCamley to retrieve her sister's personal items. It was a frustrating experience, particularly when Gordon left her standing in the street while he stood talking to someone else. She was also surprised to find Caroline's watch in the apartment. It had been given to her by Andrew Blanchette and she never took it off. They left Gordon with her diary and work portfolio, the watch, a leather jacket, bathrobe and bottle of her favourite perfume, Lou Lou. They were the only things he wanted, he told them.

By the day of the funeral, 12 June, Tony decided he couldn't face the event. He'd done the same when Andrea was buried in a plot a few rows from where Caroline would be laid to rest. He hated funerals; couldn't stand the hypocrisy of post-death plaudits. Nice things should be said during life, not in hindsight. Robert, Peter and Deanna didn't question the decision. They would stay with their father while the service at the Field of Mars, Catholic Lawn Cemetery in Quarry Road, Ryde, would be attended by Tony's extended family only. She would have no headstone, not because of indifference or neglect but until her father decided he had done enough to bury her properly.

Gordon Wood was not told nor invited. He had made his own arrangements.

The next time Tony saw him was on Wednesday, 14 June. Deanna was returning to Tokyo the next morning and Robert suddenly suggested that Gordon might want to come over to say goodbye.

From the moment Gordon arrived Tony wished he hadn't allowed him back into his home. Gordon promptly informed the grieving family that he'd been riding a dune buggy with some friends. It was yet another jarring conversation, somehow inappropriate that he was off enjoying himself less than a week after Caroline's death. Then again, maybe he was being harsh. Gordon stayed for dinner. As he was about to leave, he walked up to Deanna and pulled out his wallet. 'Here's your card,' he said without explanation before walking out the door. It was the Westpac keycard she'd lent Caroline before she left for Japan.

It was the end of June before Tony talked to Gordon Wood again. In tidying up Caroline's affairs he needed details to wind up formalities with the Taxation Department but the conversation barely touched the reasons for his call. Tony had been stewing about Peter's strange conversation with Gordon the day they'd gone to see Cindy Pan.

'Gordon, Peter told me you said it was Caroline's spirit which led you to The Gap.'

Gordon didn't demur. 'Yeah. We had this telecommunication. She knew what I was doing and I knew what she was doing even though we were miles apart.'

'Gordon, I just find this bizarre. I wish you would have had this premonition at 6 pm on the day and returned Peter's phone call when you got it. We might have been able to save Caroline.'

Gordon's tone hardened. 'Nothing could have saved Caroline. She told me once that you had to rescue her from jumping off a roof of a city building.'

'What? I haven't the faintest idea what you're talking about. Why were you so keen to marry a girl who told you that she wanted to kill herself?'

Gordon was angry now. 'If we had got married, as we'd planned, and had children then she would have done this and taken the kids with her.'

He spat the words. The anger, even at the other end of the telephone, was palpable. Tony pulled back. 'Look, okay. That's enough. I'll speak to you later.'

A week later Gordon telephoned. There was no mention of their previous altercation and Gordon quickly came to the point. 'I haven't received Caroline's Westpac Bank statement. Do they come to you or me?'

It was a strange request but Tony answered. 'To me. Caroline never changed her address when she moved in with you.'

'When you receive it could you redirect it, unopened, to me?' It was more a demand than a request.

'Okay, Gordon.'

Tony had no intention of complying, if only because he needed the document for the Tax Office. He had another reason when the statement arrived in the mail a day or so later. Tony tore it open and read with growing disgust; in the days after her death the bastard had been systematically stripping his daughter's bank account.

The statement detailed Gordon's trail from one teller machine to another, starting the day he came over for dinner and bragged about going dune buggying. It showed he'd withdrawn $400 from a Handybank in Double Bay. He'd repeated it on the 15th, the 16th and the 17th, each time taking $400 from Handybanks in Kings Cross. There was another $100 on the 23rd and $50 on the 26th, then $10 for petrol at a service station in Woolloomooloo on the 26th. In total, he'd taken $1760 out of an account that had held $1782 on the day the woman he professed to love had died.

19

WHITEWASH

Four days after his girlfriend's death Gordon Wood gave a formal statement to the police at Rose Bay. With the details of the terrible night still fresh in his mind, Gordon signed each of the five pages and they were witnessed by Constable Craig Woods. Its brevity and litany of grammatical mistakes indicated an understandable desire to get the process over with as soon as possible, but in the years to come the contents would raise more questions than answers for those attempting to link the fragments of the peculiar riddle.

The early pages traversed his relationship with Caroline in the barest of details, pausing only to reveal a discussion in which she told him of having suicidal thoughts, including an incident in which she allegedly tried to jump from the roof of a city building before being stopped by her father—an event Tony Byrne would emphatically deny.

Gordon then set the scene for the tragic events of 7 June; how he had returned from a month overseas with Rene Rivkin to find his girlfriend 'not her usual self', something he put down to the combination of the flu and starting a new job she had doubts about keeping. The couple decided to take a week off and go away together. When they returned Caroline would quit. But their plan was never realised.

On the morning of 7 June Gordon Wood said he had gone to work and returned home at 1 pm for lunch, as planned, only to find Caroline still in bed and wanting to sleep. Given that she was not the sort of person to sleep during the day, Gordon became worried and checked the bathroom cabinet. Missing were 'five or six' Rohypnol tablets—a powerful sedative—which had been prescribed to help him sleep while travelling overseas. Gordon questioned a drowsy Caroline who told him she'd been taking a quarter tablet each night to help her sleep.

Gordon left the flat and went to Ditto's restaurant in Victoria Road, Darlinghurst, to meet two mates for lunch but was called to pick up Rivkin before he could eat. After attending to his boss, Gordon stopped at Bondi for lunch before going home around 4 pm. Caroline was gone so he went back to work. She had still not returned by 7 pm. Assuming she had gone to a doctor's appointment or to visit her father, Gordon settled down to watch the television news, and promptly fell asleep for the next five hours.

Paragraph 11 detailed the next critical events:

> I woke up at 12.40 am and Caroline was still not home which immediately concerned me as she always rings me to tell me where she is and I knew that something was wrong for her not to be home at such a late hour. I got dressed and wrote a note for Caroline telling her to ring the mobile if she got home before me. I then walked to the Kings Cross parking station where our car is always parked but it was not there so I walked to Crown Street to the carpark of one of our company cars and used that car as I normally do if I need a car. I then drove to Caroline's father's building to see if the car was there. It wasn't so I drove around Bondi looking for the car and then to Camp Cove because it was a place that we both go together. The car was not there so I drove back towards The Gap and drove down a lane next to The Gap and saw the car parked in the lane but Caroline was not in the car. I parked the car and ran around the cliffs calling out

to her and I spoke to a couple of fishermen who said that they hadn't seen anyone around.

Wood then described the dramatic cliff-top search and finding Caroline's body before summing up the woman he said he loved:

> Caroline was an extremely happy person always appearing to be enjoying life. We shared everything together and were very happy together. Caroline talked to me about her problems but never mentioned to me that she would harm herself in any way, nor did I believe that she would ever take her own life. We planned a family in the future and marriage and we talked about it often.'

Then a plea for privacy:

> I feel that an inquest into Caroline's death is not required as I don't want myself or the family to have to go through it. I accept the fact that Caroline took her own life and prefer that it not be a public matter.

Gordon's official interview with Craig Woods a month later was even shorter. It began at 1.14 pm on 10 July and was over just 37 minutes later. Contrary to Tony Byrne's growing alarm, it seemed there was little that Constable Woods thought required closer attention. He asked only 21 questions, of which Gordon answered 'yes' or 'no' to nine.

The remaining questions shed little further light, mostly providing details such as his address, occupation, the type and registration of his car as well as clarifying dates. Gordon also specified the time he spent at Ditto's and the friends he met—1.15 to 1.45 pm with two photographers, Nicolas Simartis and Brett Cochrane—and then fleshed out some details about his movements during the afternoon. In fact, he'd gone to the Alife restaurant in Stanley Street, East Sydney, to pick up Rene Rivkin's lunch partner rather than Rivkin himself. Gordon dropped the man at his office 'then drove through Darlinghurst looking for somewhere to eat my lunch because it was a sunny day. I ended up going to the Lamrock Café at Bondi for a burger.'

Although it was pertinent to do so, if only to confirm events and tidy up the investigation, Constable Woods did not ask him the identity of the man lunching with his boss. But he did ask one question that, eventually, would change events dramatically.

'I've been informed by two witnesses that Caroline was seen at Watsons Bay Park around the afternoon of Wednesday 7 June 1995 with two male persons one of which matches your description. What can you tell me about this?'

'Nothing other than I wasn't with her then,' Wood replied.

Constable Woods pressed him. 'Had you and Caroline been in the Watsons Bay area around that date?'

'No. We had been to The Gap for a Sunday walk once in our whole life together, probably a year ago.'

Constable Woods tried again. 'Had you been anywhere else in the Watsons Bay area recently?'

'We had been to Camp Cove in our first summer together, two or possibly three times, for picnics.'

And that was it. The police officer given the task of investigating Caroline Byrne's death had completed his line of questioning.

'Is there anything further you wish to say about this matter?' he asked.

'No,' replied Gordon Wood. With a bold signature left on each of the three pages, he walked out of the Rose Bay Police Station.

June 16, 1995 was a busy Friday lunchtime in The Gap Restaurant, perched by the side of Military Road as it curved into the entrance of Watsons Bay. The place had recently opened and neither Craig Martin nor Lance Melbourne, who owned the place as well as the Bad Dog Café across the road, had time to look closely at the photograph of a young blonde woman being shown to them by an equally stunning brunette. Apparently the blonde had jumped off The Gap a few nights before and her friend wanted to know if anyone had seen her in the hours beforehand. At first glance they hadn't.

Kylie Watson returned to the table where her parents and June Dally-Watkins sat. It had been a long shot on an emotional morning in which they had attended the first of two planned memorial services for Caroline Byrne. It was a formal event in the Marist Chapel at Circular Quay, in sharp contrast to the second, planned by her boyfriend for 21 June, which would be a secular ceremony, held outdoors in McKell Park at Darling Point with views of the Harbour Bridge to the west and Sydney Heads to the east. Caroline, according to Gordon Wood, was not religious.

Kylie had left the church in tears, wanting to know more about her friend's death. It didn't seem to ring true that she could kill herself. Maybe it was an accident. She'd convinced her father to drive to Watsons Bay and have a look themselves. Once atop The Gap with the powerful surf below, the brutality of Caroline's death struck home. They quickly retreated, finding refuge in the restaurant at the base of the steps.

It was only after they had sat down that Kylie pulled out a photograph of Caroline and showed it to the two men. Now, as they sipped their drinks, the men returned. On reflection, they had seen the girl. And she was with two men.

One was tall, fair and athletic-looking with a brown jacket. The other man was shorter, wearing a black leather jacket and his hair pulled back in a ponytail.

Six days later, at the McKell Park ceremony, June noticed a man in the small crowd fitting the description of the second man given by the two restaurateurs. She quietly drew Kylie's attention to the man. Kylie knew him. 'Don't be silly, Miss Dally. That's Adam, the booker at the agency.'

Adam Leigh was indeed Caroline's booking agent at the modelling agency. It was his handwriting on the booking sheet for the 5 June job with Big W, eventually taken by Tania Zaetta. And according to workmates, Leigh could have been at Watsons Bay that afternoon. After all, he frequently went missing during the day and was regarded as unreliable and sloppy by his colleagues, with a bad habit of deflecting criticism by blaming others. Equally, it was highly unusual for him to be in the office after hours which made it unlikely that he was in the office around 7 pm when two faxes confirming jobs were sent out in his name. But why would he be at Watsons Bay with Gordon Wood and Caroline?

On 9 July, the day before they were due to interview Gordon Wood, police arranged for Craig Martin and Lance Melbourne to make statements about what they had seen. Martin was certain it was around lunchtime as he crossed Military Road between the restaurant and café:

> I noticed a young blonde girl approximately 20 years old with long blonde hair and quite tall. She was wearing a blue denim jacket with light [coloured] tights, walking across Military Road in the company of two males. They were walking towards the path in Robertson Park; one of the guys was short and thin build with dark hair in his mid-twenties. He was wearing a black leather jacket that looked too big for him. He was of dark complexion. The other guy with the girl was tall; probably 6'2" or 6'3" tall, reddish or light-coloured hair cut short, of slight build, Australian appearance. He was wearing a dark jacket, anorak style. I saw the three walk down the path, through the park towards the Watsons Bay Hotel.

Melbourne's was much more detailed:

> I noticed a tall, attractive girl, blonde hair wearing a blue denim jacket which came to her hips and a pair of full-length tights standing on the top of the pathway at the entrance to Robertson Park. She was very striking in appearance. She looked like a model and I wondered what she was doing hanging around with the two guys. One I would describe as tall, slim build had medium-length fair hair and he was wearing a brown-coloured suede type of jacket. The other guy was short, and had dark long hair and was wearing black clothing and long black boots. They all appeared to be

laughing and enjoying themselves. They walked through the park down the pathway towards the restaurant.

Melbourne saw them again two hours later as they walked back up the path. He watched for a while as they dallied near the corner of Clovelly and Military roads. Later, around 6 pm, he noticed a white soft-top Suzuki parked opposite what he called the rear entrance to The Gap. There were no other cars in the street. The car was still there the next morning. He peered inside to see if it was stolen.

His wife, Sandra Munro, had also noticed the car. She had been crossing between the café and the restaurant and happened to see the white car in the laneway. She didn't pay it any attention at the time because it was lunchtime, about the same time her husband and Craig Martin were admiring the woman they would later identify as Caroline Byrne.

As evident in the statement he typed at his desk in Rose Bay Police Station on 12 July, two days after interviewing Gordon Wood, Constable Woods was 24 years old and green as grass.

The six-page document constituted his final report on the death of Caroline Byrne; an investigation he'd been given simply because he was on duty at 6.55 am (he'd noted the time) on 8 June when Sergeant Gale had telephoned with news 'that a body had been located at the base of the cliffs and it was believed that it was the body of Caroline Byrne'.

The robotic language of police seemed appropriate, given that the job of investigating a suspicious death must be dispassionate, objective, scrupulous and meticulous. Tony Byrne would argue that Constable Woods' investigation was none of these things. There were several reasons for this, in particular his inexperience and that the implicit suggestion in the order of a superior officer was that this was a simple matter—a suicide.

Constable Woods and his partner had been to the morgue and the Sydney Dental Hospital to get a copy of Caroline's records.

His inquiries over the next few weeks consisted of checking restaurants in Watsons Bay in case Caroline had booked for lunch that day, and noting the bank receipts found in her wallet which showed she had bought petrol in Paddington at 3.32 pm and withdrawn cash at Rose Bay at 3.37 pm.

He had taken a statement from Gordon Wood and had several telephone conversations with Tony Byrne, who was in a fragile psychological state and unwilling to cooperate with the young copper.

He had also spoken to Cindy Pan and confirmed Gordon's story that Caroline had been due to see a psychiatrist about depression, and taken short statements from Nicholas Simartis and Brett Cochrane who confirmed Gordon Wood was with them for 30 minutes or so at Ditto's that day. He'd also interviewed Martin and Melbourne but that was all.

Andrew Blanchette had offered to give a statement but one had not been taken. Neither had the constable been able to track down the two fishermen Wood had mentioned in his statement, nor had he spoken to Rene Rivkin or any of Caroline's family or friends.

Of Tony Byrne he wrote:

> I have had numerous conversations with the deceased's father. Mr Byrne refuses to supply me with a statement in relation to the matter and informed me that he did not wish to make a statement as he accepts the fact that his daughter took her life and requests that the matter [be put] to rest so he can deal with the matter in his own way. He informed me that he does not request an inquest in relation to the matter.

When he learned of the statement and its conclusions many months later, Tony would become furious. He remembered taking two phone calls from the young officer but was in no condition to participate. The weight of Caroline's death had enveloped him and he isolated himself from friends and family. He found it hard to speak to anyone without breaking down, let alone go through the process of a statement and interview with police.

He was vaguely aware that Gordon had given a statement and told police about not only Andrea's suicide but Caroline's own aborted attempt. The story was half right, he told Constable Woods without going into any details, adding that his daughter had everything to live for and could not have committed suicide. The officer's response was that families of suicide victims often felt that way about their loved ones.

The second phone call, made as he finalised the report, was more emphatic. Constable Woods told Tony he had checked out Gordon's lunchtime alibi and believed he was telling the truth. The statement astounded Tony because the issue was not where Gordon was at lunchtime but where he had been in the afternoon and evening. And he did not appear to have an alibi. The young officer would not be moved. The report would conclude that Caroline had committed suicide:

> I believe that the deceased was suffering from depression and that she could no longer cope with this and has attended The Gap sometime after 3.47 pm [on] 7/6/95 and has taken her own life.

And what of the alleged sighting of Caroline with two men in the hours before her death?

> The statements made by Lance Melbourne and Craig Martin show that the deceased was possibly with two males at Watsons Bay around the date of her death but this cannot be proved. The deceased's boyfriend Gordon Wood states that the deceased was at home around the time mentioned in Melbourne's and Martin's statements.

As far as the police were concerned the investigation into Caroline Byrne's death had been completed. There was only one safe conclusion—like her mother, Andrea, four years before, the young model had taken her own life.

20

A FATHER'S QUEST BEGINS

It was a small book, not much thicker than a pamphlet and offered free inside Buddhist temples as an introduction to its philosophies. *How to find peace and tranquillity*, it promised on the cover. Tony Byrne wasn't searching for a higher meaning as much as a way to escape his torment. The title attracted him and its contents became his saviour.

He had collapsed, physically and emotionally, in the week after Caroline's funeral, pushing away family and friends other than his remaining children and refusing to countenance the questions of a young police officer who seemed to Tony to be intent on accepting Gordon Wood's conclusions so he could wrap up his investigation. It was all too much.

For the first time in a life attentive to optimism Tony felt the grip of what might have appeared to some as depression. It was darkness certainly, although not the same hand which emptied the bottle of booze and pills down Andrea's throat or that was now being blamed for the shove that caused his Caroline to be shattered in a crevice of rocks at the base of The Gap.

This was grief, a feeling of such despair that you wish tomorrow would never come. To his dismay Tony did not push the feelings away but embraced them like a blanket, as a warm comfort to keep out the icy torment of losing a child. How could he possibly survive? Andrea's death was a loss mixed with anger and self-analysis but this was monstrous, unthinkable, unfathomable. There was no friend with whom he could lament, no place to be distracted, no time of day or night to forget, even for a moment. He tried getting away from Sydney, on fishing trips up to Harrington in the state's north with his brother John and son Peter. But the horror followed like a shadow.

The professional help he sought from the crisis centre at the old Darlinghurst police station was kind and able to explain, at least intellectually, the stages of the grieving process. He saw a psychiatrist a couple of times who could offer little remedy beyond time—and Valium which Tony took on and off for months—to heal the wound.

Then he found the book. It was his son Peter's idea really. Worried about his father, he had moved into the Connaught and suggested Tony try meditation and Buddhism. Tony had nothing to lose. He was searching for something he could not define and which his Catholicism could not provide. He and Peter found themselves searching across Sydney, even attending prayer meetings inside private homes. They began visiting temples outside the city, the Nan Tien near Wollongong and the Sunnataram Forest Monastery near Bundanoon in the Southern Highlands. It also gave them an excuse to get away from the city for a day.

Tony allowed himself to be ushered into a world he could never have contemplated visiting let alone embracing. He didn't delve into its philosophies but the meditation was a tool and the book tangible. There was no immediate transformation but a slow climb from the pit, crafting a technique he would use for years when he felt alone and vulnerable or if he woke, trembling in a sweat in the middle of the night, to help him back to sleep.

Meditation may have been his sanctuary but it was the sting of injustice that now gave him a purpose, mending a lifetime of prudence and planning undone by greed and impulse. And, like the meditation book, words provided the tangible evidence.

On Friday 29 December 1995, the Federal Court approved the takeover of the Offset Alpine Printing Group by forcing the sale of almost 10 million shares—more than 38 per cent of the company—held by Swiss banks EBS Zurich AG and Bank Leumi le-Israel on behalf of secret investors. Most of the company had already been sold the previous month in a bidding war between two consortia during which the price boomed. Two weeks before the 1993 Christmas Eve fire, Offset Alpine shares stood at 65 cents each. They were now worth $2.72 each.

The media could not resist the link. There, grinning at Tony from the business pages of the *Sydney Morning Herald* on a Saturday morning of the worst year in his life was Rene Rivkin, cigar in hand, having made a paper profit of $8 million selling his own private shares in the company.

'To be honest with you, I don't know much about the printing business and I was always going to sell,' he had quipped to the reporter.

Behind the smile Rivkin knew that he stood to gain much more. He was one of the three secret shareholders of the Swiss bank shares. The Australian courts had not been able to force the banks to reveal that Rivkin, Graham Richardson and Trevor Kennedy were the ultimate beneficiaries of the shares which were now worth over $25 million. There were other windfall stories too. The television personality Ray Martin and his wife owned thousands of shares; prominent business people had prospered, even the Governor-General Bill Hayden. It seemed almost everyone knew there was a bargain to be had from the ashes of the printing presses.

Rivkin's grin was enough to send Tony into a spin. He had to do something about it, not for revenge but to find the truth for his daughter who lay in an unmarked grave and would do so until she got justice.

Five days later, on 3 January 1996, Tony began a quest that would dominate the next twelve years of his life. He started with the first of many letters, written in an explosion of thoughts, suppositions and events that had been bottled up inside him for six months.

The letter was addressed to the head of homicide, Detective Inspector Ian Kennedy, and pulled no punches, linking Caroline's death directly to the destruction of Offset Alpine and the subsequent sale of the company.

He went on for six pages, detailing snippets of conversations with Gordon Wood including his claims that the Offset Alpine fire was a 'set-up'. He discussed the farcical purchase of the Macleay Street flat, the fallout between Rivkin and Wood, their reconciliation and travel overseas. He wrote of Andrea's suicide and how the first flat Caroline had moved into with Wood was across the road from the pharmacy where her mother had bought the fatal drugs:

> If for some reason Caroline had wanted to end her life she would certainly, without a shadow of a doubt, have chosen the same method her mother used.

It then went on to detail the last week of her life and the contradictions in Wood's version of events. Questions peppered the ramble as he attempted to squeeze as many elements of the riddle as possible onto the pages.

> Why did he not return Peter's afternoon telephone call?
> How did he really know that Caroline was at Watsons Bay that night?
> Where were the diaries she kept so meticulously?
> Why is he lying?

Tony offered his own theory—his daughter was murdered by a hit man. In hindsight he would accept it was fanciful but not in his current desperation. Wood had taken Caroline to Watsons Bay for a waterfront lunch, he insisted. At some stage during the afternoon they had met a man at a prearranged time and place who was introduced by Wood as a business acquaintance but who was actually a contract killer. In the early evening, under the cover of darkness, she was knocked unconscious by one or both of them and thrown over the cliff.

The theory smacked of a man desperate to find an explanation, if only to deflect from the possibility that his daughter had died by her own hand. Although his thesis contained a number of reasonable suspicions, there were also several glaring inconsistencies which rendered the ultimate conclusion as improbable. Why, for example, would Gordon take a woman he intended to murder to lunch in broad daylight just 200 metres from the place at which he intended to kill her hours later? What if they were seen, which was highly likely in a major tourist spot?

Then there was motive. It had to be convincing and dire enough to pay a professional killer. Tony offered greed, that somehow Caroline threatened Wood's relationship with Rene Rivkin and his chance of wealth. Perhaps it was linked to what she'd been told by Wood about the Offset Alpine fire, the promised windfall bonuses or ownership of the disputed Potts Point flat. Whatever the secret, she paid with her life, he concluded.

Barry Blanchette, Andrew's father and a long-time friend of Tony's, delivered the letter to reinforce the message that police had given up too quickly. Ian Kennedy agreed. We've already got the brief, he told Blanchette. The coroner, Derrick Hand, also suspected foul play and wanted a new investigation and the snippets of conversations contained in Tony's letter would only heighten suspicion about Caroline's boyfriend.

Two officers, Detective Senior Constable Brian Wyver and Senior Constable Clem Scott, had been assigned to join the dots to see if they could reveal a murder plot. But, as Tony was to discover, old homicide investigations were not a priority when it came to police rostering. It would have to wait until after the summer staff shortages.

Tony couldn't wait. He hatched his own plan, printing 100 posters and sticking them up around the East Sydney haunts he knew Gordon Wood frequented. They had no picture, just bold black type which read: *In loving memory of Caroline Byrne betrayed by best friend 7 June 1995.*

Tony wanted to avoid an outright accusation but the words still conveyed a clear message and challenge to Gordon who would hear of the investigation soon enough. He posted him a copy to make sure.

Tony wanted to elicit a response that would tell him if Wood was involved in Caroline's death. An innocent man would telephone the father of his dead girlfriend and discuss the development, offer his support and help to find the truth. In the months since Caroline's death Gordon Wood had done none of these things. Neither had he heard from Gordon's mother, Brenda. There had been no visit, no phone call, no letter or even a card. There never would be. No response was a guilty response, he concluded.

There was still none a week later when Brian Wyver called to ask if he was responsible for the posters. Tony's admission only prompted a chuckle from Wyver who'd been down to City Gym to investigate after an acquaintance of Caroline's had seen them. One of the first people he'd seen at the gym was Gordon Wood who agreed to take police back to his flat where one of the posters was sitting on the dining table. Tony Byrne's message had been delivered.

21

I DIDN'T KILL HER

Newspapers rarely report suicides. It has long been an accepted principle that to do so would only encourage copycats. Dozens of people kill themselves on the city's train tracks each year, for example, disrupting the lives of the commuter masses and yet they are recorded as anonymous blips in on-time running statistics. There are exceptions of course, like the famous fallen whose personal demise makes irresistible reading or the domestic tragedy of murder-suicides, but in the main the demise of people such as Caroline Byrne pass unnoticed.

Tony was not going to let that happen, emerging from his grief to begin hammering police with his insistence that his daughter had not committed suicide but was murdered, probably by her boyfriend. And they were listening.

Finally, in the late afternoon of 28 May 1996, police sent out a notice inviting Sydney media 'to attend a re-enactment into the circumstances leading to the death of 24-year-old Caroline Byrne whose body was found at the base of The Gap in the early hours of June 8, 1995. Police hope the re-enactment may prompt witnesses to come forward . . .' The document, as innocuous as it was, would become a vital piece of evidence in the jigsaw puzzle of circumstances that would follow.

On the morning of the re-enactment the *Daily Telegraph* would publish the first of what would be hundreds of stories about the case. SUICIDE OR WORSE? PUZZLE OF MODEL'S DEATH STILL UNCLEAR, challenged the headline, under which the paper raised the obvious questions: Why would beautiful Sydney model Caroline Byrne want to take her own life?

The notorious Gap, so often the scene of grisly suicides, had become the focus of its first homicide squad investigation. In particular, detectives wanted to find two fishermen who'd told police on the night that they'd heard 'screaming or laughing'.

No-one had bothered to take statements or even names and addresses. Instead, Brian Wyver had been forced to spend several nights waiting beneath the sandstone walls of The Gap, hoping they would come back. Neither man had.

An inquisitive media throng turned up the next day to watch Mark Powderly, the rescue squad officer who had found Caroline, give a running commentary while Lisa Camwell, the constable who helped retrieve the body, was lowered down the cliff face and then clambered gingerly across the rocks to point out where Caroline's body had been found.

'Constable Camwell is now indicating the exact position where the body was found,' intoned Powderly formally, his back to the canyon as the cameras panned past him to focus on the tiny figure pointing with two hands among the slate-grey boulders at the bottom of the sheer drop. Gordon Wood, hair now shorn to a crew cut, was among the onlookers and clearly visible in the television footage carried on news bulletins that night.

In truth the investigation had been underway since March but there had been little progress, with only eleven statements taken over three months—from family, friends or work colleagues. Still it was a step forward from the effort a year earlier which hadn't even included people as obvious as Andrew Blanchette or June Dally-Watkins and her staff.

Although the coroner wanted an investigation it didn't mean police had the personnel or the time to reinvestigate an old case. The interim report of the Wood Royal Commission had been dumped like a bombshell in early February and the service was still reeling behind the scenes with news of a permanent Police

Corruption Commission to counter 'entrenched, systemic corruption' in the force. It was not a time of great public confidence in the NSW Police Force.

There was a flurry of activity in the days after the re-enactment. The fishermen, Norman Wano and Domenico Brunetta, saw the footage and came forward to confirm what they had seen and heard. Adam Baczynski and Cindy Pan also gave written statements. There were five more in June—two cops including Powderly, two friends—Narelle Cook and Natalie McCamley—and a city café owner who knew Caroline as 'pleasant and polite' and once witnessed an argument in the street between her and Andrew Blanchette which he thought might be significant. Craig Martin and Lance Melbourne each gave fresh statements which fleshed out in more detail what they had seen the year before.

But that was it. Other than a lengthy interview with Gordon Wood on 14 June, a psychiatric report commissioned to assess the likelihood of Caroline suiciding, and a forensic examination of three cars—the white Suzuki, the red utility driven by Gordon Wood to search for his girlfriend and the green Bentley used by Wood to pick up his boss—the second police investigation was over.

On 20 November Brian Wyver sat down in Bulli Police Station to type out his own assessment. It ran to only seven pages, indicating how frustrating the process had been and the many questions which remained unanswered. It wasn't a case of how many had been interviewed but how many had not been asked to make a statement. Rene Rivkin had sacked his chauffeur in February just as the investigation got underway and yet was not approached. Neither was Adam Leigh, the booker from Gordon Donald's agency, who appeared to fit the description of the third figure with Gordon Wood and Caroline at Watsons Bay that afternoon. Even so, Wyver believed he had enough to make a recommendation to the coroner. And it painted a very different picture to the conclusions reached by Craig Woods.

Caroline's friends had described her as *loyal, conscientious, serious but fun-loving and highly unlikely to take her own life*, he wrote. But their view of Gordon Wood was very different:

> They describe him as unusual. It would appear he was obsessed by Caroline Byrne and the view seems to be that even though he was living in a de-facto relationship with her he, in fact, stalked her.

As for suicide, the fourteen-page report of Dr Neil Schultz, the pyschiatrist who insisted that Tony Byrne had told him his daughter had taken her own life (Tony denied doing so), concluded her chances of jumping were low unless Gordon Wood's version of events was accepted.

And Wyver did not accept it.

> Gordon Wood appears to be the last person to see Ms Byrne alive. His version of events does not seem to be correct and is contradicted on a number of occasions. I believe that Wood has not been completely honest when speaking with police. I formed the opinion that he has not disclosed all that he knows about the last hours of the deceased's life.

A week after the first anniversary of Caroline Byrne's death, Wyver finally got around to interviewing Gordon Wood. There had been a number of conversations between them since the investigation was reopened but this was formal, taped and transcribed at the Strawberry Hills police centre. For two hours he canvassed Wood's version of his relationship with Caroline, the events leading up to her death, and what happened on the night itself. Wyver interrupted only to steer Wood's at times rambling discourse back on track. The transcript would indicate the random nature of Wood's thoughts, as if they still hadn't crystallised even a year after Caroline's death. On occasions he couldn't quite remember times and dates, critical details such as what he did after picking up his boss from lunch on the day of Caroline's death, or if he walked, ran or took a taxi to fetch a car and look for his girlfriend when he woke up to find her missing.

There was cluttered emotion mixed with clinical assessment, such as reliving the search along the cliff top, firstly with Tony and Peter Byrne and later with the police rescue team as his frustration grew about the way they scoured the cliff face with torches and a helicopter.

'I remember the helicopter flying up and down and, like, it was way away. I can remember thinking "that's ridiculous you're in the wrong area". They had these big torches that threw a square of light and I remember saying to one of the cops holding that, I said, "Have a look down there. I thought I saw something" where I thought I saw sneakers with Peter. And he shone the torch in the general direction and it lit up most of the rocks down there and I could see her legs and I said, "There, that's her down there", and he looked and somehow he didn't see it and he said, he said, "No, I can't see anything there" and he kept moving it away and I remember saying, "No, no, look back there. That's her there". And he shone the torch on her and then they could see her legs sticking up. And they radioed the helicopter . . .'

He went on, describing his mother and sister arriving, the trip to the morgue, meeting Rene Rivkin at the Lamrock Café, and then lying to friends about how Caroline had died.

Wyver changed direction, taking Wood more carefully through some aspects of his statement which appeared at odds with the reflections of others. What about the Rohypnol he found missing from his bathroom cabinet as Caroline lay in bed? There were five or six tablets in a foil given to him by Rivkin, he assured Wyver. Caroline, still half asleep, told him she'd been taking half a tablet each night to get to sleep.

But the post-mortem had revealed no Rohypnol in her bloodstream, challenged Wyver. She must have been lying, Wood countered.

And the story he told Peter Byrne as they walked to Cindy Pan's surgery the day after Caroline's death, about her spirit guiding him to Watsons Bay. Could he explain what he meant?

'This is gonna sound probably odd to you, Brian,' Wood began. 'I don't know what you believe in but I believe—I think there was some kind of spiritual communication to me that was occurring to me subliminally to go there, because if you think of that idea—if my, if my girlfriend has not come home and is missing she could've driven to Toowoomba for all I know but I look at her father's house, which is the logical place to look, Bondi, not a particularly logical place other than that's where we used to hang out, and Camp Cove/The Gap. So yeah, I'm—I mean, I've, I've sort of explained it as if there was some kind of spiritual communication.'

Wyver interrupted. 'Yeah, well Peter also said you said to him it was Caroline; "Caroline's spirit that told me where to find her" so . . .'

Wood chipped in, 'I think that, I believe that. I'd like to, I'd like to believe that's how I got to be there.'

And Rene Rivkin? They had parted ways in February, Wood conceded. It was Wood's decision to leave really, he said. What began in October 1993 as a springboard to financial security—'the deal was I wanted him to teach me about stock markets and trading and things and I wanted to learn more and more'—had unravelled after Caroline's death. 'I became pretty unhappy. I was unhappy, full stop. I was very depressed, full stop, but—just couldn't do it anymore.'

And how did Caroline get on with Rivkin?

'She was suspicious of him,' Wood offered.

'In what way?'

'Caroline had a lot of suspicions about him. The fact that he used to hang out with a whole stack of very suspicious people at the café which, I'm sure you've discovered, has a reputation for being a hangout for ex-drug-dealers.'

'You're talking about Joe's Café?' Wyver asked.

'Joe's Café, yeah. It doesn't have a good reputation. Some of Rene's closest cronies have certain criminal backgrounds, or are rumoured to have. And the fact that Rene has a high degree of interest in good-looking young men. So she certainly expressed concern about his intentions towards me.'

Wyver wondered how to handle the next question. 'Right. So are you aware of Rivkin being involved in an unusual sexual activity?'

'I, I don't—I've never seen anything exactly myself. I've heard all sorts of phenomenal rumours and I have heard first-hand from people that he has a—he plays a teasing role with them, with men, but whether he'd actually had sex with men or anything else other than normal heterosexual activity, I can't categorically say yes to.'

Wyver pressed on. 'Right. Have you ever been involved in a homosexual relationship yourself?'

Wood was emphatic. 'No.'

'Were you involved in any other sexual relationships while you were with Caroline?'

'No.'

Wyver went for the jugular. 'Now, I have been informed that on the day of Caroline's death she did not in fact attend work, but she made surveillance of you and in the course of this surveillance she caught you and Rene [Rivkin] having homosexual intercourse. What can you tell me about that?'

'Absolute lies,' Wood shot back.

Wyver asked the question, 'Okay, and then I have been informed that as a result of that an argument between her and you ensued. Is there anything . . .'

Wood interrupted him. 'No.'

Wyver persisted: '. . . and that you went to The Gap and you threw her over The Gap.'

Wood stood firm. 'No, that's not correct, not correct.'

The interview moved on, canvassing his stripping of Caroline's bank account and claims that she was genetically disposed to suicide. He defended his decision to end communication with Caroline's father because of the family's refusal to accept her death was suicide, instead offering 'different variations of what could've happened'. He could offer no explanation to claims by friends that Caroline kept a meticulous personal diary of her thoughts which had gone missing—although he conceded she'd kept a Filofax diary of her professional life which he'd read in the days after her death and which did contain notations of major events and 'uncharacteristic' references to songs by the legendary blues musician Miles Davis.

For some reason Wyver didn't bother pursuing the issue or asking for the diary, instead returning to her death. 'All right. Now were you involved in any way in the death of Caroline Byrne?'

'No.'

'Can you give me any reason why Caroline Byrne would take her life?'

Wood rambled. He hadn't considered she was a suicide risk but on reflection it may have been genetic because of her mother. Caroline's outward happiness was a way of disguising her depression which simply erupted at some point. A Professor Penny, whom he'd been to see, told him it was inevitable with such people. 'Not that it's any consolation, but she could've done it when we had two young kids or post-natal depression, something like that. He said it was inevitable.'

He'd also seen a clairvoyant who'd arranged a spiritual rescue because Caroline's spirit was still earthbound and needed to be freed to the spirit world.

'They did the session and the woman, who didn't know Caroline at all . . . or anything about her mother . . . said she saw her mother and everything and that she said Caroline had killed herself and really wanted to do it and she was really clear that she wanted to do it to be with her mother.'

'Right,' said Wyver, who'd listened without comment.

Wood continued. 'Now, again, I mean, I don't know whether I like to believe that because it sits well with me or whether that's the case but . . . if the question is do I believe she killed herself, the answer is yes.'

Gordon Wood was feeling the pinch. Losing his job with Rivkin had stung, not only for the loss of an income and the potential for riches but also for the loss of his home, as he was evicted from the flat he once hoped to own. In typical bravado he would tell friends that he was thriving outside the Rivkin world, running two or three times a week around Bondi, bodysurfing and training at the gym. He felt fantastic, he told Brett Cochrane in one letter:

> Of course earning a buck comes into that glossy portrayal of my life somewhere. Luckily for me I was not under a huge financial strain when I left Rene and wasn't under pressure to go out and work. I could probably scrape through the year without work but I've pretty much got straight down to earning. I was very tempted to cut loose for a while. I thought about going for a jaunt around the world but I thought 'no' that is what Bretty would do. That would be tempting but where would I be when I got back with no money and a mortgage to take care of, so I bought a computer for $5000 and began to trade the markets.
>
> I had no idea I had learned as much as I did until I put it to good use. I am doing pretty well. Earning more than I was when I was working with Rene plus I put together a company with two partners and we plan to manage people's funds in the futures markets. We've approached Rene to try and get him involved in a 25 per cent partnership and he has agreed. The only hitch is that he left for an overseas trip for three weeks before we got the paperwork signed so we have to hope he is still interested when he gets back. We can't progress until he signs the papers.

The police weren't interested in Wood's lifestyle when they recovered the letter but his comments about life inside the Rivkin camp and the reasons the businessman had got rid of him were intriguing:

> I hated what I was doing and having to put up with all the bullshit of the café and all those backstabbers, politicking and manoeuvring behind Rene. Rene himself is fine and I have an enormous amount of time and affection for him. It's

> the others I can't stand. Now that I am free of it all I can really say how it was for me. What freedom, what a load off my shoulders.
>
> I won't go into what brought on my departure but suffice to say I voiced my dissatisfaction with certain things and questioned the fulfilment or non-fulfilment of certain promises. The resolution that I came to was that I was unhappy and we were better off as friends. This is definitely so, and I would say that our relationship is much better now without the complication of boss and employee relationship.

The comments could be interpreted that Wood was complaining about Rivkin reneging on a promise to pay him a bonus for the success of the Offset Alpine deal.

22

A NEW BEGINNING

It was September 1997 and Tony was finally free of the Connaught. The inner-city real estate market had collapsed at the wrong time and it had taken almost two years to sell the apartment. Now he could find a new place away from the memories and wait for what he hoped would be justice.

It had been excruciating, trapped in a city he wanted to forget and forced to watch the slow, grinding process of officialdom at work. Letters to police were the only outlet for his frustrations, an uninhibited place where he could vent his feelings and observations without interruption or contradiction. Some were typed, others handwritten as he replayed the events and nuances of conversations in the weeks and days leading up to Caroline's death. He wrote to the state coroner, Derrick Hand, complaining about what he was being told would occur and what was actually happening. Hand seemed to understand the frustration of a grieving parent when he wrote back.

> I wish to assure you . . . that the death of your daughter will be thoroughly investigated and all evidence relevant to your daughter's death will be placed before me at the inquest hearing.

Tony had been buoyed when Brian Wyver told him that Hand did not flinch when told that police believed Gordon Wood had murdered Caroline. He'd come to the same conclusion, Hand replied, adding that Rene Rivkin's business and personal life may have been a motive for Caroline's death. A few years later when publishing his memoirs Hand would go further.

> Generally, when someone suicides, you can find a reason. This didn't have the hallmarks of a classic suicide. It was just suspicious from the word go. There was more to it . . .

But things had continued to drag. The case was mentioned in July and Hand had set a hearing for September. Then it was delayed again until November. Tony was glad he had something else to concentrate on in the meantime.

Cronulla beckoned with a fresh start and a new name. Well, not really a new name. He'd decided to revert to his old business name—Bill Byrne—and hope that no-one recognised the link. There'd been a burst of publicity about the case when the investigation was launched but that was sixteen months ago and, he hoped, largely forgotten. There would be more, he expected, when the inquest finally got underway.

He'd been drawn south to Cronulla because of family. Sisters Ruthie and Judy had lived in the Shire for years. He'd often take the kids there to the beach when they were growing up. It seemed an easier environment than living in the heart of the city. He was still close enough to work a few days a week at Windsor Plaza but far enough away the rest of the time to find something new to occupy his mind. It wasn't that he wanted to escape the case—that would feel like he was abandoning Caroline—but he desperately needed a diversion.

Join the bowling club, his brother John suggested, waving away Tony's protests that he'd never played the game. That's not the point; it's about meeting people, new people.

Eventually Tony succumbed. He walked into the Cronulla Bowling and Recreation Club one afternoon and was directed downstairs beneath the restaurant bar and poker machines to the clubrooms and the pleasant strip of green.

'Have you ever played before?' a member taking bookings asked. The question conveyed how new people commonly came to the game around the same age.

'No, never.'

'Well, someone will be in touch soon. We can't just let you loose on the greens.' Two days later, as promised, he got the call.

John had been right. Tony suddenly understood something which had been missing for years—a life outside work and family. The years on the farm, as glorious as they were, had been insulated from the outside world where he either drove a truck or a bus or tended horses. In between he had watched the kids grow up. There was no time for anything else. They went north to the family holiday home at Harrington but that was it. Life in the city had been the same. He'd had no time for interests beyond working and the occasional fishing trip. In Cronulla he was meeting other people with new and different lives and stories. Everyone went to dinner or bowls events or away for the weekend. It seemed like a new life.

And there was female company. It wasn't that Tony had shied away from women after Andrea's death, more that he wasn't interested in anything more than casual company and didn't want the demands that a relationship brought. If a woman got too close he fled.

But Val Clare was different. He'd first noticed her on an adjacent rink one weekend. She bowled for a neighbouring club and he asked one of his playing partners how to arrange a meeting. 'That's easy,' he replied. 'My wife and I are close friends with her and her late husband. We'll arrange it.'

It seemed like a repeat of his meeting with Andrea Jeffree 40 years earlier. This time he was not blown over by the carefree excitement of youth but a woman who made him feel at ease and secure. She was his type; neat as a pin and punctual. They were both comfortable financially and had few expectations other than enjoying the moment. It was hardly love at first sight but within six months he was considering buying a flat inside her building in another part of Cronulla.

'Please don't,' she asked. 'If you want to move into the building I'd rather you move in with me.'

Tony bought a flat in a nearby building.

Sydney was consumed by a mysterious death on Sunday 22 November 1997. Michael Hutchence, sexual king of rock'n'roll, had been found dead, naked and hanged with his own belt in his luxury suite at the Ritz Carlton Hotel in Double Bay. A maid found him after shoving open a blocked door to Room 524. She heard the body thud to the floor in a room which reeked of alcohol and cigarettes and had pills strewn across the carpet. The maid ran screaming down the corridor.

Was it death by misadventure—some auto-erotic sex game—or was it suicide? By the next morning most media outlets were favouring suicide and the probability that a man who appeared to have so much could be so depressed that he would end his life.

The parallels were not lost on the small group of family, friends, witnesses and media who assembled that morning at the Glebe Coroner's Court in Parramatta Road for the first day of the inquest into the death of Caroline Byrne. Two days were set aside but most expected it would take much longer. The key witness, Gordon Wood, was not even listed to appear.

It was not the only inquest to begin that morning. The media spotlight was on the inquiry next door into the Seaview air disaster in which nine people had died on their way to Lord Howe Island. The death of so many deserved the attention of the coroner so Derrick Hand had given the Byrne case to his deputy, John Abernethy.

Kylie Watson was the first witness. Other friends like Natalie McCamley and Narelle Cook would follow. Sergeant John Gibson, the officer assisting the coroner, quickly canvassed the parameters of Kylie's friendship with Caroline and the events leading up to her death. But he was more interested in Kylie's relationship with Gordon Wood in the months after her friend's death. She had telephoned Wood after Caroline's death, not only to see how he was faring but for her own solace. In the aftermath of the two memorial services she was looking for company and preferably someone who knew Caroline and understood how she was feeling.

They had agreed to meet at a café in Bondi where Gordon replayed the story of Caroline's disappearance and his desperate hunt in the middle of the night, including being drawn to Watsons Bay because he and Caroline had some degree of telepathic communication, like identical twins feeling each other's pain. She listened uneasily but stopped him when he began describing Caroline's injuries, as if he'd seen her at the morgue. There was no life in her because her personality had gone, he said. It was like a body with no air in it.

Kylie walked away unsure what to think. She agreed to keep contact because it made her feel safe. Sometimes they had a coffee and occasionally saw a movie. Then things began to change.

'He began coming onto me,' she told Gibson. 'He was very charming and I was very young and very vulnerable and I sort of didn't know how to take it at the time. I felt very guilty because Caroline was my friend and I didn't feel it was right so I just brushed it off as, you know, him maybe looking for comfort.'

Her statement to police in May 1996 had been more explicit. She recalled that one night he had given her Caroline's gold watch and invited her to stay when she moved permanently to Sydney from Canberra where she was still at high school.

'If you feel uncomfortable we can repaint the place so it doesn't remind you of Caroline,' he offered.

'Where will I sleep?' she asked, looking around the one-bedroom flat.

'With me,' he replied.

The compliments began soon afterwards; she had a cute arse, she was beautiful, he saw the seventeen-year-old as a sexy mature woman. Then he began writing letters, declaring his love. One was written from the snowfields barely two months after Caroline's death.

> On occasions these past few days I've missed Caroline, in my dreams or on a solitary chairlift ride but I have noticed

> in those moments an overwhelming sense of aloneness. Not just the loss of my mate but also the personal nature of my loss which cannot be reached by anyone, not completely. But these times are not too frequent nor too long. You are my frequent cure for this as your beautiful face pops into my thoughts. I think of you almost constantly; what you are doing, what you are feeling, what you're thinking of. I always hope you are happy. After our time together in Sydney I wish to have you close to me always. Canberra is so inconvenient. I think you have a good home and a lot of love from your mum and dad, so I guess that's okay if you know what I mean.

There was the occasional physical encounter, like the day he lifted her off the ground in a hug and rubbed his groin against her. His penis was erect.

'I want to make love to you now like a real man should,' he whispered.

'Not now,' she replied, loosening his grip.

There were also constant telephone calls, even during the day when she was at school. One day he phoned from the street in Kings Cross and told her people were staring at him because 'I have the biggest hard-on talking to you.'

Worse was the day in his flat when he brought out a copy of the magazine *Black and White* which featured photos of himself taken by Brett Cochrane. They were sitting side by side at a coffee table as he showed her shots of himself standing naked under a shower, water cascading over his shoulders.

'Is that really you?' she asked.

'Of course it is.'

Gordon closed the magazine and then showed her other photos which had not made the issue. One was a full-frontal shot with his penis erect. Kylie would later recall being embarrassed and overwhelmed, not knowing where to look or what to say. Gordon just watched her and smiled. Proud of himself. The confusion and embarrassment of betraying her friend became fear as his advances grew more persistent. Eventually, she stopped returning his calls.

Tony listened intently as Caroline's friends and colleagues told the same story. His daughter was not suicidal, in fact she was the opposite, relishing her life. A little confused perhaps about the future and whether to keep a full-time job, but certainly looking ahead rather than for an escape route.

There was a consistency in the recollections of Caroline's closest friends. Natalie and Narelle spoke of a young woman they knew as happy, conservative and in control. She had ups and downs like anyone else but nothing out of the ordinary. She had seemed secure about her relationship with Gordon Wood. By contrast he had seemed insecure; always checking up on her by phone, sometimes even calling friends like Natalie if he couldn't reach Caroline directly. Gordon had also unnerved Natalie by the way he had seemed to stalk Caroline, sometimes arriving unexpectedly while they were having coffee, and even watching from his car.

'He said to me that he used to like it if he saw her in a café,' she told Gibson. 'He'd drive in and sort of watch her for a while, watch what she did and while she was writing in her diary or she'd be on the phone and he'd sort of watch her.'

Gibson asked them all about the diary. If a diary existed, as claimed by her family, then it might be important in shedding some light on Caroline's state of mind in the days before her death. Wood had consistently denied that she kept a diary with personal observations but her friends insisted she was meticulous and carried it everywhere. Narelle had exchanged diaries with Caroline every Christmas since their teens and Natalie said all models kept diaries if only to keep track of their appointments and castings.

The testimony of Gordon Donald and workmates like June Dally-Watkins and Carel Clifford did not appear to offer any new answers to the mystery. No-one thought she was capable of suicide. Cindy Pan was categorical: 'I didn't think she was suicidal and she said as much. In fact, not only didn't she have thoughts of committing suicide but she didn't have thoughts of even harming herself.'

Norman Wano took the stand on the second morning. It was dark, windy and cold, he told Gibson. He had been out there on other occasions with his brother-in-law and had been able to see the other side of the chasm where Caroline had fallen. On many nights there had also been a steady stream of stragglers coming out of the pub across the park, yahooing and playing stupid games near the edge of the precipice. On more than one occasion the fishermen had warned the drunks about the dangers of skylarking and, thankfully, there had been no accidents. But on this night there was no-one about, no light to see by and no reason to be there if you were not a fisherman.

There was one admission he wanted to make to the court, just to clear his conscience. 'I've got to admit to the court I had a smoke of marijuana on the night, which I don't know if it's got anything to do with it but my thoughts still weren't impaired by it; what was going on.'

Sergeant Mark Powderly took the stand just before midday, quickly establishing his credentials as a specialist since 1982 and his involvement in more than 50 rescues and recoveries, including sixteen operations at The Gap.

Gibson wanted to know about the science of optical light and how, unlike the standard torches carried by police, let alone fishermen, the beam does not dissipate as it spreads out while being shined at an object some metres away. Even the light carried by the search helicopter had been useless against the darkness and the sea mist.

Painstakingly, Powderly took the court through his search methodology, tracing the cliff face as it changed along the arc of The Gap until he continually crossed a discolouration, which turned out to be Caroline Byrne's shoes.

Gibson posed the question: 'So would it be true to say that any suggestion that Caroline's shoes or legs could have been seen by using an ordinary torch . . .'

Powderly chopped him off: 'Not possible.'

'Not possible?'

'Not possible.' Powderly's response was unequivocal. 'Later on I had a torch brought down to me while I was waiting for equipment to be established up top and I had a torch sent down to me by rope and using one of the police Maglite torches and even down there, with the mist coming off the water, and I was at water level, it just disappeared into the mist itself, even at close range.'

'So you say even with a standard issue police torch . . .'

'Not effective, sir.'

'. . . you wouldn't expect to see?'

'Not on that night, sir.'

The point had been made. How could Gordon Wood have claimed to see Caroline's shoes and legs from the top of the cliff when police using the highest quality optical lens lights struggled to find her?

Gibson moved on. He wanted to know where Caroline landed and how she got there. 'Is it at all possible that Caroline had actually bounced when hitting the actual surface initially and then ended up in the position that you saw her in?'

Powderly had thought of it himself. Part of their training, he explained, was to treat all situations as crime scenes and to take note of detail that may need to be assessed by detectives because it was not physically possible to take everyone down to the base of a cliff in the middle of the night.

'I formed the opinion that she had gone into that crevice first landing,' he concluded. 'There were no other indications—things I examined were torn clothing, any body injuries that may have suggested bouncing off the rocks. There was no indication on other rocks. I formed the opinion that night.'

Gibson took him to a police video made for the re-enactment on 26 May 1996. How far from the cliff edge was she found?

'It was a bit difficult to correctly measure but . . . approximately nine to ten metres.'

And was it possible to judge the point from which she fell, jumped or was thrown?

'Yes. I formed the opinion that she had come from a corner point at the top of the cliffs at the northern end of The Gap as it starts to break away to head around towards The Gap bluff.'

The obvious question beckoned: 'Going back to the previous evidence of the distance of nine metres out from the top of the cliff, is there anything unusual about the distance as far as you're concerned?'

The question had bothered Powderly for more than two years. He answered carefully. 'My opinion is that it's a long way out. We found it a little bit hard to conceive that somebody with her light frame, and with an offshore breeze blowing in, could project some 30 feet out.'

'Without a decent run-up?' Gibson persisted.

'It'd want to be a good run-up, sir.'

23

THE CORONER

Craig Martin arrived at the Glebe Coroner's Court a few minutes before 10 am on 11 February 1998. He was running late, caught by the morning peak-hour traffic from Cronulla; particularly along the stretch at Brighton Le-Sands where the traffic tended to bunch into a giant parking lot.

Martin paused for a moment before getting out of the car, collecting his thoughts and replaying in his mind the phone call at home the night before. It was Brian Wyver, the cop on the Caroline Byrne case, reminding him that the coronial inquiry was resuming, just for the day, and he was wanted again; not to give evidence as he did the previous November, but to identify one of the men he had seen with Caroline at Watsons Bay that day. He had already identified the taller man who had been sitting in the court foyer on the first day of the hearing. Now Wyver wanted the second man. 'All I want you to do is look around and see if you can spot them. If you can't, that's fine.'

Martin hesitated. It wasn't that he was unwilling to cooperate, but it didn't seem the normal way they do these things. Didn't they have line-ups or something?

'Look, I know it's not perfect but this is a coronial inquiry, not a court. We just want to know the truth.'

'Is Lance going to do this?'

'Yes. He'll be there.'

'Okay. I'll come.'

Martin locked the car and walked towards the court. There were a few people hanging near the door, most of them smoking, and a couple of press photographers hovering, probably waiting for the Byrne family. He could see through the glass doors another knot of people in the foyer, maybe 30 or so. This shouldn't be too hard. He passed one man standing on the front steps by himself. Martin hesitated; the face was familiar. He walked up the steps and stopped to make sure. The bloke was on the phone, unaware he was being studied. No doubt about it, thought Martin. He had the same build and complexion. The clothes were different, a blue suit instead of black leather pants and boots, and his hair had changed, dramatically. It had been long, past shoulder length and, well, shiny in the sun when he saw the man with Caroline. Now it was short; cropped around the ears. In fact, it looked like he'd just had it cut. Martin walked inside. He didn't need to look anymore. He sought out Wyver and told him.

Tony Byrne watched as Wyver sent Lance Melbourne out into the waiting area. It was crowded now as police, lawyers, families and friends milled impatiently, waiting for the doors to two courtrooms to open. There were two inquiries today; the other was investigating the shooting of French photographer Roni Levi on Bondi Beach. Both cases had caught the attention of the media.

Melbourne made his way through the crowd. He glanced at Gordon Wood, who was sitting with his sister, and Adam Leigh, who was alongside his mother, a prim-looking woman who had given Tony a half-smile as he walked in.

Wyver ushered Tony and Melbourne back into a corridor where they could talk.

'See that guy over there,' Melbourne said, pointing at Wood who was taking off his hat and sunglasses. 'He's the tall guy I saw, and that bloke over there [pointing at Leigh] is the smaller guy. He's changed his hair too but I recognise him.'

Tony's heart leapt as Wyver shuffled his two witnesses into a side interview office to take statements. He came back a few minutes later to say that the coroner, John Abernethy, wanted to see them before the hearing started. Tony followed him through the court, up behind the bench and into a corridor behind where the coroners each had an office. Abernethy dispensed with formalities.

'Tony, it looks like we've got these blokes, at least with a positive identification. I believe we should postpone the hearing,' he announced.

Tony was aghast. 'Why?'

'I think we should allow the police to go away and bug their premises; continue the investigation. Is that all right with you?'

Tony strove to grasp what was being suggested. He was on the cusp of an important victory, as least morally, for his family and they wanted to keep the identification a secret. He was swimming against the tide of a system he could not comprehend. How was justice being served if Gordon Wood escaped public damnation?

'No. I want this out in the open. I want them cross-examined and I want the media to report it.'

Abernethy nodded. 'Okay. We'll start in a few minutes.'

As he walked back to the waiting area Tony wondered if he had made the right decision. There was no reason why the police couldn't tap their phones afterwards. He went to tell the family.

Craig Martin's evidence lasted barely five minutes, long enough to confirm he had seen Leigh outside the court and had previously nominated Wood as the other man with Caroline in Robertson Park. Lance Melbourne's time in the dock was equally brief.

'Are you certain that those two fellows are the same two fellows you saw with the female on the day that you mentioned in your statement to police?' Gibson asked.

'Well, as certain as I can be. I mean I—I recognised them straightaway so no-one, sort of, pointed them out or—I was on my own when I saw one of them straightaway.'

That was it. Melbourne was not walked through his police statements or asked to recount what and who he saw on 7 June 1995. Caroline's name was not even mentioned. Tony was perplexed.

Surely more could have been made of the identification in open court. He wanted to hear the words for himself, for the reporters, for justice.

Adam Leigh took the stand shortly after 11.30 am, hunkering into his seat in a suit at least two sizes too big for his slight frame. Tony Byrne wondered if he might collapse in fright.

Gibson began: 'You've been seated in court this morning, true?'

Leigh nodded. 'True.'

'And you've been listening to the evidence that has been given by two witnesses thus far?' Leigh again nodded: 'That's correct.'

'Both of them told us that they saw you with Caroline Byrne and Gordon Wood at Watsons Bay, true?'

Leigh knew what was coming, and stalled. 'Well, they said they saw a dark person in evidence . . .'

Gibson cut him off: 'They, in fact, identified you as being the person who was present at Watsons Bay with Caroline Byrne and Gordon Wood.'

'Uh-huh.' Leigh relented, before switching his attention above as John Abernethy intervened.

'Just to make it clear, Mr Leigh; they gave—well you heard the evidence—they gave evidence of the dark person, they indicated to Detective Sergeant Wyver that you were the person they saw at—in the park at Watsons Bay about 1 o'clock and then a couple of hours later.'

As Gibson resumed, Leigh explained why he said in his police interview the year before that he had never been to Watsons Bay with either Caroline Byrne or Gordon Wood. Perhaps, he mused, he had been with Caroline at a dinner organised by a friend, but the timing was out. Neither could he think of a reason why Melbourne or Martin might have identified him other than he had lived a high-profile life and had worked in a number of cafés.

Gibson pressed home the point. 'He observed you and the other two at a distance of only five metres. He's not identified you as being a person that he's just seen simply at Watsons Bay. He's actually saying that you were there with Caroline and Gordon Wood.'

Leigh became defiant. 'Well, I know I've never been—well as far as I can remember—I've only spoken to Gordon Wood about half a dozen words, half a dozen times.'

Gibson's interest had been raised. 'And when were those times that you say you spoke with him?'

'Okay, they were at social functions when I'd see them out and just say hello to both of them. When I couldn't find Caroline for a modelling job and I had to ring and speak to—he was the last call on the database, so he'd be spoken to. At the funeral I saw him. Whenever he came into the agency he always went and saw my boss. He never really associated with me. And apart from that, from my recollection, I've never actually—I've never known him. I've never spoken to him personally about anything.'

Gibson had seen an inconsistency. 'That's a little different to what you told us in the interview [when] you said Gordon had come into the office on one occasion and that you'd seen him at the funeral.'

Leigh squirmed. 'Well, I've been trying to think now of all the possible exposure I might have had to them and I don't think I did say that in the original interview. I don't think I actually said . . .'

Abernethy, reading the interview transcript, interrupted. 'You said "I doubt I've ever spoken directly to him". Now you're saying "Well I would have half a dozen times".'

Leigh wasn't going to concede that he'd changed his story. 'No, well, I've spoken to him as far as my job, but personally I never engaged in a conversation with him. It was always when I rang him "Hi, how are you, where's Caroline, I can't find her".'

Gibson tried a different tack. 'You indicate in your statement that you have a tendency to wear dark clothing and that you possess a pair of long black boots, true?'

'Uh-huh.'

'Mr Melbourne suggested the person who fits your description—he picks you actually—was wearing dark clothing and long black boots. So it's much more than just seeing your face, isn't it?'

Leigh mulled over his situation. 'Well . . .'

'Think about it carefully,' Gibson continued. 'He said he saw your face and he describes the nature of your clothing.'

Leigh relented. 'I don't know if I was there or that I wasn't there. What I'm saying is I cannot remember ever associating with them. If I came across them and said "hi" to them it'd be no big deal to me and I wouldn't remember it. I thought that was strange that somebody would identify me in long dark boots because you would have to wear your boots over the top of your pants to identify them as long, wouldn't you?'

Abernethy leaned over the bench. 'Did you own a pair of leather trousers at the time?'

Leigh looked upwards. 'I do. I don't know whether it was that day—at that time and I don't know whether I owned the long boots at that time either. I know . . .'

Abernethy interrupted again. 'What colour leather, the trousers?'

'Black.'

'Mr Melbourne, you will recall, says a man in black leather trousers.'

'Uh-huh.'

'Not you, though. Is that what you're saying?'

'Well, as far as my recollection, I have never been in the company of those two alone and I've never been that close to Gordon to have a conversation with him.'

Abernethy persisted. 'We're talking about probably the afternoon she died. I mean that would jog the old memory a bit wouldn't it, if you've seen her shortly before she died?'

'I saw her every day for eighteen months . . .'

'Yes, yes, yes but at Watsons Bay?' Abernethy was getting frustrated.

'Watsons Bay, yes, that's what I'm saying is that I cannot remember being there and ever coming across them.'

There was little point in continuing. Adam Leigh was excused after eleven minutes in the witness box. He did not talk to anyone as he sat at the back of the room, not even glancing at the man who had been called inside from the waiting area to be the next witness—Gordon Eric Wood.

24

RICHO'S MY ALIBI

If Gordon Wood was worried he didn't show it as he entered the room. He was either an innocent man without a shadow of guilt or a guilty man who believed he could not be caught. He was a confident presence in the witness box where he could survey the room, watching the journalists making notes of his casual dress—a 'crisp white shirt and cream trousers', as one reporter would describe his attire—to include in their reports the next day. He didn't appear concerned as he snapped answers to John Gibson's preliminary questions about his police interviews, his address and his occupation. Formalities out of the way, the dissection began.

'How well did you know Adam Leigh?'

'I don't,' Wood replied.

'Do you know who I'm referring to in that regard, know who that person is, Caroline's booker?'

Wood barely responded. 'Right.'

'The gentleman who's seated towards the rear of the court in the navy-coloured suit. Recognise him?'

'Nuh.'

'Never seen him before in your life?'

'Not that I'm aware of.'

'You don't remember seeing him at the memorial service of Caroline wearing sunglasses and crying a great deal?'

'No I don't—I don't recall it, no, but he may well have been there.'

Gibson tried one last time. 'You've never been to Watsons Bay with that gentleman and Caroline?'

Wood would not bend. 'Nuh.'

Despite his prominence in Caroline Byrne's professional life and the other man's claims that they had known each other at least casually, Gordon Wood was adamant that Adam Leigh was a complete stranger.

And unlike Leigh who pondered about his whereabouts on 7 June 1995, Wood remained firm as Gibson progressed, unaware, he said, why two men he did not know would say he was in a place with a person he had never met. He had been at lunch with two friends at a café in Darlinghurst where he stayed for 30 minutes, even ordering lunch which had not arrived by the time he received a phone call and had to leave. 'I went from Ditto's to Alife where Rene and Graham were lunching.'

John Abernethy leaned forward. 'To where?'

'Alife, it's the name—well it was the name of a restaurant in Stanley Street.'

'So you were in East Sydney, okay?'

'Yeah. And I can't tell you how long I waited around there until they finished their lunch and then I would have taken Graham into town.'

Abernethy wanted to know more. 'What is Graham's name?'

Wood didn't hesitate. 'Graham Richardson.'

'Graham Richardson, the politician—ex-politician?'

'Ex-politician, yeah. And I would have dropped him off and then I would have driven around looking for somewhere to go to lunch and probably ended up going to the Lamrock.'

So there it was. As the papers screamed the next day, Gordon Wood had named not only his boss and a couple of friends as alibis on the afternoon before Caroline Byrne's death, but former Hawke and Keating minister and Labor Party numbers man, Graham Richardson. It would be a statement left untested for another four years before it was debunked by Richardson himself.

He had not been lunching with the stockbroker but with the president of the Canterbury-Bankstown Rugby League Club, Peter 'Bullfrog' Moore. They were seen in earnest conversation at the Hilton Hotel at the time Gordon Wood says he waited to chauffeur him from Stanley Street. But neither Rivkin nor Richardson was on the witness list to give evidence. Rivkin had refused and could not be compelled to appear.

Tony Byrne had heard Wood's version of events on the night of Caroline's death many times over. He'd quizzed him on the night, read his police statements and heard others retell his stories. Now he intently watched the man who he believed murdered his daughter, not listening to the words so much as watching his body language to see if he could tell when Gordon lied, if only for his own satisfaction.

Gibson was taking Wood through the evening of 7 June; how he supposedly got home to find Caroline gone, how he fell asleep in front of the television and woke after midnight, tried to phone her, left a note, walked to one of Rivkin's garages to get a car and finally drove past Tony's own home to see if she was with him. Tony didn't believe a word of it and neither did Gibson.

'Why didn't you ring her father's address?'

'It was after midnight.'

'But this is your fiancée we're talking about here. You're concerned about her?'

'Mmm.'

'You say the most likely place she would be at that time of night is her father's?'

'Logically.'

'Logically you would ring him?'

'Well, not logically. I would think that would be the most likely place she would be but I guess that I didn't think it was the right thing to ring somebody after midnight if they weren't there so . . .'

Gibson tried to help him. 'So then from that point in time you immediately think the worst and you go for a drive down to Bondi?'

'Yeah.'

Abernethy waded in again: 'Why Bondi?'

Tony held his breath. Was he going to repeat the ridiculous line he'd told Peter and Brian Wyver; that he had been sent down there by some premonition and mind link with Caroline? He hoped so.

Wood shrugged. 'Well, I didn't know where else to go frankly. I mean I don't—Caroline and I didn't go out a lot so the only places where we sort of did go were Bondi, Camp Cove . . .'

The answer hung in the air as, led by Gibson, he recreated the desperate drive along Oxford Street, past the deserted shopfronts of Paddington before turning down Bondi Road and descending to the famous beachfront. He drove along Campbell Parade looking for the white Suzuki, heading up through Vaucluse and following the headland to Camp Cove at the far end of Watsons Bay. He had found her car by accident—as he turned back—parked in a laneway at a dogleg in Military Road, and began a desperate search along the cliff top where he talked to the two fishermen before ringing the Byrne house and driving around to pick up Tony and Peter.

Tony wondered why Gibson didn't ask more questions about the time it took for all this to happen. Gordon said he had woken after midnight, walked a couple of kilometres to get a car, driven past his house and then to Bondi and Camp Cove before finding the Suzuki and rushing around the cliff top searching for Caroline. The trouble was that he and Peter were woken by Gordon at 12.40 am, when he was already at The Gap. None of it fitted. Wood was lying and no-one seemed to be picking it up.

John Abernethy had taken over the questioning and had his own concerns about Wood's story, particularly why he didn't get a torch himself when picking up the Byrnes, why he didn't call the police and why he thought Caroline was lying at the bottom of The Gap. Wood had no answer, other than he probably wasn't thinking properly amid his panic that she was dead.

There was another burning question. How did Wood see Caroline at the bottom of the 30-metre cliff with a weak torch barely strong enough to bait a fish hook on a dark night with a sea mist rolling in from the Pacific Ocean? Wood must have expected the query but his convoluted answer left many in the courtroom agape.

'Well, I think I did explain to you that the torch, as far as it could reach, was being shined down the face of the cliff. I recall there's only one point when the fence line does a dogleg up close to the edge of The Gap which is higher up the north end of The Gap than where Caroline was found. If you lean over there facing northwards away from where Caroline as found, you can see the rock face which is, presumably, what Peter and I would have been shining at. If we'd shined the torch at the sea we wouldn't have seen the sea because the torch wouldn't have lit up the sea. So how I can—what I can—the answer to your question is I could see what the torch would light up on the cliff face which obviously wasn't Caroline's body because she was back there and down some feet—metres.'

It was hard to make sense of the answer, like everything else that night. Wood asked for an adjournment. He had a phone call to make.

Afterwards Gibson's questions kept coming. Why, in the days after her death, did Wood tell people that Caroline was killed in a hit-and-run?

The break had done nothing to improve Wood's coherency. His thoughts spewed out in a ramble, as if it had never occurred to him that these questions might be asked.

'I think it seemed like "Well, what are my options if I'm not going to say it's a suicide, what do I have to say?" and I think it happened on the—I was in the car with my mum and my sister on the way to or from the morgue here when I had a telephone conversation with Tony about that and whether he said "Tell them it was a car accident"—I don't think he did—but I think he did ask me not to tell people about the suicide and not—for there to be no—he didn't want any publicity which I agreed with and I imagine our concern was that people would make a judgment about Caroline if they found out she jumped off The Gap. However,

I mean, the only way I felt I could deal with that was probably to make sure it was a blanket suggestion to everybody . . .'

Sergeant Gibson moved on: 'You had access to her Westpac card I believe?'

'Yeah.'

'I just showed you the account, and certainly after her death you were the only person to actually access her account.'

'Yes.'

'I notice that the first withdrawal following her death was 14 June. A matter of days after her death you withdrew an amount of $400?'

'Right.'

'And then you made subsequent withdrawals in the amounts of—I think there were three other $400 and one $100 and a $50 etcetera. You can see those there?'

'Yep.'

There was no denying the obvious. The bank statement, which had been sent to Tony, showed Gordon Wood had systematically stripped his dead fiancée's account in the weeks after her death.

Then Gibson voiced the question that everyone wanted to ask: 'Why were you withdrawing all the money from her account?'

'Well, Caroline was dead. She wasn't going to use the money.'

The reporters scribbled furiously, checking with one another in case they had misheard. Gibson wasn't finished. Wood had also tried to use Deanna's keycard which she'd left with Caroline when she went to Japan. But the machine spat out the card because he didn't know the PIN code.

Wood tried to suggest that he had inadvertently used Deanna's card instead of his girlfriend's but, as Gibson pointed out, the bank records showed he had used it after already withdrawing money from Caroline's account.

Wood grasped for an answer. 'Well, I can't tell you that but I know that if I went into the account to go and get money out of Caroline's account I would have used her card and mistakenly used Deanna's because, as I'm sure you're aware, Deanna's card wouldn't work with Caroline's PIN code. So—and as I didn't know Deanna's PIN code and only Caroline's . . .' The answer trailed off.

Wood had been in the witness box barely two hours and, as far as Tony was concerned, had only confirmed his guilt. He expressed none of the outrage at any of the suggestions that one would have expected from an innocent man, nor had there been any coherent explanation about his behaviour on the night, his claims of seeing Caroline at the bottom of the cliff, why he didn't call Tony or the police, his lies about how she died, or his callous stripping of her bank account.

Now he was trying to explain why he believed Caroline could commit suicide—a woman he had believed was happy and wanted to marry. It was a combination of being sick, unhappy at work, doctors' visits, even falling asleep on his mother's couch after dinner a couple of nights before her death.

'Right up until the day she died I'd never considered Caroline committing suicide. All the characteristics I've spoken about earlier were easily attributed to her being sick and unhappy with work . . . whereas afterwards when you look at, you know, all the things you think, "Ah yeah, sure, it looks like she was suicidal".'

There was another pointer to Caroline Byrne's mental state that day, said Gibson. It was contained in her purse, found on the floor of the Suzuki which Wood agreed he must have taken away afterwards. 'Now when you went through it, you know, with Peter and Tony, can you remember how much cash was inside at that time?' he asked.

'No, not at all. I would imagine if there was any it would have been a smallish amount. I would imagine it would have been less than $50. I mean, Caroline did not carry a lot of money around with her at any time.'

Tony thought back, recalling the scene in the carpark that night; how Gordon unlocked and opened the car and took out the wallet, giving it to Peter to open. It was as if he had already rifled through it. He remembered Gordon taking the wallet back and pulling out what Tony thought was about $70 in cash, shoving the money in his top pocket and throwing the wallet back into the car without checking anything else. It still upset him.

Gibson wasn't only interested in the cash. 'I'll show you a couple of receipts. The first one I draw your attention to is a receipt from Caltex at Oxford Street, Paddington. You'll see there that the card has been used to purchase some petrol, Freddo Frogs I think . . .'

Gordon interrupted, reading a copy of the receipt: 'Freddo Frogs and milk—yeah two—yeah.'

'Do you know the time on the face of that receipt, it's three . . .'

'Yeah, 3.32.'

'Now quite obviously that would have been Caroline making a withdrawal. Do you agree with that?'

'Uh-huh.'

'Now I show you a second receipt which is also dated 7 June '95 and it's a withdrawal from Westpac at Vaucluse. See that one, and that one's actually timed at 3.47 pm?'

'Uh-huh.'

'So there's around a fifteen-minute gap between the petrol and Freddos and the $50 being withdrawn at Vaucluse?'

'Uh-huh.'

'Now that's the actual afternoon prior to Caroline's body being found at the base of The Gap, right?'

'Uh-huh.'

'Can you make any comment as to why Caroline, if so suicidal, would have been withdrawing $50?'

'No.'

'No comment at all?'

'No.'

Gibson summed up his own line of questioning: 'It doesn't make a lot of sense.'

25

AN OPEN FINDING

Court judgments are notoriously frustrating for those waiting to know their own fate or for justice. Judges, or in this case, Deputy State Coroner John Abernethy, must prepare a statement which reviews the case chronologically and the evidence logically so that the people involved can understand why a certain decision is made or a conclusion cannot be reached. Caroline Byrne was such a case.

Tony Byrne felt calm sitting at the bar table between John Gibson and Brian Wyver. He'd stayed in the city the night before at Peter's apartment, had a quiet dinner and slept peacefully considering what lay ahead, hoping that they would get some answers. After Gordon Wood and Adam Leigh had been identified outside the courtroom, the evidence showed they were, or at least Gordon was, guilty of murder.

But Tony knew deep down that it wasn't enough, at least not to charge them. He knew the brief was weak and the lack of rigour in the examination of Wood and Leigh bothered him, but he felt at sea with the process, unwilling to question what was happening in case it all collapsed without resolution. Perhaps enough doubt had been planted for suicide to be ruled out. God, he hoped so.

Abernethy launched into his judgment by describing the initial investigation as below standard, puzzled why the homicide squad hadn't been called in, given that Caroline was found so far out from the cliff top. He gave a potted history of Caroline's work and mindset; the apprehension about her career balanced by descriptions from friends and work colleagues of a normal, vibrant young woman. Even the GP, Cindy Pan, was adamant that Caroline was not suicidal but had visited her as a precaution. Abernethy doubted that Caroline wanted to kill herself.

Tony switched off as Abernethy wandered through the evidence which reconstructed the last days of Caroline's life. He had gone over the events hundreds of times in his own mind; trying to find a chink, some tiny clue which might shed light on the obvious rift between her and Gordon. There was none, and Abernethy didn't seem to be questioning it either, merely stating Gordon's version of events. Then the coroner changed course:

'One glaring inconsistency is just how he managed, of course, to see a sandshoe or a body below The Gap on a dark night with a barely operating torch. Another anomaly is why he lied to a wide range of people about how Caroline came to her death. He said the Byrnes wanted him to say that it was not suicide. That is what he finally said in the witness box but they don't agree with that. So he has told a whole range of his friends—it may not take us anywhere—but he has told a whole range of his friends that she had an accident as a pedestrian at Rose Bay until the truth had to come out, of course.'

Abernethy was clearing a path to launch an attack on Wood. But how far would he go?

'But by far the most telling [of Wood's] inconsistencies is the evidence of Craig William Martin and his business partner, Mr Lance Melbourne. They made statements in which they described a woman and two men walking in a park near the restaurant at Watsons Bay. They later identified the woman as being Caroline Byrne.'

Tony desperately wanted to turn and look at Gordon Wood, who was sitting at the back of the room, just to see the look in his eyes. But he didn't dare take his eyes off the coroner who was describing how he had adjourned the inquest to pursue the identification. Adam Leigh had been brought from Melbourne to give evidence and both he and Wood had been identified outside the courtroom by the two restaurateurs.

'I am satisfied that they saw Caroline. Both men, in a crowded foyer—we've got the Bondi Beach case next door—identified those two men, strangers to them—as Gordon Wood and Adam Leigh. Neither man has anything to gain from giving this evidence and only went to police in the first place because of a conversation with Miss Dally-Watkins and others at their restaurant a week or so after Miss Byrne's death. I mean, they were handing around a photograph asking "have you seen this woman".

'It would be totally against the weight of evidence not to accept that evidence of identification. I am satisfied that they have not got their heads together. They had no reason at all to do so. They are truly men on a Clapham omnibus as we say in the law.

'Both Gordon Wood and Adam Leigh gave evidence and trenchantly denied being with Caroline Byrne the afternoon of 7 June 1995 at Watsons Bay. Nevertheless, those of us in this courtroom well remember the convincing evidence given by Mr Martin and Mr Melbourne.'

It was a high point. Abernethy believed Craig Martin and Lance Melbourne. Caroline was with Gordon Wood and Adam Leigh at Watsons Bay in the hours before she died. That made Gordon Wood a liar and, in all probability, a murderer.

'But,' Abernethy continued. 'Even if I accept the evidence of Mr Melbourne and Mr Martin, which I am happy to do, that is not evidence that any known person was involved in the death of Caroline Byrne. It simply arouses suspicion and suspicion, of course, is not evidence. At the end of the day I can only look at evidence.'

Abernethy was winding it up but there was a remaining hurdle for Tony. Despite the evidence, he was not prepared to rule out suicide.

'In order to bring a finding of suicide, I must be able to say, on the evidence, that suicide is very probably what occurred—not probably, very probably, highly likely. It is a higher standard than what we simply call the balance of probabilities which is more likely than not, balancing the scales. I am of the opinion that the evidence does not permit me to make such a finding. That being so, there are three possibilities: that she took her own life, of course that is still there, that she fell accidentally or that she was murdered. I cannot, on the evidence, raise any of these possibilities to the status of what probably happened, let alone what happened beyond reasonable doubt. I have to record an open finding. It is to Caroline's family, and those close to her, I offer my sympathies. She must have been a very special person.'

The tears were coming but Tony held them off. He barely heard Abernethy's final words.

'With an open finding, the police I can assure you, are still interested—very interested—in it and will be seeing whether they can take the matter any further. They know that the coroner is still very interested in it and for that reason alone, will analyse the evidence and see what more can be done. If anything comes out, of course, they will follow it up.'

Gordon Wood had not waited around. As Abernethy began his statement Wood left the room, rushing to the white Suzuki Vitara and driving off before the media could follow.

Tony Byrne and his family had not noticed. Unlike Gordon Wood, Tony stopped for the media when he emerged 30 minutes later. He was relieved, he said. 'We have hoped for this for two years,' he shouted against a background of cars rushing along Parramatta Road. 'We know Caroline didn't take her own life, but a lot of questions remain unanswered. I believe there was a conspiracy and Caroline had to go. She was happy and it's unfeasible she took her own life. She was thrown off that cliff. And I believe she was killed first.'

Tony slept peacefully the night of John Abernethy's judgment. He'd had dinner with Peter, Robert and Deanna, reflecting on the events of the past two days. The open finding was a relief in a way and gave him hope.

The evidence of Lance Melbourne and Craig Martin had thrilled Tony. He had known roughly what they were going to say but had not been privy to the police statements and could not have imagined just how emphatic their identification would be.

The next morning he rushed out to buy the papers. The *Herald* and *Telegraph* had both run their stories on page 3, each with a photo of Gordon Wood, newspapers under his arm folded at the crossword page as if he didn't care, and yet rushing off to his car looking guilty as hell, at least in Tony's eyes.

Tony felt emboldened, as if the world was finally waking up to the injustice. If Melbourne and Martin were correct then Gordon Wood was a liar. Did that mean his alibi was also a lie? Rivkin and Richardson would know and yet they hadn't been called to give evidence. It didn't make any sense. Coroner Abernethy had said he wanted the investigation to remain open but nobody seemed ready to do the obvious. Were they scared of Rivkin and Richardson? Were they too powerful?

The moment seized him and Tony decided to call Graham Richardson himself. The former politician was doing breakfast radio for 2GB. Why not get to him on-air and put him on the spot in front of all his listeners?

Tony got through twice but was rebuffed each time even though he told Richardson's producer he was a freelance journalist named Bruce Marshall. The mistake was to reveal that he wanted to talk about Gordon Wood. Richardson would not take the call until ten minutes after he came off air at 9 am. The producer put him through. Tony would later make notes of the brief conversation.

'Hello, Graham speaking.'

'Hello, Graham. Bruce Marshall is my name. I'm a freelance journalist. You would remember me from Canberra.'

'Yes, I remember you Bruce. Was it you who rang earlier this morning?'

'Yes, Graham. I rang to ask you about this morning's headlines. Will you be making a statement?'

'Yes I will. My secretary is on sick leave with shingles. When she returns I will have her check my diary as to where I was that day.'

'Did you know Caroline Byrne?'

'No.'

'She was at Rivkin's 50th birthday party.'

'So were 500 other people.'

'How well did you know Gordon Wood?'

'He's a nobody—Rene's driver. He never came to lunch with us. He's a nobody.'

'Rivkin took him overseas with him.'

'If you're worth $70 million you don't carry your own bags.'

'Okay, Graham. You will make a statement as to whether you were with Gordon Wood on the afternoon of 7 June 1995 when your secretary returns.'

'Yes.'

'Talk to you later.'

As brief as the call may have been, it would arm Tony with a sense that he was fighting a lone battle to bring powerful people to account. He didn't think for one moment that Richardson was involved in Caroline's death, but the man had now been drawn into the case by Wood and should, as a prominent member of society and former cabinet minister, come forward with the truth. It was no excuse to wait for the police.

His frustration grew when staff from Channel 9 knocked on his door a few days later and announced they could arrange an interview with Rivkin and Richardson. The confrontation would make great television. He agreed to go with them and was ferried around in a car all day while all attempts failed. Neither man would even answer their calls.

Rivkin had chosen another medium, agreeing to an interview with gossip writer Ros Reines whom he would later hire to write his biography. The story appeared on 22 February, a typically flamboyant, rollicking conversation in which Rivkin described Gordon Wood as an obsessive, Walter Mitty character who, like the fictional character in James Thurber's famed 1941 short story, lived a life that flashed between fantasy and reality. But Mitty and Wood were not alike. One was a fictional character; a meek, mild man slipping into senility and imagining himself a wartime pilot, an emergency-room surgeon and a devil-may-care killer. The other was real; a young and arrogant man intent on getting somewhere in the world, stupidly passing himself off as Rivkin's financial adviser at dinner parties attended by the businessman's friends. He was a hustler and Rivkin didn't like to be hustled.

> He just got on my nerves in the end. He became very possessive of me, which I found fairly strange. He tried to become close to my family and to become best friends with one of my children. He's a very obsessive personality.
>
> He kept hassling me for money, although I had helped him make money off the stock market. In the end I got sick of the constant demands. He wanted to be a millionaire quickly. Gordon started to hustle me because he didn't believe he was getting there fast enough. I became a bit shirty with it all.

But as annoying as he was, Rivkin insisted that Wood had not murdered his girlfriend. Wood loved her, he said, while conceding that just three weeks later he was courting Kylie Watson.

Neither could Rivkin shed light on whether Wood had picked him up from lunch that day. 'Can you remember where you had lunch three years ago?' he responded when asked.

26

'DO YOU THINK I DID IT?'

Tony Byrne would call it blood money when he found out nine months after the event, lamenting he would never have agreed to participate if he'd known from the outset. But if Caroline Byrne's father had carefully considered the alternative scenario he might be less harsh on Channel 7's decision to pay Gordon Wood $25 000 to appear on a television interview two weeks after Bruce Abernethy handed down his open finding.

The fee—$20 000 to Wood, a chunk of which he promptly spent on a watch, and $5000 to a freelance journalist named Jamie Fawcett for brokering the deal—may have been questionable from an ethical perspective, but in terms of its impact on a flagging murder investigation, few television interviews would be more important than the 20-minute joust between Wood and the journalist and author Paul Barry which went to air on the evening of 4 March 1998.

Barry later conceded he was uncomfortable with paying Wood but insisted the interview was far tougher than he got at the inquest. Most who saw it agreed. It was enthralling television—a curious death, a beautiful victim and a charismatic suspect who had not only sold any rights to complain about being grilled over his alleged role in the death of his girlfriend but was willing to participate in re-enactments. Wood drove his car at night with a camera crew to describe what happened, he pretended to fall asleep in front of his television in a darkened lounge room as he said he had done on the night, he swam at Bondi in his Speedos. He even walked the cliff top where his girlfriend fell to her death.

Barry and his editors interspersed the interview with clips of Tony insisting that his daughter had not committed suicide and Brian Wyver casting doubts over Wood's story. But it was the interview with Wood which was compelling—a supremely confident man who stared down his inquisitor, did not blink and maintained his story could not be challenged, at least while the cameras were rolling.

Barry pulled no punches. 'Do you accept that you are under suspicion in this affair?'

'I'm not under suspicion by the police,' Wood replied.

Barry persisted. 'Well, the coroner uses the word suspicion. He points the finger of suspicion. He doesn't actually say it's you but he says it's your evidence that's bizarre and has glaring inconsistencies and anomalies.'

Wood didn't back down. 'Hmm. He says that suspicion doesn't amount to evidence.'

'Well there's a very strong suspicion that you're lying.'

'There may be, but I'm not.'

Barry moved to Caroline's suspicions of her boyfriend's relationship with Rivkin. Was she right to be concerned?

'She probably didn't trust him. Why is this guy so generous? Why does this guy have twelve good-looking young men hanging out on his boat in the afternoon? Those are probably thoughts she had.'

'Were you one of his good-looking young men?'

Wood smiled, his answer disingenuous. 'I don't get up in the morning and think I'm good-looking.'

Barry pushed the issue further. Was it true that Caroline had sprung him and Rivkin having homosexual sex?

'It is utter, utter garbage; I mean there is no evidence to support that Caroline had hired anybody, or that Rene had homosexual sex or whatever with me or anybody.'

'Police went on to say that that's why you threw her off The Gap.'

'The same comment; utter lies.'

And so it continued. The possibility of suicide, his lack of an alibi after 1 pm, how he was identified by Melbourne and Martin as having been in the park. 'They identified the clothes you were wearing that evening. They picked you out of a crowded foyer at the Coroner's Court. The coroner said we should believe them. If they are to be believed then you are lying.'

'If they are to be believed . . . supposedly Caroline and her booker and I were wandering around laughing and having a good time.'

After canvassing Wood's story about getting home at 6 pm to find Caroline missing and then falling asleep in front of the television, Barry questioned why he had not called anyone about a woman he felt was in trouble, and had not replied to a message left on his machine by Peter Byrne.

'What did you think when you woke up at 11.30 or 12 and she still wasn't there?'

Wood: 'That something major had happened to her. That she was in big trouble.'

Barry: 'Why didn't you ring her father?'

Wood: 'Why would I?'

Barry: 'Because you thought she was there.'

Wood: 'I hoped she was there.'

Barry: 'Why didn't you ring him?'

Wood: 'I went around to visit him.'

Barry: 'You didn't go in?'

Wood: 'No.'

Barry: 'Why not?'

Wood: 'The car wasn't there.'

Barry: 'Why didn't you ring him?'

Wood: 'Well, I was looking for my wife.'

The other compelling issue was how Wood claimed he could see Caroline's body under faltering torchlight.

'I certainly don't know she's down there, but I would want to find her, I imagine; I just want to find her. Maybe I wanted to find her on a ledge, injured but okay. But the fact of the matter is if the torch can't reach the bottom of The Gap [then] how could I have seen her? So I would have had to have been pointing the torch at something else, not so far down.'

'Or maybe knowing that she's down there already.'

'I'd be a bit of an idiot, wouldn't I, to point to everybody where she was if I had killed her. That would be a little bit dense.'

'Well you're a bit of an idiot if you say you can see something when you can see nothing at all.'

And so it wound down, Wood insisting that only Caroline could answer the question of how she died. 'The only person who can answer the question, completely, utterly and categorically, is Caroline, and she didn't leave a note and nobody saw her jump. So we can never prove it.'

Barry: 'Did you kill her?'

Wood (quietly): 'Of course not. Why would I kill her?'

Barry: 'Did you?'

Wood: 'No.'

Barry: 'And have you lied?'

Wood: 'Not once. I wouldn't sit here, in front of a television camera and put myself at the mercy of editors if I had to say anything but the truth. So all I can do is hope that truth is going to win over at the end of the day.'

Barry: 'Okay, you're pretty cool.'

Wood: 'I have no reason to be anything but. I've got absolutely nothing to hide.'

Barry: 'Okay, thanks.'

The interview had finished but the camera kept rolling. Gordon Wood leaned forward, took a sip of water and popped a lozenge into his mouth.

'Okay, no worries. So, do you think I did it?' he asked, leaning back and fixing Barry with a stare.

'I don't know; I'm like the coroner,' Barry replied, out of shot.

In metrological terms the 19th of March usually marks the last day of summer across the Southern Hemisphere although for Tony Byrne, the summer equinox of 1998 was the beginning of something rather than the end.

Brian Wyver called in the morning. He had good news. A man had come forward to say he had seen three people—two men and a woman fitting Caroline's description—out at Watsons Bay on the night of her death.

Tony was dumbstruck, as if he hadn't heard properly. He asked Wyver to repeat what he had said. A man had come forward after watching the *Witness* program on 4 March. It prompted his memory of watching a tall, pretty blonde woman crying in the street below the window of his Military Road studio around 8 pm.

There were two men, one tall dressed in suede and the other, dressed in black and standing back in the shadows, watching. Tony's blood froze as Wyver detailed what he'd been told over the phone. This man was describing Caroline, Gordon Wood and Adam Leigh. He must have been the last person to see his daughter alive. And he had seen her killers.

Tony didn't think to ask for the man's name in his babble of questions that followed, or why Brian Wyver hadn't rung before now and told him. Apparently the man, a painter of some sort, had telephoned Crime Stoppers on the night of the program, more than two weeks ago. Brian Wyver had even spoken to him the same night yet had said nothing. More to the point, why hadn't he been out to formally interview the man? Surely that's what the police should do. Wyver dismissed Tony's concerns. His bosses wouldn't give him the time to drive up from Wollongong for a couple more weeks. Besides, there was plenty of time. The guy wanted to help and Wood was going nowhere.

In fact, John Doherty's recollection had been prompted first by an article published in the *Sydney Morning Herald* in February. A neighbour, friend and fellow artist named Fairlie Kingston had read the story and remembered having a conversation with the Irishman in the street a couple of days after Caroline Byrne's death during which he mentioned having heard her scream. She showed him the article and they watched the *Witness* program together, after which he decided to go to the police.

It was just before 7 pm on 9 April before Brian Wyver telephoned Tony to tell him the interview had finally been done—36 days after the *Witness* program was aired and the man came forward. The interview had been a frustrating process, Wyver said, even down to providing his own witness—a colleague from Wollongong—because homicide wouldn't provide anyone to help him. But it had been worth the wait.

Wyver began slowly. 'Tony, the man is an Irish artist. His name is John.'

Tony didn't respond so Wyver continued. 'John is a very credible witness. He knows where Caroline was and who was with her. I believe I now have enough to put Gordon Wood before a jury.'

It was about as much as Wyver would divulge. He didn't offer Tony the man's full name and Tony, relieved that the interview had finally been done, didn't think to ask.

The story was in the papers 48 hours later. It revealed barely as much as Wyver had told Tony but it was enough to spark a new rush of media attention. By the following day the new witness had not only been identified as John Doherty but he'd been found, interviewed and even photographed. So much for police secrecy, Tony thought.

Apparently Doherty, who liked to paint at night, was disturbed by an argument on the street below his studio apartment. He looked out the window to see a young woman sitting by the side of Military Road within sight of The Gap, moaning loudly, her head in her hands. Across the road, a tall blond man was shouting and gesturing at her. Another man was standing in the shadows further along the road. The article quoted Doherty:

'I have one very distinctive memory and that was of the big guy crossing the road to the woman. I can see him. Tall, blond. I can see his jacket; it seemed to be black leather. That memory has stuck with me.'

Tony studied Doherty's photo closely, trying to assess the man. He appeared resolute; a fit, youngish-looking man for his 49 years, leaning casually with one hand on his hip against the wooden fence at the top of The Gap and gazing out to sea.

Tony went back to the artist's words and they filled him with some hope: *'If what I saw can help her family, of course I want to do that.'*

He then looked at his own words at the bottom of the story—*'Now it seems the case will be reopened and we may have the truth. It is wonderful to see justice slowly unfolding.'* Tony wept. He had learned to accept, even embrace the moments when emotion overcame him. Stoicism was no use at these times and at this moment he didn't feel so alone in his quest.

His hopes would be dashed quickly when a friend telephoned two days later. She worked, by chance, with a woman who lived next door to Wood in Bondi and had noticed a For Lease sign in his window. Gordon Wood had fled.

Tony called Brian Wyver in a fluster. What the hell was going on, he demanded. Why were police sitting on their hands while their main suspect fled the country? Wyver tried to calm him. It was nonsense, he insisted. Wood was still in his Bondi flat. It was just a ruse to confuse the media who were now camped outside his house.

Wyver was wrong and it was the media, again, which provided the answers. Wood had sold his possessions and left Australia. He had flown out the day before Wyver interviewed John Doherty.

He was now in Barbados in the West Indies, having told friends he was taking an extended holiday because of stress. But the move seemed far more permanent than a holiday. Wood had sold his car, cut off his phone, given his dogs to his sister and broken the leases on his Paddington office and Bondi flat. He had no intention of returning.

Was it coincidence or had someone tipped him off about Doherty?

There would be no mystery, at least initially, of where Wood had gone or what he was doing. Just two months after leaving Sydney the *Woman's Day* published a double-page story, purporting to be an investigation in which the magazine had tracked down Caroline's 'haunted lover' to the Bahamas.

The magazine story had actually been fuelled by Wood himself and offered for a price. He had already blown the $20 000 he'd pocketed from the *Witness* program interview and, by his own admission, was spending money like water.

The article was garnished with grinning photos of Wood on a luxury yacht in the company of two young American women and snorkelling around the island of Nassau in the Bahamas. He was with Jamie Fawcett, who had brokered the *Witness* deal and who had met Wood in the United States.

The story gloated over details of him 'living in the lap of luxury', lounging by the pool at the historic Riverside Hotel in Fort Lauderdale before inspecting apartments, cars and motor yachts, all the while not forgetting a daily gym workout. He and Fawcett had met 'Elizabeth and Jackie' in Nassau and taken them on a snorkelling cruise in a hired yacht.

The reality was very different. Fawcett had been in the United States completing a documentary. He arranged to meet Wood who was in Miami struggling to come to terms with where to go and how to pay for a life that appeared to be on the run. Fawcett reckoned there might be a few more dollars in the story. Channel 7 agreed and suggested hooking Wood up to a lie detector. It would make great television. The problem was that the reporter, Paul Barry, was overseas on another assignment. The idea fell through.

Instead, Fawcett, who paid Wood's hotel bill, hit on the photo idea. He bought a throwaway camera, found a couple of pretty girls, and got his cameraman to take the photos; a bit of harmless fun to help pay for the cost of the trip. They got $10 000.

In the *Woman's Day* article Fawcett painted a picture of a troubled, solitary man who wanted peace:

> I think he feels a great deal of pain associated with Caroline's death. He seems to be carrying this heavy burden all the time; the sleeplessness, the nightmares. He claims he has come to terms with what happened but I don't think he has ever got over it. It's like a dark cloud hanging over him. Gordon wants to cling to ordinary people. He needs friends but he's also very solitary. He wants to start his life over again, some place where people don't know about Caroline's death, where he is not recognised. It's a sad plight, I guess, for an intelligent, good-looking man like Gordon. He's out there on a limb, trying to find a way to come back.

It sounded more like a man fleeing the truth, rather than a man seeking public sympathy and redemption. And that's the way it appeared to police and the media; a story of triumph and challenge as if Wood was saying 'come and get me if you can'. Although Wood would later complain of being hounded by the media, it was this story which laid the groundwork and rules of engagement for the chase to come. Wood's quotes were brief, but poignant:

> I don't get much sleep. I wake up in a cold sweat, night after night. I have terrible dreams. I'm in a courtroom, facing my accusers, people asking me what happened to Caroline . . . I'm being handcuffed by the police . . . then I wake up. The nightmare has no end. It always stops with the handcuffs being fastened around my wrists.

Gordon Wood didn't know it, but his endless nightmares would play out for another eight years before they came true.

Fawcett would also have several serious conversations with Wood, mostly as they lounged around the motel swimming pool. He tried to steer the conversations towards the death of Caroline Byrne, in the hope he might find out what really happened that night, but Wood stuck to his story. Instead, the conversations drifted back to Rene Rivkin and, specifically, the Offset Alpine fire. Wood believed the fire had been deliberate although he had no evidence to prove it. He even named the man most likely to have struck the match and listed the directors and others who would benefit from the blaze.

Fawcett scribbled down the names and how they fitted into the complex conspiracy offered by this strange man who must have realised what he was saying. Wood even contributed to the document; his tiny, careful handwriting clear in contrast to Fawcett's when the document was examined by police years later. In itself, the document proved nothing other than Gordon Wood believed his former boss had much to hide and he was happy to help hide the secrets. Most serious was the rift it had caused in his relationship with Caroline Byrne in the last days of her life.

Tony and Andrea: Young, just engaged and dreaming of the future. (PHOTO: TONY BYRNE)

Life on the farm: Three-year-old Caroline looks on as Tony and older brother Peter feed a lamb. (PHOTO: TONY BYRNE)

Siblings Peter and Robert in their school uniforms hover over younger sisters, Caroline and Deanna. (PHOTO: TONY BYRNE)

Young Nasho: Tony as a young man before family life. (PHOTO: TONY BYRNE)

The schoolgirl: Caroline at sixteen and on the cusp of being discovered as a model. (PHOTO: TONY BYRNE)

Caroline at seventeen with Andrew Blanchette just before moving to the city. (PHOTO: TONY BYRNE)

An early modelling shot.
(PHOTO: TONY BYRNE)

Caroline the beauty queen, at age seventeen, winning the Miss Spirit festival in Camden.
(PHOTO: TONY BYRNE)

Caroline: Hauntingly beautiful. (PHOTO: TONY BYRNE)

Gary Redding shows off his physique and tattoos in a fashion shoot. (PHOTO: FAIRFAX)

On his way home: Gordon Wood, head bowed, on a Qantas flight after being extradited in 2006. Paul Quigg accompanies him. (PHOTO: ANDREW MEARES, FAIRFAX)

The tiny ledge from which Caroline Byrne, almost certainly unconscious, was pitched to her death. (PHOTO: FAIRFAX)

A grim-faced Gordon Wood walks past reporters on his way to court. (PHOTO: FAIRFAX)

Tony Byrne and Associate Professor Rod Cross, the physicist whose evidence was critical to the case. (PHOTO: FAIRFAX)

The two combatants: Winston Terracini and Mark Tedeschi inspect The Gap at the beginning of the trial. (PHOTO: FAIRFAX)

Paul Quigg and Paul Jacob discuss the case outside the court. (PHOTO: FAIRFAX)

A family celebrates: Brothers Peter and Robert Byrne, father Tony, sister Deanna and Robert's daughter, four-year-old Sheenah. (PHOTO: FAIRFAX)

Paul Jacob and Tony Byrne toast the end of their journey after Gordon Wood is convicted. (PHOTO: FAIRFAX)

27

IRONDALE

John Abernethy wanted the homicide squad to cast fresh eyes over the Caroline Byrne case, or at least the new witness who had come forward. It was worth another look but in the jumble of ongoing cases and fresh overnight crimes it seemed a small job, hopefully taking a couple of weeks at the most.

Paul Jacob, one of the state's most experienced detectives, made his way to see Abernethy and grabbed the file of transcripts and witness statements. It was impossible to miss the case. The mere mention of Rene Rivkin's name was enough to attract front-page publicity, let alone the ruckus over Wood's television appearance.

Privately, Abernethy believed Caroline Byrne was unlikely to have killed herself. She was killed and the most likely killer was Wood, but there wasn't enough evidence to take it to court and he didn't have the power to compel witnesses like Rivkin who'd been approached in the street by police but wouldn't cooperate. Abernethy's hands were tied unless something more compelling could be produced.

Jacob went back to his office at Strawberry Hills. Perhaps the job wasn't so simple after all, he thought as he sat down with a cup of coffee. A couple of hours later he knew it wasn't going to be an ordinary case and couldn't be handed back to Abernethy without answering the dozens of questions buzzing around his own head.

As he read into the night Jacob's amazement turned to anger. The witness interviews were pathetic—simplistic, rushed and lacking any real detail. Was it laziness, incompetence or simply that the uniformed police who had handled the case weren't trained for detective work? On reflection, Jacob would choose the latter. From the moment Tony and Peter Byrne walked into the Watsons Bay Police Station with Gordon Wood to report Caroline missing, there was a presumption that she had killed herself.

Rene Rivkin may have moved on from Gordon Wood but not from his bizarre entourage choices. As police quietly prepared to publicly announce the formation of a new team to reopen the Caroline Byrne investigation, Rivkin was showing off his latest employee—a giant convicted armed robber named Nathan Jones. Rivkin took Jones to lunch with him one day in early June where the broadcaster John Laws described the 207-cm-tall monster as stronger than an acre of garlic. Jones flexed, Rivkin grinned.

No-one was quite sure why Rivkin needed a bodyguard who was dubbed Colossus of Boggo Road (Prison) because he could lift a 400-kilogram car and was capable of breaking handcuffs. Rivkin didn't, of course; it was just more show, like the cigar and the fleet of cars, not to mention his fortune. Everything about Rene Rivkin was built on perception, except his family who suffered as a result of being real. The businessman would realise his mistake far too late to redeem himself.

While Rivkin preened in the shadow of his behemoth servant, the state's so-called super cop Clive Small, who had headed the investigation into the Ivan Milat backpacker murders, revealed the new strike force called Irondale, a computer-generated word meaningless other than being the name of a stream of coal running beneath the Blue Mountains near Lithgow and a couple of tiny US mining towns. Small, the Crime Agencies commander, announced the six-person team to be headed by Jacob who had worked on some of the city's most infamous cases.

'There are a number of factors that have brought us to the position,' he told assembled journalists. The 'glaring inconsistencies' in Gordon Wood's testimony at the coroner's inquiry, the statement of John Doherty, and the untested alibi of Wood that he was picking up his boss, Rene Rivkin, and Graham Richardson from lunch in East Sydney around the time that two men say they saw him with Caroline and another man, possibly Adam Leigh, at Watsons Bay.

Tony Byrne said little in response beyond welcoming the development. There was no point. The fact was they had already been working for several months behind the scenes reinterviewing witnesses, some for the third time. Police investigations could be like that; going back and back and back to talk to the same people as new evidence emerged or, in the case of Gordon Wood, as new questions emerged from their confusing account of events.

In this case, the need to revisit some people was more about the inadequacies of the first two attempts. Constable Craig Woods couldn't be blamed; not only was he young but his superiors had written off Caroline's death as a suicide from the moment they reported her missing at The Gap. Brian Wyver had tried his best, Tony thought, but he'd been given no real support or time to conduct a proper investigation.

The formation of Irondale was a step forward, if only because it was formal acknowledgement that time and resources were needed to do the job properly. And senior police now believed there was a case to answer. Still, Tony wasn't kidding himself. Caroline had been dead for three years and some of the prime suspects had not even been interviewed.

It would be another fortnight before Tony met the cop who would be his last chance for justice. There was no great fuss, no speeches and no promises. On reflection, Tony couldn't even remember being offered a cup of coffee when he went to the headquarters at Strawberry Hills to assess Paul Jacob, for that's what it was—an assessment of character for both men. They sat inside a small interview room with a token photograph of Caroline pinned to the wall. It had been taken at a Westfield's parade a few months before her death. It wasn't Tony's favourite but, like any photo taken of his daughter, she was beautiful; regal, almost, and serene.

Jacob let Tony speak first.

'I know Caroline was murdered,' he began. 'I knew from the moment Gordon Wood came into my apartment the next morning and wouldn't look at me.'

He could still recall Wood standing at the window, staring across Hyde Park. Tony could only see his profile but his expression said enough. He was cool and calm, completely at odds with the frantic man a few hours earlier calling out like a lunatic that he loved Tony like a father. Any man who'd lost the woman he claimed to love would be an emotional wreck, desperately seeking an explanation. Not Wood. He was hiding something and they both knew it.

It was a tough case, Jacob acknowledged when Tony had finished, but there was enough to suggest that Caroline was murdered, and they wanted to get to the bottom of it. He introduced the detectives who would work with him but didn't offer any information about himself or the cases on which he'd worked, like the Granny Killer on the city's north shore or the mindless, bungled killing of the heart surgeon Victor Chang.

It was clear that Jacob was an understated man. He exuded calmness rather than a policeman's steel and was hardly the mental picture Tony had built up in anticipation of the meeting. He'd expected a smaller man, fit, athletic and aggressive, but Paul Jacob was the opposite. A big man who tried to lessen the impact of his double chin with a goatee and whose white shirt was constantly threatening to escape his belt. He stooped slightly, as if carrying the weight of the world on his shoulders but his smile was reassuring and his presence comforting rather than over-powering.

Tony decided Paul Jacob was fair dinkum and somebody he could talk to when he needed for the next twelve months he reckoned the investigation might need to reach its conclusion. Jacob felt the same. These cases tended to become personal, though neither man considered it would still be a consuming part of their lives nine years later.

28

KISS-KILL

Tony baulked as he stepped out of the elevator then cautiously entered the third-storey office above Chinatown. It was a cold empty room on a winter's night, just like the people invited to fill it for the monthly meeting of the Homicide Victims Support Group. He felt alone in a place designed to make him feel the opposite; part of a select group of people who understood what it was like to have a member of their family murdered.

Paul Jacob had encouraged him to join and had taken him along to meet two civilians, Martha Jabour and Di Beckett, who ran the group which was funded by the NSW Health Department and supported by senior police, who would often attend meetings.

In truth, Tony saw the group as a means to establish better links with the police investigation rather than to help him with his grief. It may have been a touch naïve but he was desperate. Standing in the cold room only confirmed his sense that he did not belong, not because he was any better than these people but that he'd already learned to cope and had the investigation to lean on as a crutch.

Still, he'd promised so he would try. A knot of people stood making themselves a coffee, their conversation so low that he could hear teaspoons clinking against china. One of the men saw him standing in the doorway, could sense his indecision and walked over to introduce himself. Tony recognised Gary Lynch, father of the murdered nurse Anita Cobby. The others were parents and siblings from equally notorious cases, as if the group was torn from the pages of the tabloids.

Tony moved inside and made himself a coffee, avoiding any further contact and dreading the moment he would be asked to introduce himself. Within half an hour there were 30 or more people who, when called to order by Martha Jabour, formed a circle in the centre of the room where they sat, coffee cups in hand. It was time to share.

Tony couldn't help feeling he was in the middle of an Alcoholics Anonymous meeting. He knew it was a harsh judgment but as the baton was passed around the circle he could sense there were those who had told and retold their stories for years. He wanted to escape, not entrench the misery.

Each in turn told their story and expressed their grief, which was inevitably followed by anger or frustration. It was a common theme. When it came to Tony he declined. Not tonight, he said, and the baton was passed on. Tony had made up his mind. Although he would continue to attend on occasion and sometimes spoke, he always came away from meetings feeling down rather than comforted.

People dealt with grief in different ways. A range of emotions was normal, according to the literature handed out. Many of them burst out crying as they shared their stories. Tony would hear them all, some many times because they never seemed to change.

Tony didn't want to be ruled by the case any longer than necessary. In the meantime though he realised the group meant he would always have support if he needed it, not only from the group but from Paul Jacob. He was lucky. Some didn't have a police officer they could call at any time. Even the use of the word homicide was encouraging.

Consoling the family of victims was a necessary part of the job for a homicide cop. Paul Jacob reckoned it made him a better detective to understand the humanity of such crime and its effects on the human spirit, even his own soul. People like Tony Byrne were victims themselves and needed constant reassurance, particularly when investigations seemed to be going slowly.

The telephone was the easiest tool of communication. He could talk when he had a few spare moments to ensure there was a ready excuse to end the conversation or he could talk at night, after the kids went to bed, and while he had a smoke and a beer out the back.

He liked Tony. He liked his gentleness, his innocence. Somehow, despite all that had happened to tear apart his carefully nurtured world, including his wife's suicide and now Caroline's death, the man did not seem capable of anger or hatred. He spoke of injustice rather than revenge and wanted answers to questions so he could move on.

It was 8 pm on 4 May 1999, the kids were tucked in, the house was quiet and Tony was on the phone. There was time tonight to let the conversation wander. Irondale was nearly a year old and although there had been a lot of work they were still trying to get through the obvious people—family, friends, the fifteen police officers out on the cliff that night—this time in scrupulous detail, before they started the painstaking process of seeking out those who had not come forward. It was going to be a long process.

'What do you think they argued about out there, up on the cliff that night?' Tony asked.

Paul had wondered himself. What happens in the minutes leading up to such a catastrophic moment when one human being takes another and hurls them over a cliff? Was it about money, was it about Wood's sexuality, was it because his relationship with Rivkin was threatened?

He could only answer part of the question. 'Caroline wanted to end their relationship?'

'So it was a moment of madness, as we all have with arguments with our wives and girlfriends?'

'Yes. But we wouldn't have gone as far as Wood did.'

'What about Adam Leigh? Why was he there and who paid him?'

'Tony, I can't answer that. We think it was Adam Leigh but I'm not convinced yet. It could have been someone else.'

Paul wanted to get inside, away from the case for the rest of the night, and relax with his wife for a while. Police work was a killer for relationships and families. He had to swing the conversation back to something positive, to give Tony a reason to say goodnight and maybe feel better.

'Mate, we've got ten volumes of evidence against him now and there's more to come.'

Tony hadn't finished. 'What about Rene Rivkin?'

'We're not frightened of Rivkin. When we're ready we will talk to him.'

Paul tried again to end the conversation. 'Look, Irondale is going at 100 miles an hour, buddy. There are a lot of resources being thrown at this investigation and they wouldn't be doing that unless they expected a result.'

'Yeah, but they've buggered it up so much already.'

'True. If we had been called in on that night things might have been different.'

'How can you be so certain?'

'Tony, there's one thing I'm certain about: people who suicide don't scream.'

Jacob said goodnight and hung up, squeezing the last shred of tobacco from his cigarette before retreating inside to try to forget about work for a few hours. It was impossible to compare cases but there were always aspects which had similarities. The Byrne case was like no other but for some reason it made him recall his first murder investigation. It was easily solved and, if anything, a little mundane—a man stabbed to death at the front door of his flat in Surry Hills. But its detail provided a chilling insight into the human psyche and one that would remain with him.

The victim was a young man playing loud music with a friend inside a flat, the assailant an older man downstairs peeling an orange in his kitchen who, annoyed by the sound, climbed the stairs, knocked on the door and asked if they could turn down the music. The younger man refused and an argument ensued during which the older man suddenly plunged the knife he'd been using to peel the orange into the other's chest. The victim died instantly.

The attack was unplanned and if he'd stabbed his victim anywhere else on the body the man would have lived. It showed Jacob that humans were capable of almost anything on the spur of the moment.

The Byrne murder appeared to have many of the same elements. Gordon Wood did not plan to murder his girlfriend. Quite the contrary. He took Caroline to Watsons Bay to save his relationship. That was obvious because anyone planning murder would not take the victim to the chosen site in broad daylight and lunch with them where they would be seen. Whatever his motives—love, infatuation, greed or, more probably, a combination of the three—he desperately wanted Caroline to stay. When, after hours of cajoling, pleading and finally threats he had snapped, hit her and then in a moment of fury and desperation, hurled her from the cliff top.

Kiss-kill, they called it.

29

AN EXCELLENT CHAP

Gordon Wood was back in Sydney and, as usual, the first Tony knew about it was from the media. A journalist rang to say that Wood had flown back into Sydney on 15 December 1999, to spend Christmas with his family. The police were confirming he was in town but little else beyond insisting that the investigation was continuing. Did he have any reaction?

Tony resisted commenting and hung up. Of course he had a reaction—pure outrage at the notion of Wood having Christmas with his family while Caroline lay dead. A week later Gordon's picture was snapped at the airport returning from Adelaide with his mother where they'd spent a few days with one of his sisters. *Discreet entrance / Dead model's boyfriend returns*, it read across the front page above a photograph of Gordon, wrapped in sunglasses, cap and upturned collar like some rock star. The story was galling to read. He looked untouchable and it certainly seemed that way. Paul Jacob wasn't going anywhere near Wood as far as he knew. In fact, Paul seemed to be avoiding Tony's phone calls.

Somebody was talking though. Probably the police justifying themselves, assuring everyone else they were on top of the investigation when the truth was they were foundering. The newspaper reports were full of detail about Gordon's life in London; a personal reinvention of sorts, with a high-paying job, luxury cars and a jet-setting life around Europe while police had supposedly monitored cash transactions made from Australia into his account with Barclays Bank in London. The papers said the money probably came from his family but Tony was suspicious.

He waited until early afternoon on New Year's Day to call Paul Jacob, angry that he was being inundated with calls from the media wanting interviews. Tony had refused, mainly because he didn't know anything.

Paul was apologetic, calling him 'buddy' as usual and insisting he'd been running around 'like a fart in a pickle bottle'. Tony wasn't sure if the sentiment was genuine or just a way to fob him off. The call didn't last long.

Tony was out later when Paul called again and left a message. Wood had left town early and without being interviewed. Apparently the newspapers were running a story the next day accusing police of bungling the case yet again. An opportunity lost.

Paul didn't think so. There was no guarantee that Wood would talk to them, he argued, and there was a covert operation going on behind the scenes which might bear fruit. Then his oft-repeated line:

'You know what I think happened to your daughter, buddy. The worst-case scenario is that it will go back to the coroner. If that happens I will get in the witness box and say what I think happened.'

It was wearing thin but Paul Jacob was Tony's only chance.

Gordon Wood may have earned an economics degree at Sydney University but in the years after he graduated in 1986 there was no evidence of having used those skills in a professional sense. Instead, he worked as a ticket collector in the Surry Hills headquarters of the Sydney Opera House before striking out as a gym instructor and personal trainer—a career move that brought no great financial reward if Caroline Byrne's frustrations with him being a layabout were any indication. He then spent three years as Rene Rivkin's driver and gopher—personal assistant and manager, friend and trusted adviser as he boasted to others—before trying his own hand on the stock market after being given the flick by his benefactor. The records of his company, Jakuda Pty Ltd, showed little success when it was finally deregistered years after he left town in a hurry in April 1998.

Yet when he arrived in London seven months later Wood walked straight into a management position with a printing firm which earned him the equivalent of $400 000 a year. Why?

Glyn Harris, the man who recommended him for the job as an executive director, refused to explain his decision years later when asked by *Australian Financial Review* journalist Neil Chenoweth. Harris, a credentialed management consultant, told the board of PressTech Controls he had worked previously with Wood. When challenged by Chenoweth, he said Wood had come recommended but wouldn't say by whom. Glyn Harris was Wood's maternal uncle so it seems the answer was nepotism. Not only did he get a job but he moved into the Harris home.

PressTech Control, a printing company based in Hertfordshire, about 60 kilometres north-west of London, specialised in providing technical expertise for publishers needing high-calibration printing for printing bank notes or securities, even lotto forms.

It had been operating for more than 50 years but in 1998 the company was in trouble. A combination of the Asian crisis and the surging British pound was destroying the value of its international business and the company financiers decided to call in experts to rescue the ailing organisation.

Glyn Harris was their man; a so-called turnaround specialist whose job was not only to find cost savings but new ways of doing business. Harris had the business pedigree, having been a senior manager at BP, a finance director for a commodities brokerage, and a director of a shipping company and an energy company. He arrived at the company offices in the city of Hemel Hempstead with Wood in tow, introducing him with a fictitious CV as a financial controller who had worked in previous turnaround projects and put him on the board. He was put on a three-month contract paying £500 a day.

The job continued long after the three months expired as Wood became involved in debt collection, according to the company's executive chairman who described him as 'an excellent chap'. But many of his office colleagues, who regarded him as brash and inappropriate, were less impressed. His ability to turn on a show of anger was also noted, apparently trying to bully clients on the phone which some saw as calculating behaviour, premeditated for maximum effect.

And Wood's tales didn't ring true. He claimed to have been a broker in Sydney, describing how he sat trading shares on Bondi Beach with his laptop and drove luxury cars like Ferraris around town. The car bit was true, although he failed to mention that they were owned by another man and that he was a paid man-servant.

Wood even imported one of the games he and others at Joe's Café used to play. He called it 'Would you do something for a million quid?' and it was usually based on sexual favours, starting with £1000, then £10 000, £100 000 and finally £1 million. 'Gordon was the sort of guy who would do anything for the right money,' one player remarked.

There was another bit of horseplay which was more disturbing. One executive told Chenoweth of the day he was speaking to the managing director when he noticed Wood standing on the other side of a glass panel.

'I could see out but the managing director couldn't. Gordon was standing next to this glass strip waving his cock at me. He was standing there with his dick out. When he saw me he waved it at me. Then he put it back in and walked away. He did it twice. He had a sort of funny grin. He was flopping it around. It was bizarre.'

But Wood's world would change dramatically when he returned to London from his Sydney trip. The media tracked him to PressTech and started calling the company for confirmation.

Colleagues began to notice that Gordon would not answer the phone unless he knew first who was calling. He was hysterical one day after a telephonist put through a call from a journalist without his knowledge. 'I never have and I never will have anything to say to you. Never call me here again,' the journalist reported him as saying before slamming down the phone. In her subsequent story she also reported that Wood had moved out of the Harris home and was now living in an exclusive suburb of west London and driving a silver five-series BMW.

'He just simply lost it,' a colleague later recalled. 'He went out of the offices, went into his own office and shut the door. He said later, when he came out, "Don't ever tell anybody I'm here if they don't have an appointment". He was pretty well always looking over his shoulder.'

Around the same time Wood began mentioning to colleagues that he liked a well-known ski village named Megeve in the French Alps, near the Swiss border. He'd first been a few months after arriving in London and again after he got back from Sydney, bragging about taking company cars across for the weekend and then claiming expenses. He was so enamoured with the place that he'd bought a chalet or at least a share in a chalet. Few believed him.

30

RICHO'S DIARY

Paul Jacob seemed on edge. He and Tony sat having coffee near Windsor Plaza. It was mid-July 2000, six months since the missed opportunity to interview Wood in Sydney. Little had been said so far. Tony could tell he had more bad news. More delays, more excuses.

In March John Abernethy had approved a summons to allow Paul to interview Rene Rivkin but it was delayed for a month. Then April rolled around and the interrogation was delayed again. It would have to be May. In May it was changed to June and in June . . . well Tony had given up.

Each time he had bad news Jacob would spice it up with some snippet of information to show he was doing something. Rather than give him heart, such details only made Tony more despondent. It was five years since Caroline's death and from what Tony could tell they should have had enough evidence to put Wood on trial and at least publicly embarrass Rivkin. Why were they so reluctant to go in and finish the job?

'We've got two options,' Jacob said finally, breaking the tension. 'We can call on Rivkin next week and question him about his actions and statements but we know he will not speak to us. The second option is to wait until after the Olympics in September.'

Tony didn't feel like backing down. He wasn't asking for miracles, just to be told the truth. If he couldn't keep a commitment then don't pretend. It just made the wait worse.

That was the problem. Jacob knew he couldn't promise anything. He wanted to protect the guy but he couldn't bullshit about what was happening and how long it would take. He also had to be mindful of how much to tell him, given he might one day be an important witness. The balance was difficult and words had to be chosen carefully. He already worried that Tony was seeing his answers in black and white when the reality was far less certain.

Jacob was being stuffed around as well but Tony wouldn't understand. There was constant pressure inside the force for him to simply take what he had back to the coroner and let them make a decision which, at this stage, would have been to drop the matter. It was such an old case and they were snowed under every week with something new. Resources were strapped and manpower was limited. When he started he was given six officers and now he had two apart from himself—Matt Moss, who'd been there at the start because he was the assigned detective from Rose Bay and the systems analyst Bianca Comina, who was not even a police officer. She was a shy but fantastic young woman who'd taken the job on a whim and was responsible for everything from managing documents to producing timelines and establishing profiles. Mossy was an old Special Weapons and Operations Squad (SWOS) detective who had been give permission to do what he could when he had the time. It was an untenable situation, and impossible for Tony to appreciate. He felt like the pig in the middle.

A few weeks later the pair met again at the same place. They'd finally interviewed Rivkin and Paul could hardly contain his excitement. Rivkin had 'bagged' Wood, he said. Wood had defrauded him of $70 000 amongst other things, and he was going to give them the evidence. Richardson was next.

Tony listened, perplexed. The interview had been done onboard Rivkin's $7 million boat, *Dajoshadita*, which meant it was conducted on Rivkin's terms, his home turf rather than the austere and uncomfortable surrounds of a police station where the cops would have the upper hand psychologically.

Paul seemed to read his thoughts. They'd had no choice, he said. The businessman had changed the venue on them at the last minute. It was frustrating but they had to press ahead given the opportunity. Paul had sought approval from his superiors before he agreed. Still, they'd got what they wanted.

It took less than a fortnight for news of the Irondale interviews with Rivkin and Richardson to reach the media. Less than a month before the world's eyes turned to Sydney for the 2000 Olympic Games, the mayor of its athletes' village was being questioned over a murder investigation.

The papers were quick to point out that Richardson was not a suspect as such, but could throw light on Gordon Wood's alibi—that he had picked up Richardson from the Alife restaurant in Stanley Street, East Sydney, where he had been lunching with Rivkin, and taken him either to the Rugby League headquarters in Phillip Street or to the Park Street headquarters of Australian Consolidated Press, where the former Labor minister was employed.

If Richardson corroborated the story then it destroyed the evidence of two key witnesses, Lance Melbourne and Craig Martin, who insisted that around the same time Gordon Wood was actually at Watsons Bay with another man, possibly Adam Leigh, and his girlfriend Caroline Byrne just hours before her death.

Tony hoped the publicity made both men squirm. It was more than two years since Wood had given evidence before John Abernethy and neither man had come forward voluntarily to tell police what they knew. They deserved whatever bad publicity came their way, and to think that Richardson was once a senior minister in federal government.

Paul Jacob telephoned. 'Richardson's diary shows he was lunching with Peter Moore that day, and he'd got a credit card receipt to prove it.'

That meant Gordon Wood had been caught telling lies, Tony thought as he hung up.

Within days of the media stories Gordon Wood had resigned as a director of PressTech in London. He would remain with the company for a few more months but the writing was on the wall. By Christmas he had been sacked, although he stayed in touch with his workmates.

'He used to phone me quite frequently,' one said later. 'He'd say, I can't tell you where I am, but I'm sitting in a café in the sun.'

It wasn't actually sun. Gordon was in Megeve, figuring out how to craft a living in a ski resort town even though he'd had no real experience in the snowfields. He was all but destitute, with no job and no car because it had broken down on the way to France and he had no money to fix the damn thing. He sought refuge in the only place he felt in command—the gym—and it was here his luck would hold yet again as he struck up a conversation with an Englishman named Simon Butler who, by chance, not only owned a ski chalet with a spare bedsit but was a successful tour operator in the French Alps. The pair formed an immediate friendship. Butler lent him a car, gave him a room and found him a job as a photographer taking shots of the rich guests as they played in the snow. It was hardly the life of a playboy, but Gordon Wood had landed on his feet once again.

31

A GUT FEELING

Some memories on the job are impossible to erase, like the moments cops realise their decisions, good and bad, have lasting consequences. Sometimes they are fatal.

Paul Jacob had nightmares about John Wayne Glover, a former pie salesman dubbed the Granny Killer for his murderous spree across Sydney's north shore between 1989 and 1990 during which he bludgeoned to death six elderly women.

Jacob was a young constable then. It was his first really big case; part of a team trying to find the killer before he could strike again under the glare of constant media attention. Glover had been in their sights for weeks when they watched him enter the home of his mistress, Joan Sinclair, at Beauty Point on 19 March 1990. They assumed he was picking her up and taking her somewhere, possibly for a meeting with his solicitor but after 30 minutes neither of them emerged.

Eventually a uniformed officer was sent forward to investigate. He retreated as soon as he saw a bloody hammer lying on the lounge room floor. Glover had killed again. Jacob entered the house with the others, his gun drawn; they ignored Joan Sinclair's bloody remains as they searched for Glover who was still in the house. It was Jacob who peered into the bathroom and saw him, lying chin deep in water, with spittle dribbling from his mouth. Glover had taken an overdose. He survived, was convicted and sentenced to life. His last victim might have lived if the police had intervened earlier.

More than a decade later Jacob and his then boss, Denis O'Toole, still lived with the consequences of that decision. O'Toole occasionally drove out to Dubbo where Glover was jailed, hoping he would break and tell them about other women he probably murdered over the years. O'Toole reckoned, for example, that Glover might have killed the famous Sydney artist and socialite Florence Broadhurst, who was found bludgeoned to death inside her apartment in 1977. Glover had met her at his brother's wedding in 1972. There were others too, some in Sydney and some in Victoria. It seemed to O'Toole and Jacob that if Glover admitted the crimes they might free themselves of some of their own guilt.

In the first few days of January 2001, O'Toole made his last trip to see Glover. Paul Jacob went along. O'Toole was retiring and he wanted the murderer to know there would be no more visits, probably in the hope that he would finally give up his secrets. Glover stayed mute and the pair headed back to Sydney.

Jacob told Tony about the visit a few days later, hoping he might understand a little more of his own dilemmas. Instead, the conversation turned angry once again. Both were on edge. It had been months since the Irondale team had managed to make headway on the case. The Olympics had got in the way and then his over-worked officers needed time off. Paul was as frustrated as Tony but it was inevitable that the conversation would end badly.

Despite Jacob's assurances, Tony could not shake the belief that Rivkin was in some way involved in Caroline's death. Neither was there any evidence of a homosexual affair with Wood. Rivkin's staff and colleagues had dismissed the notion. Tony was not convinced. Of course his friends and employees would stand up for him.

The conversation deteriorated further, Tony's anger fuelled by an interview in which Rivkin described Caroline as having been obsessive, 'no angel', and had cheated on Gordon Wood. It was a vicious lie and yet, from his perspective, Paul appeared to be going soft on him.

There was something going on; Tony was sure of it. There were politics in play here. Gordon would never be charged or brought before a court because it would be too embarrassing for Rivkin and his powerful friends.

Just as the *Witness* program had three years before, Rene Rivkin's performance on *60 Minutes* on 21 June 2001 once again heightened public interest in the case. Rivkin was at first defensive, telling journalist Richard Carlton that he wished he'd never met Gordon Wood.

'Do you think he did it?' asked Carlton.

Rivkin didn't hesitate. 'No, as a matter of fact I don't think he did it. My gut feeling is that he was there but he didn't do it.'

'So, a pretty unsavoury character then?'

'No, I said he was there but didn't do it. Why does that make him unsavoury?'

Now Carlton had to defend his line of questioning. 'Well, because you are associating him with her death.'

'No, not at all. Either you don't understand or you are choosing not to. What I'm arguing is they might have been strolling, they might have had an argument and she might have jumped to her death. All I can tell you about him is that in the years he worked for me never once did he criticise her and three to five times a day he told me he loved her, so I doubt very much that he had anything to do with it.'

'But he's shot through now, hasn't he.'

'Well, if you were an O.J. Simpson-type character, and didn't do it, there'd be every inclination and every advantage to shoot through.'

Carlton moved on. The interview was about Rivkin rather than the Caroline Byrne murder, but the impact was significant. Tony Byrne watched the program with mixed emotions. He couldn't stand the prancing eccentric businessman and his money but the man's huge ego had exposed new information. Here was Wood's former boss, on national television, saying he believed his chauffeur was with Caroline when she died.

32

CUNNING RAT

The US President George W. Bush was at Buckingham Palace lunching with the Queen the week NSW homicide detectives Gary Jubelin and Jason Evers flew into London. Less than two months later the world would be in shock over the terrorist attack on New York, but in the balmy mid-winter of July 2001 the biggest media events in Britain were the protests over Bush's stance on global warming, and the jailing of author and politician Lord Jeffery Archer for perjury in a libel case against a tabloid newspaper.

Jubelin and Evers had left behind a wild Sydney winter for their secret visit to interview Gordon Wood. The trip had been planned ever since he'd left Sydney a second time. When he wasn't in Megev with Simon Butler, Wood was living in a modest apartment in Chelsea since but no-one was quite sure how he was surviving financially. They decided against arranging an interview in case Wood reacted badly. Instead it was best to just confront him and hope he would cooperate. After all, they weren't here to arrest him—not yet at least.

Wood was almost at his front door when the pair jumped out of a car. His instinctive response was to refuse. He'd already been interviewed twice by police and then again in the witness box at the coronial inquest. He had nothing more to say and wanted to forget about the whole thing and get on with his life.

But Jubelin wasn't taking no for an answer. This was a new investigation with new information and new questions. It wouldn't look good further down the track if he refused. Besides, an innocent man had nothing to lose. Wood agreed to meet them the next day at a local police station.

The transcript would be the biggest document in the police brief; almost six hours of a see-sawing conversation as Jubelin and Evers sought to find a chink in Wood's story and he, in turn, maintained his story and alibi.

Much had happened in the three years since Wood gave evidence at the Coroner's Court. Telephone records had been scoured which enabled police to track Wood's movements on the day of Caroline's death as he moved around the city and the eastern suburbs, fetching and carrying for Rene Rivkin. During the morning he made calls to people and businesses between Waverley, Annandale and the city where Rivkin was working in his George Street office. Just after midday he rang Alife restaurant—one of his boss's favourite lunch haunts—and booked a table. Rivkin lunched there at least once a week before walking around the corner to the flat he and his crew used for his usual afternoon nap. By coincidence, the Alife owner Michael Jaggard lived in the same building and knew Gordon and Caroline from City Gym across the road.

At 1.18 pm Wood called his mate Brett Cochrane who he met with Nick Samartis for lunch after being rebuffed, he claimed, by a drowsy Caroline who was still in bed dosed on pills. But was the call to arrange the meeting or was it made after he left his friends to allegedly pick up Rivkin and Graham Richardson from Alife? Wood couldn't recall, he told them.

His afternoon phone calls again ranged from a golf driving range in the city owned by Rivkin to his boss's home in Vaucluse. Then at 5.14 pm the phone was suddenly diverted to his paging service.

'Under what circumstances would you divert your phone?' Jubelin asked.

'Private time. Pretty much after work I'd always divert it,' he replied. 'If Rivkin needed me he'd come on the pager.'

Wood didn't know it but police had records of a page sent by Rivkin to Wood around the same time, asking him to come to The Sanctuary, as they called the flat, and bring another of the team, Gary Redding.

Wood had clearly received the message because he'd called Redding, a man he described to Jubelin as 'a hopeless case'. He called Rivkin back at 5.48 pm to confirm. It was the last call Gordon Wood made until 4.44 am the next day when he telephoned Tony Byrne to confirm that Caroline Byrne's body had been found at the foot of The Gap.

The communication blackspot appeared suspicious for a man so wedded to his mobile and who worked for such a demanding boss. And why was his phone off when two pages were received—both from Rivkin—at 7.38 pm and 8.33 pm?

Was he asleep in front of the television as he claimed or arguing with his girlfriend at Watsons Bay, observed, by chance, by an inquisitive artist named John Doherty?

Jubelin also wanted to probe Wood's apparent discrepancies about the time he claimed to have awoken in front of his television. Was it 12.40 am as he told police four days after Caroline's death or around 11.30 pm—more than an hour earlier—as he would later say in subsequent police and television interviews?

'Now 12.40 is quite a specific time. It's not 12.30 or around 12. Can you tell me why you were so specific?' Jubelin asked.

Wood was nonchalant. 'I would guess that if I woke up on the sofa and Caroline wasn't at home then that is a major event in my life and I would absolutely check what time it was. That would make sense to me.'

And the later estimates of '11ish' and '11.30ish', Jubelin continued.

Wood stood his ground. 'If you mean did I change my story, no. I could have easily got the time wrong. That doesn't bother me. I would say that a year later I did not have an absolute recollection of what time I woke up.'

Jubelin wanted clarity. 'With time for reflection and the fact that I have made you aware of those varying times, what time do you think you woke up?'

'I would believe the time I said closest to the incident. If I said 12.40 four days after she died then that would have been what I remembered most correctly.'

It was a critical point. Wood had to justify how he had time to walk several kilometres to get a car from Crown Street, drive through the eastern suburbs to Camp Cove, run along the cliff tops looking for Caroline and then drive back to the city to pick up Tony and Peter Byrne, particularly when the Byrnes claimed his call to wake them was made at 12.30 am—ten minutes before Wood said he even woke up.

Back in Sydney Paul Jacob was ecstatic. Not only had the interview gone well but he'd just been promoted to Detective Inspector. Things were looking up, he quipped, handing Tony one of his new cards as they sat drinking coffee in the Windsor Plaza coffee shop and running over the events of the past month.

Tony wanted to know what Wood had been up to since leaving his high-paying job. Jacob shrugged. Probably still living off his severance package, or maybe he was back doing personal training at a gym. He didn't really care. What really mattered was they'd had more than five hours of interview with him. It was detailed and it was damning; fantastic he said, even though they regarded him as a cunning rat and he had not deviated from his original statement, even his afternoon alibi, insisting that Graham Richardson was wrong.

They were on a roll now, Paul said, with plans to interview George Freris, Rivkin's right-hand man who was now living in Tasmania, before going back to Rivkin and Graham Richardson to firm up their interviews and statements.

For the first time in eighteen months Tony finished a conversation with Paul Jacob feeling positive, as if his hopes of a resolution might be met. Their meetings and conversations were more frequent now, sometimes several times a week through September and October. Each time something new seemed to have happened.

Detectives had also tracked down Adam Leigh, the booker who was supposedly with Caroline and Wood during the afternoon. He was now in a mental institution in Melbourne and unlikely to ever come out, let alone present credible evidence in a court. Apparently the man was paranoid, wrapping himself in silver foil and wearing a silver cap because he believed everyone was out to get him.

And Gary Redding was now suspected of being the second man at The Gap that night. Tony knew the name; he was one of the Joe's Café mob and part of the Rivkin group, a strange man with bulging arms and tattoos coupled with a hot temper. Caroline had mentioned him a few times as a friend of George Freris. Paul wouldn't say much more other than Redding was in New Zealand and Paul was waiting to get permission to go and interview him. Redding was unlikely to admit to anything but at least they could get a sense of whether he might be involved.

Martha Jabour, from the HVSG, joined them for coffee one morning in late October, mainly because Tony was now considering establishing a memorial at the Randwick Children's Hospital and he wanted to get her approval. As usual the conversation meandered back and forth, revisiting old theories and questions and how they fitted into the new information. But it always ended up at the same point: was there enough to convict Wood?

Paul insisted they were progressing. He hesitated to give a date but he hoped to have the brief put together and forwarded to the DPP by next June, the next anniversary of Caroline's death.

'Is an open finding the best we can expect?' Tony asked.

Jacob shook his head. 'I would tell them from the witness box that I do not believe Caroline took her own life. I'll say that our investigation showed that she was killed.'

Tony had decided long ago that he might have to be satisfied with something less than a guilty verdict. A public declaration by police that they believed she had been killed would be enough.

'Paul, after all these years my family and I would be satisfied with that statement.'

Martha chipped in. 'I think that's the worst-case scenario.'

That night Tony called his children together for a family dinner to tell them about the conversation. He'd kept them away from the detail of the investigation most of the time because it was his load to carry, his daughter and his fight. They were young and needed to move on with their own lives. But this was different.

A few days later he sat down and wrote to Martha:

> It is now six years and five months since her death and I find it hard to believe at times that I still have my health and my sanity. As Paul pointed out for many victims there is no light at the end of the tunnel. I am well aware of how fortunate I am to have Paul working on my case.

33

NEW PRIORITIES

By January 2002, the case had stalled again. The entire Irondale team had been scattered to various parts of the state on new murder cases and it was going to keep them away from the Caroline Byrne case for a while. There simply weren't enough investigators to handle everything.

Even Jacob had been called out, directed to head an investigation into the disappearance of a 31-year-old Bathurst woman named Janine Vaughan who was last seen just before 4 am on 7 December 2001 getting into a car in the main street.

Local police had got nowhere and now Sydney homicide had been called in. It would be an investigation filled with regret, not only because it remained unsolved six years later but because it would publicly question his skills and, more importantly, his ethics.

Tony Byrne didn't sound convinced by the news: 'But we're so close. You can't stop now,' he protested.

'Sorry, buddy, but when we're on callout and these things happen your daughter's case is the first to suffer. I know it's painful for your family but if we don't get these cases straight away there will be a queue of 20 or more Tony Byrnes down the track. As it is we've got 300 unsolved murders in NSW. We don't need any more.'

Tony couldn't disagree. As infuriating as it was Paul made sense. 'Paul, how long before you get back on the case?'

The answer was one he would dread: 'How long's a piece of string?'

Tony wasn't about to let the matter drop. He had little choice but to take his case directly to the politicians, he warned. It was nothing against Paul but how could police expect to solve complicated crimes if they didn't have enough detectives?

Two days later Jacob was back on the phone. His boss, Detective Superintendent Nick Kaldas, wanted to meet with Tony to try to dissuade him from going public. Kaldas seemed reasonable and genuine but the message was the same. The homicide squad was supposed to have 80 detectives but there were only 38, a shortage he blamed on the fallout from the Wood Royal Commission. It would take time to replace the ranks of experienced officers who left, either forced out or demoralised by its impact.

'Tony, I am the head of Crime Agencies and I intend to be here for some time. I'll make this commitment to you now. Caroline's case has not been downgraded and never will be. It is not an unsolved murder. It has not been put in the big box with the other unsolved murders. Caroline's case is active. I promise you that as soon as resources become available Paul will complete his report, the brief will go to the DPP and the prosecution process will begin.'

Tony stewed for a week before writing a letter. Although he appreciated Kaldas' candour, the commitment on resources was open-ended, and although he would never question Paul Jacob's integrity it was clear that he was not able to keep his promises.

> I do not know what to do, I have reached the end of the road, the frustrations and the suffering some victims have to endure is unreasonable. I believe I have a duty and a responsibility to raise these issues with the Minister. The shortage of resources in crime agency and the impact that is having directly and indirectly on the community is unsatisfactory and must be addressed.

* * *

It is rare for a late-night sitting in the Legislative Council of the NSW Parliament to attract public attention. Law is not made here, in the Upper House as it is informally known, but reviewed and occasionally amended to satisfy the gaggle of minor parties needed by the government of the day to win approval of its legislation crafted through the Legislative Assembly, or Lower House. Even the MPs have no constituents other than the party members who granted them their spot on the ticket every eight years.

Ron Dyer had been a lawyer and party hack before he took his place on the assembly's red leather seats in 1979. Dyer did not cut an imposing political figure, either physically or in demeanour, yet he not only survived but thrived in the double-dealing world of the NSW Labor Party. Now, 23 years and three elections later, he was in the shadow of retirement; a one-time cabinet minister whose longevity had made him 'Father of the House'.

At the end of each sitting day an adjournment debate occurs. It is largely procedural but gives MPs an opportunity to make a speech, either of an issue which has bothered them such as communication from a concerned elector. On the night of 30 October 2002, it was Dyer's turn. Hansard records would show it was 10.39 pm when he rose to his feet.

'At the request of Mr Tony Byrne of Cronulla I wish to raise some concerns regarding the police investigation into the death of Mr Byrne's daughter Caroline,' he began before summarising the details of the case and the investigation which, despite Paul Jacob's hopes that it would be completed by the seventh anniversary of Caroline's death, was in limbo. Nothing had happened since Tony's meeting with Nick Kaldas eight months before. Irondale remained stalled because of the problems of running a police force stretched by resources, time and political imperatives.

Dyer concluded: 'Due to his anguish and concern at the now lengthy delay in completing the police investigation and forwarding the papers to the Director of Public Prosecutions, and especially having regard to the reason given for not completing the matter, that is, a stated lack of resources, Mr Byrne has requested that I raise this matter publicly, which I have now done. On behalf of

Mr Byrne I call for an early conclusion to the police investigation.' With that the chamber emptied for the night.

Tony had telephoned Dyer in desperation as the investigation floundered into its eighth year. He'd finally grown tired of the promises and excuses that seemed at odds with the political veneer of a police force assuring the electorate they were being well served. In truth they were not. The number of officers posted on government websites and in ministerial media releases was a bureaucratic smokescreen to cover the fact that there weren't enough police to investigate the city's crime, from simple burglaries and housebreaks all the way to violence, rape and even murder.

It left him feeling helpless yet again, embarrassed to tell his kids that he had failed Caroline and them by not getting a result. As much as it would hurt and embarrass Paul Jacob, Tony felt he had no choice but to go public although his choice was by chance rather than design.

He'd chosen Dyer on the spur of the moment after getting a political flyer in the mail one day in late August. It was a newsletter spruiking the merits of the NSW Government's budget, including a promise that 'police will be given more resources in the fight against crime'. The wording angered Tony because he was being told the opposite by the police themselves. He underlined the phrase and turned the page. There was an advert: 'NEED HELP?' it asked in capital letters above a photograph of Ron Dyer. He decided to call.

Dyer listened with a fresh, sympathetic ear. It was scandalous, he said, and promised to seek answers from his colleagues. When none came after several months of letters with the office of Police Minister Michael Costa, Dyer took it to the floor of the House and made the issue public.

Four days later the speech found its way into the media in a more dramatic form: *Detective shortage stalls Gap killer hunt*, declared a Sunday newspaper, launching into a tirade about Sydney's most intriguing murder mystery which had been left unsolved and a family desperate for answers by a lack of staff.

'It is a terrible day, for the victims of crime and for the State of NSW, when a family is told that the investigation into their daughter's homicide has stalled because of the shortage of homicide detectives in Crime Agencies,' Tony lamented to the journalist.

The Police Minister Michael Costa immediately denied the claim, insisting the delay was due to 'limited leads not limited resources' but, once again, it was the potential for public embarrassment that would force the authorities to act.

Behind the scenes Costa was more conciliatory but continued to defend the investigation and its resources. For significant periods, he wrote the day after Dyer's speech, there had been up to eight detectives on the case, spending thousands of hours of police time and even travelling to the UK.

> The investigation has been required to balance its objectives with other important case demands. The high intensity of the investigation has, on occasions, been intermittent. However, this is not to suggest the police attention to the case has been anything other than constant and focussed.

But, he argued, the problem was evidence.

> The publicity has generated widespread speculation as to the involvement of several well-known people. However, the deputy commissioner informs me there is still insufficient evidence to establish the culpability of any one person.

There was another contribution to the delay. The senior echelons of the NSW Police Service had been in a state of flux because of a major restructure under which nine major crime squads from robbery to drugs, fraud and homicide would come under a single command. But the search for a commander had turned into a farce when the five candidates were all rejected, effectively leaving the state's elite detectives rudderless and at least 120 members under-strength—exactly the criticism now being denied. A month later the government announced that 520 new detectives were being rushed through training to fill the breech. It was too little too late for Tony Byrne.

34

BAM-BAM-BAM

When Robert Byrne had moved to Sydney from Camden one of the first things he did was buy a yacht. He found a mooring near the Iron Cove Bridge behind Balmain and weekends became a water adventure in a city built around an extraordinary harbour. Brother Peter was most often his companion; mates as much as brothers, they spent time together cruising from bay to bay around the harbour, having lazy lunches and indulging a spot of fishing.

Other family members came as well; Tony, Deanna and Caroline, even Gordon Wood on rare occasions, although the boys didn't offer their prospective brother-in-law a place in their club. They never questioned their sister's choice in boyfriends but secretly hoped she would find someone else. There was something odd about him.

When Caroline died their dad stopped coming out on the boat, at least until Robert found a mooring at Red Leaf below the Woollahra Council Chambers where he worked as a town planner.

Tony reasoned that the memories weren't quite as tough because Caroline had never been there. Other than lawn bowls it was one of the few ways to take his mind off his elder daughter. Every few weeks he would head out with Robert and Peter for a few hours of peace on the harbour where the conversation could drift from the tide of injustice.

The one thing he hated was the journey home, forced to drive through Double Bay and past Rene Rivkin's office. The office dominated the street: RIVKIN, it trumpeted beneath a giant clock, as if customers had found their financial Mecca. And there was the jowled businessman, grinning from giant posters in the front windows. Under the banner *Join the Smiling Club*, Rivkin was pictured in a bright yellow shirt reclining in the back of an open-topped sports car being driven over the Harbour Bridge, his eyes behind sunglasses and a cigar clamped between his teeth. The face seemed to mock Tony, as if to say 'Here am I—untouchable, famous and making money while you suffer'.

He could not be sure if Rivkin was personally involved with Caroline's death but Tony remained convinced he knew what happened that night and was protecting Wood, even now.

What made it even more galling was that despite all the promises, Irondale remained suspended. Paul Jacob was still in Bathurst on the Janine Vaughan case and nobody had worked on Caroline's case for more than a year. Even the speech and letters of Ron Dyer had ultimately failed.

The only thing which kept Tony sane was Rivkin's battles in the courts. He had lost a defamation case against Fairfax which had cost him millions in legal fees and then won a similar case against Channel 7, over the *Witness* interview with Gordon Wood, and was awarded $150 000. Then he was charged with insider trading, accused of buying Qantas shares after being told of a plan by a small regional airline, Impulse, to sell out to the iconic giant. Rivkin was assuring his investors there was nothing to worry about, describing the court proceedings as 'free entertainment'.

As Tony and the boys drove home one evening in March 2003, Peter pulled over in Double Bay to pick up groceries for the night's meal. While Peter and Robert were inside the supermarket Tony walked back along the street towards Rivkin's office. He had no idea why or what he would do if Rivkin was inside but he felt compelled to get close, as if to show he wasn't afraid. He walked past the front door, paused and then turned left into a side street. Even in the laneway every window had a poster with Rivkin's annoying smirk. Tony wanted to wipe it off, make him feel vulnerable instead of protected.

Tony had sometimes joked about knocking off Rivkin. He had wondered how other parents would feel in his shoes, if they had fantasies where they allowed themselves to think crazy things they would never intend carrying out. It was a defence mechanism, he told himself; a way of feeling powerful at least in his own mind. As if he could do something if he chose. But, of course, he never would.

But standing in front of Rivkin' office he thought there might be something less dramatic he could do. Tony stared at the poster in the laneway and wondered what it would be like to fire six slugs through the window. That'd wipe the smile off Rivkin's face. He turned away and went back to the car before he was recognised, ashamed and yet thrilled.

Over the next few weeks his thoughts turned into a plan. He would drive into the laneway late at night, roll down the window. BAM-BAM-BAM. Then drive off before anyone was the wiser. The cops would turn up the next day, there'd be a huge fuss in the media about threats against Rivkin and Tony would be accused, or at least questioned. It would be like the posters he and the kids pasted up around East Sydney only this time he wouldn't admit to anything. And there would be no harm other than a smashed window. The notion was real and powerful.

But before he could act Rene Rivkin was convicted of insider trading and sentenced to nine months weekend detention in prison. The reason for Tony's frustration had disappeared.

There was something surreal about Rivkin's demise, not because of his conviction but because he had made so little out of a deal that had the potential to destroy his professional life. The 50 000 Qantas shares had made a profit of just $2000 for his company and $346 for himself.

Six hours after being sentenced on Thursday 29 May 2003, Rivkin was in the ABC studios taping an interview for the Andrew

Denton show *Enough Rope*. It was patent he was still in shock over the decision and that the notion of prison hadn't quite sunk in. Still, the audience of 150 could sense his fear behind the bravado.

'Going to Silverwater on periodic detention doesn't worry me because I like the average person and of course that's presumably the sort of person you meet at Silverwater. Now in addition of course, I'm sure that I'm going to be able to teach about the stock markets on weekends.'

Rivkin spent the next fifteen minutes arguing about his sentence, accusing the legal system of treating him like a nineteenth-century witch. It was they, not he, who understood the meaning of insider trading.

But the interview was heading in another, more personal direction. Rivkin's scheduled first weekend behind bars would begin on 6 June—his 59th birthday and 30th wedding anniversary. His wife, Gayle, was visibly upset in court, slumping forward and cracking her head on a wooden balustrade when Justice Anthony Whealy announced that jail was the only appropriate sentence, then crying out, 'My life is over,' when the sentence was announced. Whealy was also well aware of Rivkin's fragile mental state and raised the concerns about an attempted suicide in jail.

'Has this thought ever crossed your mind, suicide?' Denton asked.

Rivkin didn't blink. 'Oh suicide's been on my mind for 20, 30 years, and have I thought about suicide in the last week, yes.'

'And why is that?'

'Well injustice, I can't stand the injustice. Can't stand injustice, just cannot stand it.'

'And when you've had these thoughts what have you done with them?'

'Well let me tell you if I were a single man I would have done it by now. But I'm not a single man, I've got a wonderful wife and five wonderful kids and I can't do it to them . . .'

The conversation drifted first to his family's reaction and then to whether he would appeal the conviction and sentence.

'If you take it to appeal and you lose, what's that going to mean?' Denton asked.

'I don't know what it's going to mean. I'll probably go to the High Court then.'

'And if you lose there?'

'If I lose there I'll probably commit suicide.'

'Seriously?'

'Why not?'

'What about your wife and kids?'

'Well they don't really want to live with a convicted criminal.'

'Is that what they've said to you?'

'No, but that's my suspicion.'

There was another anniversary that weekend. The second day of Rivkin's incarceration was also the eighth anniversary of Caroline Byrne's death. Her father sat alone in his lounge room watching the Denton interview. Rivkin had no right to talk about injustice, he thought.

Where others may have had compassion for a sick man Tony felt only vindication. The net was tightening. Maybe justice was still possible. He thought back to the family dinner the night in 1998 that delivered an open finding in Caroline's death. They'd all known the coroner did not have enough to say that she was murdered. There had to be more, they couldn't give up.

'Kids, I need your help,' he announced at the table. 'I don't know how or when but I'm going to destroy Rene Rivkin.' Instead, Rivkin was self-destructing and all Tony had to do was sit back and watch it happen.

35

THE WRONG SPOT

After five years and hundreds of interviews, there was still one problem that remained unresolved—how could police prove that Caroline Byrne did not commit suicide and, therefore, had been murdered. It was a vital issue because no matter how strong the witness statements about Gordon Wood's strange behaviour and his phoney alibi, they alone did not amount to proof of murder.

Brian Wyver had telephoned a physics expert named Rodney Cross in 1998 to gauge his opinion about whether it was possible for Caroline to have leaped to her death. The short answer was yes, the University of Sydney academic had responded. Given a decent run-up, the average woman could run fast enough at take-off to leap over nine metres off a 30-metre-high cliff. It was all theory of course, and did not take into account the terrain, a moonless night, the offshore wind or Caroline's sporting ability. Wyver took it no further.

The first Paul Jacob knew of it was four years later, in December 2002, when Cross phoned the coroner's office to complain that his bill had still not been paid. He wrote to Cross to apologise, arrange to pay the bill and ask Cross if he could get a written report to include in the brief being prepared for the DPP.

By September 2003 Jacob was becoming confident the evidence could be strong enough to charge Wood. They'd done a lot of work during the year, helped by a new copper who'd joined the team and was putting in a lot of work. Paul Quigg, or Quiggy as he was typically known, was a bit of a legend in cop footy circles where he'd built up a reputation over the years. He was also a mate of Andrew Blanchette's, Caroline's former boyfriend, and immediately felt part of a close group of investigators.

What was needed now was the clincher; something which might be definitive amongst the tranche of circumstantial evidence. He contacted Rod Cross again.

The position of Caroline Byrne's body at the base of the cliff had been a significant issue during the 1998 coronial inquiry, he wrote, but without expert evidence on the physics of falling nothing could be proved one way or the other. Police wanted an authoritative answer of the likely scenarios of her death.

Cross accepted the brief and began experimenting by hurling sand bags on the lawns of the university to get a sense of how fast an object could be thrown. Mannequins roughly the same size and weight as Caroline were then made and thrown by students in local parks and into swimming pools. He organised running and jumping tests to get a sense of acceleration over short distances. Cross filmed everything, as rudimentary as the experiments were, but it was a start.

The problem was a mathematical equation as much as a physical one. Just how fast would Caroline have to be travelling when she left the cliff edge to end up less than three seconds later more than ten metres out from the base 30 metres below? The answer, Cross decided, was a horizontal velocity of 4.05 metres a second, the equivalent of 14.6 kilometres an hour.

The assumption was that she had been thrown from an area at the main curve of the bay where police sometimes landed helicopters. There was a clear 20 metres of flat ground where anyone of average fitness could build up enough speed to leap a distance that would not be possible on flat ground—even for an Olympic athlete, given that the world record long jump was less than nine metres.

But she would have had to be running at top speed in near total darkness and into a sea breeze before jumping from a cliff edge she could not see. And the ground rose sharply towards the ledge which would significantly affect her speed. Cross had his doubts but he needed science to prove it.

He told Paul Jacob about his qualms before filing his report. Don't worry about the conclusions, he said. I want to do more tests. Jacob was glad he got the call before he read the report's summary which seemed to rule out his theory that Caroline Byrne was thrown:

> I concluded the most likely cause of death was that Caroline Byrne ran over the edge of the cliff in the dark . . . A less likely option is that she was thrown by one or two people.

Bushfires, Steve Waugh's last Test at the Sydney Cricket Ground and Rene Rivkin's health. It was a typically slow summer's day on 8 January 2004 as Paul Jacob and Paul Quigg sat in the Irondale office at Kincumber catching up on paperwork. It was just the two of them plus Bianca Comina on the case at the moment, mainly coordinating Rod Cross's new work to do a more comprehensive analysis of the scene. They wished his report, completed in late November, had been conclusive and ruled out jumping but it did the opposite. However, it kept open the possibility that she might have been chased and leaped in fear. And that led to the nagging question of who was out there with Wood that night.

Although they had discounted him from the investigation, Rivkin remained a figure of interest. They pored over a newspaper article about the businessman's latest attempts to stay out of jail on weekend detention. He'd been convicted eight months ago but had only spent two days in jail before collapsing after being asked to submit to a body search and was carted off to hospital to be treated for bipolar disorder. The bloke had then undergone brain surgery to remove non-malignant tumours and then had his gall bladder removed and received treatment for deep vein thrombosis. In December, another doctor's certificate had been produced which would put off a decision until next month. He was either a very sick man or this was a bloody scam.

Jacob turned his attention to an email sent by Cross. Two days earlier he'd gone out to The Gap with Mark Powderly, the rescue squad cop who'd recovered Caroline's body. They wanted to go back to scratch and recreate the scene as accurately as possible, including measurements critical to a proper scientific calculation. And Powderly had some theories about launch points which Cross should hear first-hand.

That same afternoon Cross had sent Jacob an email in which he appeared to question where they were concentrating on as a take-off point:

> Paul, we spent four hours at The Gap this morning and took lots of photos. I'm only 70 per cent convinced but it looks like Mark P is probably correct that a point south of the corner post was not possible given that CB's head was not smashed to bits. Entry from the south would probably mean entry head first into rocks on one side of the cavity. Entry from a point slightly north of the corner post would allow her head to enter the cavity with the first point of impact being her shoulders.

Maybe they should be looking from the north ledge as an alternate spot. It was much further to the landing point which would have made it impossible for Caroline to have jumped, even based on the theoretical speeds.

This new email didn't say much but it had some photos taken out at The Gap attached. Jacob pulled up the series of photos, the first of which showed an officer in white overalls standing with an orange marker in the crevice in which Caroline Byrne had landed. He had long ago steeled himself against thinking about Caroline's fall but the photos were a stark reminder of her fate. The others were of the same scene, taken from above and at various angles around the hole.

Back in Sydney Bianca was looking at the same email. She'd been sent a copy as a matter of course, and would add it to the growing file, but as she stared at the photo she realised that something was seriously amiss—the rocks looked different.

She looked more closely. The shapes were definitely different to the photos she remembered being on file. She pulled the file just to make sure then checked and rechecked the running sheet to try and work out how the mistake had occurred. The next day she drove to Kincumber to tell Paul Jacob.

In all the years since Caroline Byrne's death, no-one had thought to go back to Powderly, the man who'd retrieved her body, and check the accuracy of the place they assumed she'd landed. There was a statement in which he appeared clear about her landing place; they had photo-geometrical maps and a video that was made a year after the tragedy. Could they all be wrong, using the same, flawed mentality of making assumptions rather than checking?

Jacob rang Powderly. The big square cop, now back in his hometown of Dubbo, recounted standing on the top of the cliff watching officers below insert a mannequin into a rock cavity among the jumble of grey boulders.

'I said, "What are you doing over there. It's the wrong spot",' Powderly recalled. 'It's further north a few metres, near Pyramid Rock.'

Jacob felt his blood run cold. Not only did they have a problem proving that Caroline was thrown but they had just handed Wood's defence team a free kick which might get him off. If he was ever charged, that was.

Tony Byrne was quite specific at times when marking his diary. Not only was the date important but also the time of the call or meeting. Monday, 23 February 2004 was such an entry. *Paul Jacob telephoned at 2.45 pm*, he wrote. Tony knew the call was important if only because Paul was standing in the middle of Taylor Square at the crest of Oxford Street in Darlinghurst. By night this was a seedy neighbourhood filled with late-night bars and secretive sex haunts, legitimised once a year when 500 000 people line the street for the annual gay Mardi Gras. Its daytime role in the city was far more mundane but necessary; a noisy, jostling junction box of traffic travelling in and out of the city.

Jacob said he had been dragged from a murder trial court in the Darlinghurst Courthouse to take a call from head office. Now he had exciting news: 'We're off to the DPP, buddy.'

There was that word again. Tony ignored it. 'Why, what's happened?'

'I didn't want to get your hopes up but our legal boys have had the brief for a month. They rang me today to say they reckon we've got enough to charge Gordon Wood with murder. This is a major step.'

Tony was stunned. He'd spent so long expecting something to happen. 'That's fantastic,' he spluttered. 'What happens now?'

'If it wasn't for this bloody murder trial I'd be back in the office working on the Irondale stuff. We've got to put the finishing touches to the case before we hand it in.'

Three weeks later the media got wind of the development: POLICE WANT RIVKIN'S DRIVER FOR MURDER, the headlines screamed. The story would spark a storm of publicity:

> Police, after consulting with their legal services branch, have recommended in their report that there is sufficient evidence to charge Mr Wood with Byrne's murder based on circumstantial evidence. It is understood police will tell the DPP that a jury, properly instructed, could find Mr Wood guilty of murder.

36

MEGEVE

Gordon Wood was gobsmacked. A newspaper reporter was standing on his doorstep. All he could do was stand there wondering not why the guy was here in the French Alps town of Megeve but how he had found him. It was 9 March 2004.

The previous day Wood had been alerted by friends back in Sydney that police wanted to charge him with murder and had handed seven volumes of evidence against him to the NSW Director of Public Prosecutions. It was nothing new. The Irondale detectives had made it clear they thought he was guilty and he was even sure they had tracked him since he left Australia. It didn't really matter and hadn't really hindered him from going anywhere he wanted across Europe, the US, even Canada. The only reason he hadn't been back to Sydney since his ill-fated trip in 1999 was the bloody media. And now they had found him again.

Wood closed the door, shaking his head at questions about imminent charges: 'No worries, mate,' he repeated several times as he locked the door and retreated to collect his thoughts.

The answer to how he had been found was less complex than Wood might have thought—the internet. According to some accounts, a neighbour near Wood's rooms at the Chalet Arnica, a spare three-storey wood and stone apartment block, had seen media coverage and emailed a newspaper, telling them Wood could be found in a chalet at the base of two ski runs in the middle of the famous ski-resort town, an hour out of Geneva.

Wood knew he had no escape. These journalists were not going away until they got their story. Like some cat and mouse game, they had tracked him sporadically over the years, writing some bullshit about his supposed high life in the UK, but it stopped when he abandoned London for Megeve. Suddenly he was anonymous again in this winter postcard paradise: the creation of the Baronne Noémie de Rothschild who, having become disenchanted with the resorts of St Moritz, opened a hotel here in the 1920s. More than 80 years later the travel magazines might have described the town as enchanting or authentic with its cobbled, narrow streets and sleigh rides in the town square; a huddled architectural mix of medieval, art-deco and restored kitsch against a backdrop of Mont Blanc. It remained one of Europe's favourites, a discreet winter destination with a network of slopes and lifts linked to neighbouring villages like Saint-Gervais-les-Bains, St. Nicolas de Véroce and Combloux, creating an overall skiing domain of almost 450 squared kilometres. Here, where surnames were less important than how you filled out a ski suit in an Après bar, he was just known as Gordy or Gordo. But it was all over now. After several hours of negotiations, he relented and agreed to meet with and talk to the journalists.

Of all the places in a village of the well-to-do with its quaint cafés, bakeries, bistros and restaurants, Wood agreed to meet them at the local McDonald's restaurant. Perhaps it was his reluctance to be seen, not by the media but by the locals, few of whom would be aware of his problems. The meeting was arranged by Simon Butler, whose friendship had been cemented over the past three years. Their age, gym and golf seemed the only things the pair had in common. Wood had always been a grafter while Butler was a driven entrepreneur who had been running his successful business here for more than 20 years and housed his guests in two chalets; one a five-storey hotel called Soleil d'Or in town opposite a small casino and the smaller Chalet d'Antoine, in the foothills of the ski slopes.

Wood seemed unconcerned about the developments in Australia, but refused to discuss what he called 'the case' and insisted on no photographs or taped interviews. 'I don't have a high regard for you [media] guys. I do not have a very favourable view for the media in Australia so I just get on with life. I can't change any of that.'

So what are you going to do? the reporter asked. 'Go skiing,' Wood replied with typical nonchalance.

After all, what else could he do? He'd already declared his innocence and willingness to go back to Australia if necessary to defend himself. But as much as the media liked to portray him as a fugitive from justice, Wood was nothing of the sort. Sure, he'd fled from the place where he really wanted to live, but that was a bid to hide from notoriety not justice. He could not be described as 'on the run' because he'd never been charged with an offence and always cooperated with police, but there was a sense he was overseas because he was avoiding speculation and, therefore, somehow in hiding if not in a legal sense.

What about his life? It appeared to be comfortable—a spacious if not spartan chalet in an expensive French ski-resort town, late-model four-wheel drive, golf trips to the US, flitting back and forth between France and London, and days at the gym maintaining his impressive physique. But it also smacked of a hand-to-mouth existence, living off odd jobs and the goodwill of friends. Asked about how he financed his travels, Wood said he made a living doing massages at 50 euros per hour and a bit of photography: 'I don't do much and I can't do much while this situation [in Australia] goes on. I do a bit of massage. I'm a photographer, it's a hobby but I might make a bit of a business out of it. I do it on savings, make some bucks on the side, don't have high overheads. Practically none.'

And the future? Wood was contemplative: 'Honestly, it has never crossed my mind. I haven't thought about it. Maybe back to Australia at some point, go back, see what's going on. I miss it a lot, it's a great place.'

The furore that surrounded his life and associates, he said, no longer meant a thing to him. 'I don't bother looking at the net. I don't even follow the news . . . I don't worry,' he said.

Butler, who had negotiated the meeting with the reporters, intervened: 'I've read just one thing about all this and I can tell you it's absolute rubbish. I give him [Wood] the keys to my house. I trust him implicitly and totally.'

The reporters changed tack. Did Wood still talk to Rene Rivkin? 'I don't work for him now, and no, I have no reason to keep in touch with him,' Wood snapped. Likewise, the death of Caroline Byrne: 'I've never been near that one. That's enough on that.'

With that Wood retreated again—this time to the gym with his mate, across Route National 212 and the snow-lined roads which lead up to Butler's second chalet. There would be fleeting conversations the next day as more reporters appeared but Wood offered little else of detail other than tips on skin care in the snow. Then he disappeared once more; evicted from his flat, so Butler said, because the ageing owners were disapproving of the media throng now setting up camp outside.

But the reporters kept coming, eager to splice together the life of this talented Mr Wood whose French was passable, if accented, and apart from the local tolerance of smoking, seemed to fit snugly into the easy pace of alpine life.

It was not difficult to find people in the village who knew Wood and, as usual, he had created a variety of impressions. A few close friends were sympathetic, having heard his version of Caroline's death and description of his arrival in Megeve as 'tucking myself away from the world'.

But others were less so, accusing him of scrounging—a 'cash man'—as one woman described him, who recounted Wood's not infrequent road trips across the border to Geneva where he visited a bank, compounding rumours of Wood's Swiss accounts fed by Rivkin.

'We've heard he has a bank account there,' she said, adding that Wood, with whom she'd obviously had a falling out, had once told her he'd been engaged but that his fiancée Caroline committed suicide.

'He has kept to himself. I don't think he has had a girlfriend here for the last three years. When I read the story I thought, "Oh, my God, that's Gordon Wood". He just got back from Florida. He told me he went from there on to Canada to visit his mother.'

A neighbour described him as 'a really nice guy, very polite. I would say that he fitted in well here.' Another was aware of Caroline Byrne's death: 'He mentioned his girlfriend had committed suicide and he seemed quite sad. He also said there was a story that he would tell us some day, but he never did. He doesn't give much away, Gordo, he holds his cards close to his chest.'

Others weren't as kind, like the hotelier who described him as a devious character: 'He's rubbed a lot of people up the wrong way,' she said. 'He plays people off against each other.'

A ski-shop owner was another critic: 'He is a snake, he asks for a lot and he gives nothing. He came into my shop in the low season three years ago and promised to bring me lots of business. So I gave him a really good deal on a pair of skis and *voilà*, I never see him again. He is a very, very good liar.'

A bar worker at a popular drinking venue, Cocoon, said Wood pretty well kept to himself. 'He doesn't drink and he doesn't smoke. He hangs out with the sporty people, goes to the gym a lot. When he first came to town it was like he was trying to know everyone. All you heard was Gordon, Gordon, Gordon. But recently we haven't seen much of him. I get the impression he's not in the good books about something.'

A week of publicity back in Sydney had stirred two things—political interest and a media war of who could make the next break on the story. There was a chorus of demands for Wood to be dragged home, led by Tony Byrne who was on every radio and television station with his appeals for justice. The NSW Premier, Bob Carr, felt compelled to join the fray, saying there appeared to be 'a good prima facie case' while comments by former NSW Coroner Derrick Hand that he never believed Byrne had committed suicide were dredged up and a former senior police officer claimed that the initial investigation lacked proper funding and resources. Wood's friends, like the photographer Basquali, now living in New York, proclaimed Wood's innocence and new police witnesses even emerged; flushed out largely by the media frenzy and competition for the story.

Photos suddenly appeared of Wood and Rivkin relaxing on a luxury boat in the Whitsundays with other members of the Joe's Café set. The photos, taken in early 1993, included Rivkin's right-hand man George Freris and the tattooist Garry Redding, whom Paul Jacob believed was most likely to have been the second man at The Gap when Caroline was killed. This immediately raised another question for Tony: Where was Redding and why hadn't Irondale detectives interviewed him?

37

GARY REDDING

Once again the media got there before the police. Three weeks after confronting Gordon Wood in Megeve, Gary Redding was tracked down to a house in the town of Maidstone, deep in the buttercupped countryside of Kent, an hour outside London.

Redding had been expecting to be found by someone—the cops, he'd assumed—and it made no difference when it was the media instead who knocked on his door. He was still ready to talk with a story that only confirmed suspicions about Gordon Wood. Caroline Byrne did not kill herself, said Redding. And Wood was her only problem. The front-page revelation was yet another embarrassment for investigators who were desperately trying to hose down expectations amid the continuing media frenzy.

Unlike Wood, the man suspected of being his accomplice at The Gap did not live in luxury at an exotic location. In fact, Redding lived with his mother, Maureen, and her second husband in a two-storey, two-bedroom townhouse in a quiet estate on the outskirts of town.

Neither had he landed on his feet financially after leaving Sydney, first for New Zealand and later to the UK. While Wood drove a sports car and enjoyed the London high life, Redding lived on an unemployment benefit of £54 a week and spent much of his time, alone, walking or taking public transport around a town and people he did not know, seemingly without a future. The heady days of Sydney and Rene Rivkin's generosity were far behind. When the media caught up with him he was about to begin a six-month government-funded job-training program.

Far from the tough, short-tempered, tattooed thug he was rumoured to be, Redding would give several interviews over the next week as the media war in Sydney grew. In each he would deny any involvement but implicate Wood for two reasons—he was 'slimy' and Redding didn't believe Caroline had killed herself.

He was home, alone in the Victoria Towers at Potts Point the night of the death, he claimed. The first he knew of the tragedy was the next morning when George Freris telephoned. Rivkin's inner circle habitually met their boss each morning at Joe's Café around 9 am, just as they often met in the late afternoon at Rivkin's apartment across the road from the City Gym in Crown Street.

Redding was surprised when the phone rang, as he explained. The conversation went something like this:

'So, I wakes up, put the coffee on, just about to jump in the shower and George Freris phones me. "Gary?" "Yes."

'"There's been a tragedy."

'"Who? What?"

'"Gordon's girlfriend Caroline was killed last night."

'And I said, "What?" I said, "How?" And he said, "a car accident". When I got there, I was told Caroline had been killed. You naturally think of a car accident, but later, when they said suicide, I thought it was strange. We all did.'

As time went on, and he had time to think about it, it became even more obvious that it just did not make sense: 'I don't know what happened, but I do not believe it was suicide. She had everything going for her. She was intelligent, beautiful, elegant; she had a good job and came from a nice family. She only had one problem—her relationship with Gordon—and that was not a big enough problem for her to kill herself.'

As for the police, Redding insisted he had been only too willing to talk. He had nothing to say, of course, except that he didn't do it and he didn't know who did. He was perplexed about the fuss because he'd lived in Sydney, in the same flat even, for five years after Caroline's death and yet the police had never made contact.

He then went to New Zealand where he lived for another three years before deciding to go back to the UK and live with his mother who he had not seen for seventeen years.

Then early the year before, just as he planned to leave, local police told him that the Sydney cops wanted to see him and were planning to make the trip within six weeks. It was around the same time that Paul Jacob was telling Tony Byrne about their plans. But they never happened. Instead, Redding got sick of waiting and left.

Now he was in Maidstone and if police officers wanted to talk to him they would have to travel further. It was their fault, not his.

'I am quite happy to talk to the police,' Redding said. 'If I was going on the run, I've watched enough crime programs to know not to turn up at my mother's. I obviously want to clear my name and every aspect of it. It's scary that anyone could link my name to something as serious as this, because I'm just a peaceful, non-violent person.'

What about his relationship with Rivkin, the reporters wanted to know. Had Rivkin given him money and gifts and why had he left?

Yes, confirmed Redding, Rivkin had financed the ill-fated business Skins and Needles but it was a business proposition. And he did hand out money at times, not the thousands rumoured but a few hundred dollars here and there to help him meet bills. The Harley-Davidson was not a gift, as he'd initially thought, but a loan but, yes, he had been given a Rolex watch, a Hugo Boss suit for his brother's wedding and a couple of group holidays with the gang.

He did little in return other than wash Rivkin's cars a few times but that was about all he offered. Redding assumed Rivkin was being a friend, showing him some support given that both men suffered from recurring bouts of depression.

Was that all? Why did an overweight middle-aged man enjoy hanging around young men, none of whom could have helped him with his finances?

'I asked him that myself once,' he admitted. 'Rene said it was because he never had a real youth and his job made him hang around with boring businessmen in suits. I never saw anything funny.'

And why did he leave in 1997 if things were so good?

Redding suddenly turned sour. The others were getting more out of Rivkin. Others were driving cars like Porsches and Lotuses while he got to drive around town in a second-hand Commodore. 'I was treated like a bit of an idiot because I wasn't money hungry. I was out to enjoy myself, enjoy the lunches, the goes on the boat. I was really only ever on the fringe of that group. I didn't fall out with Rene; I just decided my life was going nowhere so I wanted to move away from it.'

And Gordon Wood?

'Out of everybody in that group, I disliked him the most, purely because he mocked me of my intelligence and my education because he felt he was really educated. I didn't like him. So why would I go to The Gap with him?'

Tony Byrne read the media reports in disbelief. Redding was the man Paul Jacob had mentioned as Gordon Wood's possible accomplice, but that was three years ago around the time police had been over to the UK to interview Wood.

He flicked back through his diaries to find the notation. There it was—2 September 2001—when he and Paul had one of their rambling conversations over coffee at the Windsor Plaza. They'd spoken about Adam Leigh running around a mental hospital with silver foil on his head and Paul's promise that, if nothing else, he would get into the witness box and state that police believed Caroline had not killed herself. Then he'd mentioned Redding. They knew he was in New Zealand and were waiting for permission to go and interview him. Now, three years later, they still hadn't done it.

Jacob had been equally frustrated by the delay which was caused by a combination of hindrances including budget restraints—which cast a dim eye on overseas travel when there were doubts about if the target would even talk—and diplomatic delays. They couldn't just waltz into another country and start interviewing suspects. Redding was gone by the time they were organised.

For once Tony didn't have time to ponder. On 28 March, as the media continued to compete in the war of one-upmanship, he became a grandfather. Sheena Caroline Byrne, daughter of Robert and his wife, Mellony, was born at the Prince of Wales Hospital at Randwick.

It was difficult to sort one emotion from another as Tony held the tiny child a day or so later. He cried quietly, contemplating Robert's tribute to his sister. It wasn't meant as a replacement, he knew, but marking the beginning of a new life with a reflection on another that had passed all too quickly.

Within weeks his resolve would be tested yet again. Val Clare, who had battled firstly with breast then bowel cancer and seemed to have won, almost collapsed as they walked home one afternoon. The diagnosis was brutal—five inoperable tumours on the brain, three months to live. She died on 22 June and Tony Byrne was devastated and alone once again.

38

SPEAR THROW

Rod Cross had been working on the case for nine months before Tony Byrne even heard his name. One day in July 2004 Paul Jacob telephoned to say he'd just come back from the Goulburn Police Academy where an exciting experiment was being conducted by a physics professor named Cross from the University of Sydney. Apparently they'd tested eleven female recruits, some of them having at least represented their high school in athletics, to see if it was possible for Caroline to have jumped to her death. They had run and jumped repeatedly inside the academy's gymnasium, using a mathematical equation to determine how far they had to jump on a flat surface to emulate the leap she would have had to make.

There was another test in the academy swimming pool. Three male officers with roughly the same upper-body strength as Gordon Wood, according to a survey of his former gym associates, had been throwing a female officer the same size as Caroline from the diving board to see if they could make the distance.

Under what he called relaxed conditions and with no adrenaline, as Wood might have had on that night, one of the officers was able to throw the woman the right distance. By contrast, none of the women were able to jump the distance.

'Not even close,' Paul said excitedly.

As Tony listened he flinched; what Paul was describing was Caroline's murder being replayed over and over again. He tried to block the thought from his mind as Jacob recounted the scene with glee. As grisly as the notion was, Tony was dragged along by the excitement of the discovery.

Two weeks later he sat with Paul inside the Irondale room out at the Parramatta headquarters. As they glanced around the room lined with cartons of files, each tagged with the name of the investigation, a young policewoman walked past. Tony was immediately struck by her resemblance to Caroline. Same height, same build, same blonde hair . . .

'Carmella. Come in here. Meet Tony Byrne,' Paul yelled across the room, interrupting Tony's thoughts. The young woman turned.

'Tony, this is Carmella. She was the girl thrown into the pool during the tests.'

Tony looked at Carmella in shock. This was too real. 'Gosh you look like my daughter,' he stammered.

Carmella looked at him. 'I'm a little bit older actually, but thanks.'

Rod Cross's work was far more exciting than Paul had let on. The puzzling aspect of his early tests was that none of the obvious throwing techniques, such as being swung by two men or flung by one, could achieve the right speed to launch Caroline Byrne off the cliff and reach the crevice near Pyramid Rock.

Cross had pondered the problem for months until he came up with a possible alternative. What if the throw was done from shoulder height, using the muscles of the chest and shoulders to launch the girl through the air like a missile or a spear. It made more sense because the thrower could also use his own speed to add to the momentum.

The experiment with the men had proved his theory. It was a tough ask to get a female volunteer to be picked up by the throat and crotch and tossed into a swimming pool but this was important, and Carmella had consented provided she was wearing a wet suit to at least limit the personal embarrassment. Even though the biggest of them, who could bench-press over 100 kilograms, only achieved the throw speed once, it was enough to prove she could be thrown as his second report on 26 July concluded:

> The new data is consistent with only two possible conclusions. The most likely is that Caroline Byrne was thrown at high speed from a small ledge on the north. The throwing test results indicate that, if she was thrown, then she was probably 'speared' head-first at high speed onto the rocks below, either by a single male adult or possibly by two male adults. That launch method would account for both the high-speed launch and the head-first impact on the rocks below.

It was a summer day to cherish in more ways than one for Tony Byrne. The temperature was climbing steadily into the early 20s, fluffed by a sea breeze, as he left Cronulla at 9 am to drive up to the Central Coast village of Kincumber. There was something important to do. It was 6 January 2005, and Paul Jacob had invited him for the day to see for himself the revised brief of evidence they were about to present to the DPP. Paul had been at his hideaway for two months to finish the brief.

Tony had waited for the morning traffic to clear before making his way up the Pacific Highway to Gosford, skirting the edge of Brisbane Waters and heading towards the beaches at Avoca. Kincumber lay halfway. He spent the 90-minute journey contemplating what he was about to read. He knew the document wasn't the finished product but it didn't lessen the sense for all of them that the job was done.

Tony found the police station in the main street of Kincumber and parked his car out the front. The station wasn't open to the public or even manned so he rang the buzzer and waited a couple of minutes before Jacob flung open the door.

'Gidday brother,' the big bloke grinned.

Tony grinned back. Up here, out of the hurly-burly and politics of Sydney police, Paul Jacob was a different man. Gone were the quiet, stern demeanour and the big black suits. The man before him looked relaxed and content in his shorts, thongs and open-necked shirt.

He followed Jacob into the bunker. It had been a full police station until a few years before when, like a lot of other village stations, the staff was pulled back to the regional office at Gosford. As the villages of the coast merged with the massive population growth, so did the bureaucracy. It was now used mainly by plain-clothes detectives who wanted to get a bit of peace and quiet, maybe interview a suspect away from the busy main office.

Paul had picked the best of the offices, dominated by a big timber desk and a headboard stacked neatly with a dozen ring-binder files all inscribed in heavy black pen with one word—IRONDALE. The only other thing he noticed was one of the newspaper articles pinned to the middle of the headboard—*Father seeks answers*, it trumpeted alongside a photo of Caroline. It made him smile, if a little sadly.

'Let's go and get a coffee,' Paul said. 'I'll bring the brief with us so you can have a look.'

They left out the back door, circled back through the small carpark and onto the main street. The place was all but deserted in the middle of the day and they settled into a table at a café at the entrance to a shopping mall and ordered coffee and sandwiches. Jacob handed over the file and then lit up a smoke and leaned back to watch Tony. He was relishing the moment.

The file was 70 pages thick; merely a summary of the thousands of pages of statements and expert opinions which made up the case. Tony didn't know where to start. In truth he would be happy reading a single sentence that would state simply that the evidence proved Gordon Eric Wood had murdered Caroline Therese Byrne on 7 June 1995.

Jacob watched in silence as Tony flicked pages, stopping occasionally to read a statement. When he reached the section which explored Rod Cross's tests Jacob reached over and drew his attention to a series of photographs.

'I could show you a series of videos but it's all science and a bit hard to follow but have a look at these. They'll give you an idea of what we think happened.'

The photograph was of a man posing as Wood. He was holding a young woman at head height, his extended left arm on her chest and his right hand under the crotch, about to push—like propelling a torpedo out of a submarine, or shooting a basketball.

Tony stared at the image. Although the faces were different he was, in effect, looking at a re-enactment of his daughter's death. Even though it was almost a decade after the event, it was hard to see it without his throat locking up.

Tony had assumed that Caroline was thrown by two men each holding an arm and a leg, swinging her and then releasing her. But this explained what Paul had meant by the possibility of one man doing the killing.

Tony closed the file and handed it back to Jacob. It was everything he could have asked for, and more. They settled into small talk but it was inevitable that the discussion would drift back to the case. As they chatted a woman with two boys sidled up to the table. It was Jacob's long-suffering wife, Debbie, and his twin sons, Mitchell and Blake.

It suddenly struck Tony how much time had passed in this quest. When he first met Paul Jacob his kids were four, maybe five. Now they stood shuffling their feet and looking like typically uncomfortable teenagers. When would it ever end?

39

CROSS PURPOSE

Sunday 1 May 2005: Rene Rivkin is dead, found in a bedroom at the back of a flat owned by his mother, a plastic bag over his head and his mouth taped shut. Television cameras are there to record the ignominious sight of his bloated body being taken outside beneath a pale-blue bedspread.

It looks suspicious but a thorough and quiet police investigation would show the businessman had finally made good on the suicide threat he'd voiced on many occasions. A fortnight after moving out of the family home and declaring his marriage to Gayle was finished, Rivkin had taken an overdose.

In life Rivkin had seemed impervious at times, almost godlike in his ability to make and spend money. But in death the image was shattered and the reality of Rivkin's dishevelled life exposed. His financial empire proved to be merely a carefully balanced paper shuffle of deals and counter-deals held together by a few gems like Offset Alpine. It was as fragile as its maker's mental and physical health, and had come tumbling down when the only real jewel in his life—his marriage and family—had finally given way under the strain.

It was difficult not to pity such a man. Even Tony was torn although Rivkin was the antithesis of his own moral compass. Rivkin had enough pity for himself, he thought, reading the glut of media coverage about the life and times of his nemesis. No,

Tony's pity lay with the man's wife, Gayle, and his five children, who had lost their husband and father years before to greed. Still, he wouldn't wish such an end on anyone, particularly given his own experiences, but neither did he care much and wondered if it would simply impede his daughter's case.

In fact it probably helped, removing the expectation of an imminent decision by the DPP. Behind the scenes there had been more difficulties. Mark Tedeschi, QC, the senior Crown prosecutor who would head the case, had wanted peer review of Rod Cross's work but it had been a messy affair as he firstly appointed two women who were not even qualified and then someone from the Lidcombe campus of Sydney University. When he fell through they settled on a professor from Western Australia named Bruce Elliott. But it was worth the wait. Elliott confirmed Cross's conclusion that Caroline could not have killed herself and was likely thrown by one man:

> The most logical conclusion is that Caroline Byrne was speared from the top of The Gap. Professor Cross's references to potential body rotation during flight is at all times logical and linked to appropriate literature. His mathematically derived figures enable sound conclusions to be drawn based on data. His conclusions based on mechanics fit the injuries sustained by Caroline Byrne. It is therefore clear that Caroline Byrne neither stepped nor ran from the site.

'We've been waiting a long time for this. This call is the sweetest news,' Paul had told Tony one day, telephoning from Kincumber when he remained on extended leave. They would meet a few days later in the city for coffee as Jacob triumphantly returned the updated brief to the DPP complete with Cross's and Elliott's deductions, and sun themselves in Sydney's autumn afterglow.

But how quickly things would change. Four days after Rivkin's death Paul Jacob was back in Tedeschi's office to discuss the revised brief. He left with more work to do. It was no good producing clear scientific evidence that Caroline could not have committed suicide if there was doubt about where she actually landed. They had to find an explanation for the error.

Paul also needed to find some way of telling Tony about the new problem without worrying the poor bloke. He settled into a table at the Museum Towers Café where they'd celebrated just two weeks before, ordered a tea and sucked on a Marlboro Light.

What a week. Rivkin's death had thrown him a bit, but in reality it did little to dent the Wood case apart from raise media interest yet again. He could deal with that although the DPP office seemed to leak like a sieve. It seemed that every two or three months one of the papers would get a quote from Cowdery's office, giving the impression that a decision was imminent. Why couldn't they just shut up?

He stubbed out his smoke, took a swig of hot tea and dialled Tony's number, hoping he would not be there; out playing bowls maybe, or fishing with Robert. Then again, it would just be delaying the inevitable.

'Hello.'

'Tony, it's Paul. Thought I'd call you to let you know I've just left Mark Tedeschi's office.'

'What did he say?'

'He's asked us to do some more work, technical stuff mainly, on the point of impact—the exact spot where Caroline landed.'

Tony had questions but he didn't want to ask. What did he mean by point of impact? They already knew she had landed in a crevice between two boulders. 'So, you're happy?'

Paul wanted to be reassuring. 'Yep. What I like about this, buddy, is that the DPP is pushing us. They've asked us to do a little more work so the brief will be perfect.'

The phone call played on Tony's mind for the next week. He knew that Paul sometimes softened the news for him, kept something back, but he could tell by the tone that something wasn't right. It was confirmed when he got a call from a reporter telling him that there would be a story in the paper the next day. It would quote Cowdery saying what he already knew: that Paul had been asked to do some more work. What perplexed him though was that according to the reporter, Cowdery had said the investigations had now been completed and they were about to make a decision on whether to prosecute Wood.

He left a message on Paul's mobile in the morning. It was after 6 pm when Paul called back. Tony told him about the story and Cowdery's comment and waited for Paul's response.

'We're going at 100 miles an hour to do what the DPP has asked for. I had a meeting with the scientific people on Tuesday—'

Tony cut him off. 'What exactly do you have to do Paul? I'm a bit worried.'

It was time to come clean. 'We've got an issue with the point of impact. The problem is that the scientific branch was never called on the night of the murder. Nobody took a photo of Caroline. I don't know why.'

He was telling Tony something he already knew. 'But Mark Powderly has said where she landed. He told the coroner's inquest—'

Now it was Jacob's turn to interrupt. 'Yeah, well they made things worse when Powderly did the re-enactment with Brian Wyver back in 1996.'

Tony thought for a moment. He'd seen the video. It was played at the inquest when Powderly gave evidence. 'What do you mean, Paul? It was just a video made for the media.'

'Yeah, well they made a big mistake. They put a police officer down at the bottom. You can hear Mark Powderly giving a commentary and saying she is now pointing to the exact place where Caroline landed. It was wrong.'

He paused, not wanting to go on but knowing he had to. 'Tony, it was the wrong spot.'

Each year on the 7th of September—Caroline's birthday—Tony did his best to find a distraction. 'I'd go mad otherwise,' he told those who inquired. 'I think about it every day. It would eat me up if I didn't force myself to move away occasionally.'

Lawn bowls was normally the outlet of choice, a social game followed by a few beers and a quiet dinner just as he did each June on the anniversary of her murder. Tony even avoided family on these days because it would be impossible to sit around a table with his kids and not think of their dead sister and mother.

But this year, on what should have been Caroline's 35th birthday, Tony had no choice. He'd been out at Watsons Bay helping the Irondale team do some tests and, to make matters worse, he had a funeral to attend. Try as he might, he could not take his mind off his daughter; what she might have been doing if she was still alive, whether she might have married and had children. The thought made him angry and he rang Paul Jacob.

Paul was away but Bianca was happy to chat. The news was promising but complex, she said. The team had met with Rod Cross the previous week to arrange some new photo-geometry plans of the site. The tests had been conclusive, she said. There was a seven-degree incline at the edge where Caroline had gone over, enough to affect anyone trying to run and jump. Anyone trying to leap would be propelling themselves upward and could not reach either point of impact. Paul was going out to Dubbo next week to get one final statement off Mark Powderly to clear up once and for all just where he had found Caroline's body.

After he hung up, Tony made his usual careful notes of the conversation. He was well into his second full diary now and, if anything, he was writing in more detail as they got closer to a goal he at times thought would never come. He flicked back over the last few months. It echoed the panic inside the investigation about the problems caused by that bloody video made essentially for the media to launch the Wyver investigation back in May 1996.

Paul Jacob had explained that the police making the video had for some reason pointed to the wrong point of impact. Instead of focusing on a group of boulders clustered around one they'd called 'Pyramid Rock' which was where she pitched head-first, a young female constable was videoed pointing to another crevice, a couple of metres away and closer to the main cliff face. To complicate matters, it was being narrated by Mark Powderly, the rescue-squad officer who found Caroline's body, who was standing on top of the cliff. He could be heard on the tape confirming the policewoman was pointing to the correct spot.

Tony had argued with Paul about the value of the video in a court and that Powderly could simply give a statement saying it was the wrong point.

'He already has,' Paul retorted. 'I've got five statements from him but it's not enough.'

The DPP was apprehensive about the impact of the video. Powderly wasn't a detective. He was a rescue officer doing a re-enactment for the homicide squad who wanted to use it as a media tool. And yet what he had done might be enough for a good defence lawyer to create doubt in the minds of the jurors.

Paul was fuming. 'Powderly is our main witness on this. Honestly, it's the most frustrating situation I've ever encountered. All we needed was one bloody polaroid shot of her on the night and we would have nailed him.'

Instead, new tests had been ordered. Six policewomen had been taken out to The Gap to simulate running and jumping on uneven ground. Rather than worry about a courtroom argument about where Caroline had pitched, they wanted to know if she could have reached either places. If not, then the video didn't matter.

The wait for Rod Cross's fourth report was excruciating. The only blessing was that the media coverage had died down after Rivkin's death, other than the occasional decree from a Sunday paper that the DPP was close to making a decision. Tony wished they were right but the truth was that Rivkin's death, the confusion over the impact point, and another long-running murder case over the death of Sydney woman, Kerry Whelan, was only lengthening the process.

The one bright spot was Deanna's wedding on 14 October. Paul Jacob phoned just after the ceremony had been completed. He'd just finished taking Powderly's final statement and was in a triumphant mood. The case was almost done, bar a couple of checks over measurements at The Gap.

'It's all done, buddy. You're going to get justice,' said the copper, brushing off Tony's attempts to praise him.

'The only praise we're interested in is from you,' he said, hanging up.

A few weeks later, on 1 November 2005, the Cross report landed on Paul Jacob's desk. It was hard to contain his excitement as he read it but by the time he rang Tony with the news, he was circumspect, careful not to overplay his hand.

'It all checks out,' he said quietly. 'I'll give you the details one day.'

Jacob might have read the professor's conclusion to Caroline's father, but he didn't. It was simple enough:

> It is now clear that Caroline Byrne could not have jumped or dived into either of the two cavities identified by the police, but she could have been thrown into either one. In that respect, the identification of the correct cavity is somewhat irrelevant in terms of whether she died as a result of suicide or homicide.

40

'THEY'VE GOT HIM'

Sydney media had been on tenterhooks ever since the 'discovery' of Gordon Wood in Megeve but when the decision to arrest him was finally made it happened swiftly and without public fanfare. On the morning of 1 March 2006, after an evening pondering yet another revised brief, Cowdery agreed there was enough evidence to charge Wood with murder.

At 11.45 am Tony Byrne walked back into his Cronulla apartment to find a coded message on his answering machine. It was Paul Jacob.

'Tony Call Jaco at Parramatta.' Something had happened.

Paul answered on the first ring. He'd been sitting by the phone, hoping Tony wasn't far away. He tried to maintain a policeman's stilted formality as he broke the news.

'Tony, you are my first call. The Director of Public Prosecutions has just advised there is sufficient evidence to charge Gordon Wood with the murder of your daughter, Caroline.'

Tony burst into tears. 'Paul, that is the sweetest news,' he spluttered but Paul Jacob had already moved on.

'Tony, we've got a lot of work to do. We have to find out where he is. There is a covert operation on at this moment.'

'Paul, the only words I can think of are I am very relieved and very grateful.'

'I'll ring you back later, buddy.' And Paul was off.

Tony felt strangely calm. He wanted justice—for Gordon Wood to be held responsible for Caroline's death—but the most important was a public declaration that his daughter had not committed suicide. The combination of Jacob's conclusion and the DPP's agreement was enough. A conviction would be icing on the cake. Tony telephoned his three children to share the news.

When Jacob called him three weeks later to say that things were progressing at a snail's pace, Tony began to get agitated. Jacob had always insisted the police could locate Wood quickly, he presumed through a combination of passport checks and maybe telephone and credit card or emails. He couldn't understand why Jacob was hesitating when they spoke about Wood's whereabouts.

'We know where he is but we need to find his exact location,' he said. 'The wheels of justice are turning slowly; it's just a matter of time.'

In fact, Jacob knew exactly where Wood was living. On 24 March London police stopped him under the pretence of a routine traffic check. Wood gave them an address in Ellerslie Road, Shepherd's Bush, opposite the Queens Park Rangers soccer club, where his motorbike was registered to but it was not where he was actually living. A few weeks earlier when he reported his motorbike stolen, Wood had given a different address—the Hilton Hotel near London's Docklands. Wood made one other mistake that day: telling police he was planning to travel to Australia on 7 April. In truth, he had plans to travel to New York on 14 April on a one-way ticket. Technically, it made him a flight risk. Police now had a reason to get a warrant for his arrest.

Cree House stands at the corner of Creechurch Lane and Mitre Street in the heart of London's financial district. In its former days as a tea warehouse during Victorian London, the five-storey building would have been a prominent part of the landscape. Jack the Ripper might have hugged its shadows while making his escape after killing his fourth victim, Catherine Eddowes, in

Mitre Square 20 metres away, in the early hours of 30 September 1888. Tourists follow the bloody trail every day although in a modern city, the building is now in the shadows of a spectacular glass construction known as the Gherkin and surrounded by office buildings.

Wood, or 'Mr Gordy' as the managing agents knew him, appeared to be one of the few permanent residents. He was better known around the corner at Caffé Nero on Leadenhall Street where his customary jeans, black boots and casual shirt stood out from the suited crowd, as did his attitude to the barista if they didn't pack the coffee into the canister hard enough. He hated weak coffee and wasn't afraid to let the staff know that when he ordered his customary small latte with an extra shot.

As usual, Gordon Wood created a mixed impression with people he met. The coffee shop manager Anna Kwiatkowska thought he worked in construction. His clothes said as much if his manner did not. The young Polish woman also wondered if he fancied her, smiling as he came in most mornings, almost always alone. He was flirting, there was no doubt, but he was not her type, and slightly strange.

Wood didn't care. He wasn't interested either. Flirting with women was a practised art, particularly in an environment where he felt comfortable; in control. This was a city where he could be anonymous, at home in the warm environs of a café, choosing the morning's hot pastries.

Wood would begin most days the same way: strolling to the café from his apartment before walking to a nearby gym, Lamb's Health and Fitness, or to the head office of LA Fitness, not far away in East London, where he was employed as a consultant on a lucrative contract. At other times he took the tube from nearby Aldgate station. His Kawasaki motorbike was chained most of the time, outside the converted warehouse where units ranged from lofts to two-bedroom apartments renting for around $1300 a week.

On Thursday, 30 March 2006, Wood emerged later than usual from his flat. Adam Mclean, a freelance photographer for the

Sydney Morning Herald, was watching from across the road. The paper had got wind of Wood's imminent arrest within hours of the DPP's decision but instead of publishing straightaway, had spent the past month tracking him down to his London flat. The paper was banking on being there for the arrest—one of the biggest police stories in recent times.

McLean discreetly shot a couple of frames as Wood, dressed in his customary jeans and boots but carrying a large backpack, made a call from his mobile. He then strode off towards the tube station. McLean didn't follow, fearful he might be spotted.

Four days later—3 April—police made their move with the street still in the darkness of an early English spring morning. Back in Sydney the *Herald* had been making plans. If Wood was arrested before mid-afternoon London time then the arrest would be emblazoned across its front page within a few hours. If not, then it would almost certainly be announced by police in Sydney the next morning.

The problem was that Wood was not at home when Scotland Yard banged on his door. He had been on his way to France when McLean took his photograph and had not returned. The police withdrew. It would be several hours before they established that Wood was on his way back and had agreed to meet them at his flat.

It was past 11 pm in Sydney. The main edition had gone but the paper could still stop the presses and catch as many papers as possible. There were two hours at the most after which the story was lost. The place was on edge.

At 12.30 am and half a world away police arrived back at Cree House. Ten minutes later the phone rang in the Sydney newsroom:

'They've got him. Push the button,' was the message. Gordon Wood had finally been arrested for the murder of Caroline Byrne.

41

A REASONABLE PROSPECT

Winston Terracini, SC, was not happy and he didn't care who knew it. Where were everyone's manners, grumbled the diminutive yet imposing barrister as he stomped into the courtroom, struggling with a large mobile trolley designed to carry briefs of evidence. And why had the committal hearing of one of the state's most controversial murder cases started without him? His juniors sat at the bar table, heads bowed to dodge the salvo.

Magistrate Jane Mottley looked up, surprised, momentarily speechless at the interruption. Mark Tedeschi, QC, who had been explaining a photograph showing where Caroline Byrne died at the base of a cliff, also stopped but was not alarmed. He withdrew the photo, leant on the bench and tapped his nose with a finger, amused, even admiring the antics of his rival. Welcome to courtroom drama Sydney style.

It was 12 June 2007 and the justice system had finally cranked into gear more than a year after Gordon Wood's return from London. The extradition process had been a media circus after his clandestine arrest. Reporters crammed into the Old Bailey courtroom to watch Wood's initial resistance then consent to return to Australia and face his accusers. Even his flight home was media managed, as Paul Jacob and Paul Quigg were forced to parade Wood in handcuffs surrounded by cameras across the Heathrow Airport tarmac and onto Qantas Flight 32. The media followed them onto the flight, hoping to get footage on the thirteen hours to Singapore for the next night's news. One photographer, Andrew Meares from the *Sydney Morning Herald*, managed to snap Wood in his seat alongside Quigg while Jacob glared at the intrusion. Locked inside one of the plane's bathrooms, Meares immediately transmitted the shot back to his newsroom in Sydney. The photo was published on the front page as the plane took off fifteen minutes later.

There had been similar scenes on Wood's arrival and at his court appearance where, gaunt and silent, he was granted bail while the long process began. Others charged with murder might be jailed while they wait their turn in the crowded courtrooms but Wood, with Terracini in command, was allowed to live with his mother.

In the ensuing months there had been brief appearances and skirmishes over which of the Crown's witnesses could be cross-examined at the committal. It was even delayed because the mother of the appointed magistrate had once employed Caroline Byrne in her dress shop as a work experience student back in the 1980s. A new magistrate had to be found to avoid any perception of bias. But here they were, five days after the 12th anniversary of Caroline's death, in a Burwood courtroom where most of those in the crowded waiting room were used to the disappointments of suburban life rather than celebrity excess.

The hearing to decide if there was enough evidence to send Wood to trial had been sent outside the city for space reasons, but it was an uncomfortable crush which forced two desperate families together. On the first morning as they waited for the court to open Tony Byrne found himself in the toilet with Gordon Wood. Neither said a word, although Tony suspected he saw fear in his adversary's eyes. Whether it was fear of justice or retribution he couldn't tell nor care.

Things were little better inside the courtroom where Tony sat with his children on one side of the cramped room listening to

Tedeschi's opening address while Wood sat behind his lawyers scribbling incessantly in a large notebook while his mother and sister, Jacqui, peered over his shoulder trying to read his notes.

The next hour would be the only time Tony was allowed inside the courtroom for the three-week hearing, until the decision. He would be a prosecution witness at any future trial and wasn't allowed to hear the testimony of others, but he was permitted to listen as Tedeschi outlined the case contained in twelve volumes of evidence stacked on the bench next to Magistrate Mottley. Although he had been in frequent contact with Paul Jacob he had not read the file. Wisely so, he thought.

Tedeschi spoke without much emotion, his style in sharp contrast to Terracini who had the reputation of a brawler and a man quite comfortable with reducing witnesses to stammering fools if necessary in defence of his clients. It worked on some occasions, less so on others.

Tedeschi saw himself as more of a storyteller, taking a jury through a sequence of events to lead to a logical conclusion, at least as the prosecution saw the evidence. At committal, his job was less about persuasion and more ensuring there were no errors. They were a contrast in more than courtroom style. In his spare time Tedeschi was a promising photographer and art lover, Terracini a rabid supporter of the Manly rugby league club who couldn't help himself but drop a cricketing analogy during a conversation. And yet there were some strange connections, other than both being of Italian heritage, of two men regarded as among the best of their professions. Tedeschi's son Simon was a famed concert pianist and Terracini's older brother, Lyndon, an opera singer of some repute. They had faced each other numerous times over the years, most famously in the various trials of infamous crime boss and murderer Arthur 'Neddy' Smith and more recently the misdemeanours of radio announcer John Laws. The magistrate was only concerned with the likelihood of Wood being found guilty, whether or not there was 'a reasonable prospect' that a jury would convict. The prosecution did not have to prove their case, particularly given only a small, but critical portion, would be discussed here.

The main thrust of the evidence against Wood, Tedeschi intoned, was an explosion of rage late at night on the cliff top, caused by Caroline's insistence she wanted to end their relationship and in doing so potentially expose him to the wrath of his rich boss, particularly as he told his girlfriend about the destruction of Offset Alpine two years before. Wood had blabbed and boasted his way into danger and if Caroline was cut loose then it spelled trouble. And there was evidence from sporadic conversations with friends that she was becoming fearful of a man she was considering marrying. Who was with him? Perhaps they'd never know although the evidence would point to at least two suspects. In the end, the evidence would also say that one man threw Caroline to her death—a tall, strong athletic man whose long limbs acted like levers to hurl his girlfriend from shoulder height; a man like Gordon Wood who could bench-press at least 100 kilograms.

Peter Byrne cried silently as he listened. Like Robert and Deanna, he had not heard the details of the case and had never imagined the real horror of his sister's death. By contrast Robert Byrne bristled, constantly glancing at Wood who continued to write as if to calm his nerves. It was all Robert could do to keep in his seat and not leap across the narrow walkway to confront the man who had thrown his sister like a spear, according to the physics expert now on the stand.

Professor Rod Cross was a man of questions. He even looked quizzical; a lean and angular man who took every question with bemusement, as if it had implications far beyond the simplicity of the question posed—or the poser.

Everything had a nuance, a possible angle that might change the outcome. His career had been built on taking a question and finding an answer through science. For almost three decades he worked in the plasma physics department at Sydney University. Now in retirement, he'd combined his knowledge of physics with his passion for tennis and become an expert on, among other things, how and where to hit a tennis ball.

Cross would be the only Crown witness shepherded by Mark Tedeschi; his evidence was critical to the case because, no matter how irksome Gordon Wood's behaviour, without an unequivocal science-based opinion, there would always be doubt over how Caroline Byrne died.

Could she have killed herself, Tedeschi wanted to know. Simply run and jumped from the cliff in the dark because she was depressed after accepting a job she didn't really want, as Wood contested.

Cross was emphatic: 'No, it was not possible.' The courtroom fell silent as the reporters—and Wood—scribbled.

The puzzle had been not if Caroline was thrown but how. Was she shoved, heaved or swung by two men? No, he concluded after videoing police officers throwing female colleagues into swimming pools. The obvious throws did not generate enough speed to have reached the place where she landed, so far out from the cliff edge.

He'd eventually solved the 'how' after months of considering what made sense scientifically. Clearly, more power would be gained if an object was thrown from chest or shoulder level rather than the waist; a bit like a shot-putter or javelin thrower at the Olympics. His theory proved correct, at least at the pool where one strong officer was able to reach the 'throw speed' of 4.5 metres per second.

But it wasn't just a question of how she left the cliff top but from what point along its length and where did she land. There was no room for doubt on any of these matters. Cross had written four reports over two years, each refining the last or answering new questions as they arose.

There were only two possible places from which she could have gone over, one to the south where there was plenty of room for a long but uphill run-up line to a crumbling edge. The other point—almost certainly, according to Cross—was at the northern end of the curve, from a small ledge which would allow a run-up of no more than two metres; enough to launch a body.

In the end, he concluded, it didn't matter from where she was thrown nor where she landed—the 'incorrect' rock identified by

Police Constable Lisa Camwell in the 1996 media re-enactment or the 'correct' spot claimed by the rescue-squad officer Mark Powderly—because they were too far for a person to have leaped, even an Olympic athlete, let alone a fit but barely average athlete like Caroline Byrne. Science said it was not possible.

Determining in which crevice she landed was answered by Caroline's horrific injuries. Her shoulders, not her head, had taken the force of the fall, wedged into the elongated fissure, her head split open on a rock at the base of the hole but largely intact, not exploded into pieces as police would have expected to find if she had struck head-first. If she had landed in the other opening, as shown in the police video, then her shoulders would have been torn off. It was not possible, he said.

But had she actually landed closer to the cliff face and bounced off another rock into the crevice? No, said Cross. The key was her legs. They were not only uninjured but her leggings had not even been torn. If her body had struck a rock face the laws of physics say her legs would have whipped over her back at up to six times the speed of her fall. And she had been falling at a speed of more than 80 kilometres per hour. She had landed, fortuitously for those seeking redemption, directly into the hole.

Winston Terracini's job was to undermine; to challenge the veracity of Rod Cross's methods and conclusions and, if necessary, his motives and credibility. Abrasion was his hammer and he used it often but Terracini began quietly, offering Cross a guilt-free exit from the witness box and responsibility for the police screw-ups if he agreed the case was full of holes. It was clear from his first report that no-one could prove what happened that night. Even his own words which Terracini read out slowly, triumphantly:

> I concluded the most likely cause of death was that Caroline Byrne ran over the edge of the cliff in the dark . . . A less likely option is that she was thrown by one or two people.

Paul Jacob, sitting at the front of the court, knew the question was coming but winced anyway. This was just the beginning.

Terracini would explore every crack and flaw, every shadow and every mistake. There were many, some because of the nature of the case and others because of police incompetence. It was the reason the DPP had waited so long before approving the case. He hoped it wouldn't be the cause of justice denied.

Jacob knew, as did Terracini for that matter, that it was reasonable for an expert to write several reports and change his opinion over time as new information was discovered. It was the final report which mattered most and it would be supported in full by another eminent biomechanics expert.

The terrier-like lawyer was now testing his prey, describing the academic's studies as 'cock and bull' and accusing him of 'boosting' the Crown's case. They clashed over Newton's law of motion, and split hairs over the difference between Caroline's sporting activity and her actual ability. Terracini brandished a document from a gymnasium, which detailed Caroline's self-assessment in which she considered herself excellent in basketball, swimming, rollerblading, ice- and rollerskating; good in diving, trail-bike riding, windsurfing and bodysurfing; and fair in horse riding and jet-skiing. She also had six years of jazz ballet and funk classes. But Cross was unimpressed. The document was a self-assessment for a gym membership. He preferred statements from two of her high school teachers who said she had less-than-average athletic ability.

Sergeant Mark Powderly was as big and unflinching as the rocks at the base of The Gap where he had retrieved 20 bodies for the police rescue squad over the years. He sat, unmoved, as Terracini growled and snapped at his credibility for botching a police video re-enactment in 1996 in which he concurred that the landing point was a cavity towards the northern end of the curved jumble of rocks that make up the city's most notorious suicide spot. Powderly insisted that he had no knowledge of the mistake until 2004 when he stood on the cliff top and watched colleagues below place a mannequin into a rock hole to indicate where she had landed. The mannequin didn't fit in the hole and he'd moved them to the right spot a couple of metres further north, near a triangular mass he'd called Pyramid Rock.

But the terrier wasn't buying the story. 'You must be kidding,' he bellowed, when Powderly said he had been facing the camera with his back to The Gap when his female colleague was filmed pointing with two hands at the 'exact location' 30 metres below. And he scoffed at Powderly's claim that he 'wasn't paying attention' when watching the video during the coronial inquiry in 1998 and still did not realise a mistake had been made.

Powderly, whose evidence consisted mostly of clipped 'yes and no sirs' remained impassive throughout, acknowledging only that the initial mistake had been made because it was not a forensic exercise but a tape made for publicity. His demeanour did not change at Terracini's derisive snort and claim that police simply changed the spot because a report 'didn't suit their purposes'.

Tony Byrne had lasted three days sitting outside the Burwood courtroom before he took a day off to play bowls. It was too wet and he ended up pacing his lounge room. The next day he was back on the turquoise carpet outside courtroom No. 2, chatting with Irondale officers or dragging Paul Jacob around the corner for a decent coffee. He couldn't bear the tension, not being able to watch the testimony inside, and yet he couldn't stay away. His only window was the opinion of others—the non-committal lawyers, the nervous police officers, the jocular media enjoying the spectacle.

The newspapers gave him some detail but it wasn't the same as being inside as Wood's family were allowed to be. He'd tried to catch Brenda Wood's eye a few times. He could see her distress and instantly forgave her coldness after Caroline's death. She still hadn't written. The truth was that while Sydney watched this saga of money, power and death, there was a human reality to the tragedy: two families, one hoping justice would be delivered despite police bungling, and the other hoping that it would not be denied.

Even the venue seemed wrong, the glamour and intrigue of the case lost in the cramped suburban court set among the clustered red-brick flats and the multicultural shopping strip of Burwood. It should be at Downing Centre in Liverpool Street, a few metres from Tony's old home, within sight of the gateway to the whitebread eastern suburbs where the dangerous glitz of the emerald city's glamour begins and his daughter's tragedy unfolded.

As much as Tony was frustrated about being outside the courtroom, Wood's mother and sister had to sit uneasily inside; watching him scribble, leaning over occasionally to offer reassurance, sometimes responding physically to an excited exchange at the bar table, as if it might mean salvation for their son and brother.

There were friends too who had to run the gauntlet of media cameras outside to support a man they believed had been unfairly chased halfway across the world to answer for a death in which he played no part.

Each morning the papers covered the events of the previous day; the witnesses Tony had met outside but could not hear, like John Doherty, the elfin-like artist whose revelations after the 1998 inquest that he had seen two men and a woman arguing beneath his window that night had reinvigorated the investigation. Like Lance Melbourne and Craig Martin after him, Doherty insisted he had seen a man he identified as Gordon Wood with a young woman who resembled Caroline Byrne, and no amount of heckling by Terracini was going to change his opinion. This was not the arena in which credibility would be decided. That was for a jury, if it got to the next stage.

The same would apply to witnesses like Christine McVeigh, who managed the City Gym and recounted watching Wood and Garry Redding standing over Caroline Byrne in the days before her death. 'He said, "You're a fucking idiot, Caroline". It appeared to be an attack. She looked quite fearful. Gordon seemed to be talking to her in an aggressive manner.'

McVeigh also said she had been approached by Wood at the gym a few hours after her funeral. He should have been distraught but instead wanted to transfer the remaining three months of Caroline's membership as a credit to his own membership.

Why hadn't she come forward earlier, Terracini demanded. Why wait twelve years to make such grave accusations? McVeigh's answer was simple: she feared the repercussions of people associated with Rene Rivkin. She only dug in further when Terracini dismissed her fears as rubbish. Another club member, Frederick Dowdle, felt the same way. He'd finally come forward after Wood's arrest in 2006 with his questions about Wood's coldness after Caroline's death. Dowdle had spoken to him in the gym because he looked worried. Wood first told him his girlfriend had been hit by a car and was in hospital, then a few days later that she'd died. When Dowdle asked how he was feeling, Wood replied: 'She's gone. I've got to get on with my life now.'

The journalist Paul Barry had the same uneasy feeling about Wood when he interviewed him in 1998 for his television program, but his concerns were expressed in a statement to police rather than in his courtroom evidence which only lasted a few minutes.

As each witness appeared Magistrate Mottley released his or her police statement from the massive file. Barry told of sitting with Wood in the Bondi Beach restaurant Ravesi's waiting to begin the interview, for which Wood wanted to be paid. The pair began chatting broadly about the case and his boss, the late Rene Rivkin.

What struck Barry, according to his August 2000 statement, was Wood's lack of emotion: 'While he was speaking with us he never showed any emotion. Here he was, talking about the death of his girlfriend, who died under very tragic circumstances and not once did he cry or even look like crying. He was cold-faced and told it like it was just a matter of fact.'

Instead, Wood spoke about how good he was in bed: 'He kept talking about how good he was and how Caroline adored him. Caroline was the one who always wanted to have sex with him and their sex life was fantastic.'

The trickle of statements became a torrent when Mottley agreed to release the entire contents of the Irondale brief as journalists all but ignored the court evidence in favour of the untested statements collected over the years by Paul Jacob. There was little that Wood's lawyers could do but steam as accounts emerged of Wood's claims that he had been dudded by Rivkin on a bonus payment for 'the Offset Alpine deal' or the day Wood claimed Rivkin asked him into his bed.

There were reams of gooey love letters between Wood and Caroline and copies of Wood's sickly missives to Kylie Watson after Caroline's death. Then there was Wood's alleged demand to morgue attendant Kenneth Nichols to 'look at her tits'. The claim exploded in the media. Wood's denials—through Terracini—were drowned out in the appalled reaction.

It was a bad sign for the defence. Despite the enormous amount of information—or perhaps because of it—Jane Mottley had not deliberated for many days when she reconvened the court on 6 July. It was clear to those who clustered into the courtroom that her decision had not been difficult and it would take a brave or foolhardy lower court magistrate to prevent such a case from going to trial. Besides, the Director of Public Prosecutions would have been within his rights to overrule and send it to trial anyway.

Winston Terracini made his final, colourful pitch, describing as 'bordering on insanity' the motive put forward by the Crown that Caroline Byrne was murdered by Wood because of a dark secret about the Offset Alpine printing factory fire, and the 'insurmountable hurdle' for the prosecution to prove that Caroline could not have committed suicide when there was 'compelling evidence' that she did. As for the critical evidence of Professor Rod Cross, Terracini all but spat his derision at the academic's 'inherent bias' against his client.

Gordon Wood took the stand but his response was succinct rather than impassioned: 'I think all I can say at this stage is what I've said for the past twelve years, and that is to maintain my innocence. I have absolutely no knowledge or involvement in Caroline's death.'

It was not enough to dissuade Mottley. Although the experiments and calculations of Rod Cross were 'unusual', she said, so was the case. More to the point, 'there has been no scientific attack on his conclusions'.

And although there were what she called 'live issues' in the complex web of facts and circumstances, these issues including motive, opportunity, the admissibility, reliability and credibility of witnesses should be determined by a jury: 'I'm of the view and am satisfied there is a reasonable prospect, that a jury, reasonably instructed would convict,' she declared.

Wood, his mother by his side, stopped briefly outside the court, ashen-faced but defiant: 'I accept I have been committed for trial, but since I am innocent I know I will be vindicated at trial.'

Tony Byrne emerged a few minutes later, flanked by Paul Jacob. He had spent the previous night worrying about how much or how little to say. In the end it was little: 'Can I just say my family and I are very pleased with the court's decision, and I would like to thank the NSW police, the commander of Strikeforce Irondale and his excellent team of homicide detectives.'

Vindication was still more than a year away.

42

COURT NO. 3

August 25, 2008: The Roman numerals etched into the handsome sandstone walls of the NSW Supreme Court at Darlinghurst—MDCCCLXXXVIII—seemed appropriate for the trial about to begin. Just like the case, it took a while to solve the puzzle but was wholly satisfying when you did. The year 1888—presumably the date when the section of the grand building in Taylor Square at the top of Oxford Street was completed—is the longest Roman numeral, just as *Regina v Gordon Eric Wood* would be the longest and most expensive murder investigation and trial in the state's history. More than thirteen years after the horrific event, there was to be an accounting for the death of Caroline Byrne.

The interior of courtroom No. 3, which once hosted the Petrov spy case, had hardly changed in 120 years either, although the recent paint job—careful layers of salmon pink and beige interspaced with several shades of green—had restored it to a pristine condition unrivalled since its opening amid the celebration of the state's centenary year. The woodwork was varnished to a gloss that only encased and highlighted the names carved into the straight-backed benches which circled the room, mainly by journalists wanting to say 'I was there' when such and such happened. This would be one of those cases, the media entranced by the showdown to follow.

Gold-leaf signs pigeonholed each section of the room, from the judge and associate in a raised podium at the head of the room to the bar table below in the centre and the accused in his own box at much the same eye-line as the judge.

The jury box was along the wall to the judge's left. Behind was an area, long unused but still marked for *Governor of Gaol*, should he happen to want to sit through a trial for a potential inmate in the now defunct prison at the back of the court complex. On the other side of the room there were boxes for the media, the sheriff and places for prospective jurors when required. On numerous days in the coming months these areas would be packed with onlookers, many with a reason to witness proceedings and many there purely out of curiosity.

There were two floors for the public gallery at the back of the room where Tony Byrne now sat with Paul Jacob, waiting to hear the opening address by the Crown prosecutor, Mark Tedeschi, who was flanked by his legal team prosecutor Ken McKay and solicitor Meaghan Fleeton. He knew the details, if only because he had heard it a month before in the same venue, but he was happy to hear it all again.

Tony also wanted to watch the man in front of him—Gordon Wood—squirm with embarrassment, not only at the accusations of Tedeschi's measured address but the fact he was aware that Tony was sitting behind, staring at the back of the man he was convinced had murdered his daughter.

The traditional silver wig gave Justice Graham Barr a somewhat grizzled appearance, matching the colour of his neatly trimmed beard and contrasting the crimson gown which immediately established both the formality of the proceedings and his all-powerful judicial position. He had aborted the first trial after four days when one of the jurors contacted a radio journalist asking for advice about a group of them visiting The Gap after dark to see the site for themselves. The woman had indicated that another panel member had already declared Wood to be guilty after hearing Tedeschi's address and Tony's evidence-in-chief. The prosecution had protested but, in truth, Justice Barr had little choice if he wanted to avoid an automatic appeal by Wood's lawyers if he was convicted. The process of justice runs a precarious and precious line in favour of an accused person.

Tony had cried during his testimony. It wasn't intentional. It always happened when he talked about the day he questioned Caroline about her relationship and she assured him that Gordon wouldn't harm her. Some of the jury members had cried too, but it was all for nothing. And now he had to do it again.

He had mixed feelings of course. He felt sad because it brought all the memories to the surface. But it was also a wonderful moment, he told the media, trying to capture the gratefulness he felt that the day had actually arrived where he could answer the questions; where someone else could tell him if he was right and that his fight had been worthwhile.

The wait since the coronial inquiry had been softened by the arrival on 8 April of a letter from the Victims Compensation Tribunal. It was succinct, heavy on bureaucratic formality and qualifications but it said the right thing:

> This claim arises out of the tragic death of Caroline Byrne on or about 7 or 8 June 1995 at Watsons Bay in the state of NSW. I note the protected history of this tragic matter before both coronial courts and criminal courts. I note that the police have charged a suspect with the murder of the deceased and that a magistrate has found (after a very lengthy committal) that on the available evidence the accused should be committed for trial.
>
> On this basis, on the evidence before me, it would appear (to the requisite standard) that the deceased Caroline Byrne died as a direct result of the unlawful act of another.

It went on to award his family $50000 but the money was irrelevant and would go towards the memorial fund he'd established at the Randwick Children's Hospital. The words were what mattered to Tony. It meant he could finally order a headstone for Caroline's grave out at the Field of Mars Cemetery in Ryde. He'd been there only once, some time after the funeral which, just like

Andrea's—who was buried a few rows away from her daughter—he couldn't bring himself to attend. Now he could acknowledge Caroline's death with words straight from the letter—'Died as a result of the unlawful act of another'.

That 'other' was sitting in front of him now. He couldn't tell what Gordon was thinking but he looked hunched and uncomfortable. If he'd admitted what he'd done then Tony might have forgiven him, at least in his heart. Now it was too late. He didn't hate Gordon, it was much worse—he felt nothing.

By late afternoon they had whittled the jury panel down from 400 to fifteen members, the first time in 220 years that NSW courts had used such a large panel. It was new legislation brought in to overcome the problem of long cases losing jury members. This time fifteen would hear the evidence expected to last sixteen weeks and then three members would be balloted out, leaving the traditional twelve to make a decision, either unanimously or, at worst, by 11–1. If not, it would be declared a hung jury with the prospect of having to do it all again. Tony hoped not but was prepared to come back as many times as was necessary.

Justice Barr was addressing the jury, explaining the judicial process, how evidence would be presented and cross-examined and warning them against paying attention to media coverage or discussing the case with anyone outside the panel. He would be the judge of the law and they of the evidence:

'It is important that you approach the matter quite dispassionately, without any prejudice or emotion. Because you are human beings, you may have prejudices of one sort or another against or in favour of various kinds of persons in the community. You may react emotionally to the evidence. It is important that any such prejudice or emotion play no part in your decision in the case.'

Mark Tedeschi was on his feet now. He would take the best part of two days to tell the jury what the case was about. Tony particularly liked the analogy Tedeschi used to explain its complexity. It was like a giant jigsaw puzzle of Sydney Harbour, he told them: 'There might be some pieces of water; there might be some pieces of sky; there might even be some pieces of the bridge and the Opera House missing, but you can still look at it and say, "I am satisfied beyond a reasonable doubt that that is a picture of Sydney Harbour, the bridge and the Opera House".'

After Tedeschi had finished the jury would be taken out to Watsons Bay. The police wanted the jury taken to the bottom of The Gap to see the rocks where Caroline had landed but Justice Barr had refused. It was too dangerous and might limit the age and spread of jurists. Instead, a giant scale model of the cliff had been built and positioned in front of the jury. Tony avoided looking, even when passing it to take his place in the witness box. The model was bad enough but it also included a representation of Caroline in the hole when she'd been thrown, her legs splayed.

Tony had been able to shield his emotions from most things, but there were limits. He wanted the jury to see The Gap at night. It was one thing to walk around in broad daylight and see where everything happened—the rock where the fishermen had sat, the ledge from which Caroline was thrown, John Doherty's window and the Bad Dog Café—but it was another to be there when it was dark and cold and envisage how Caroline must have felt in the hours before she was killed. Before the end of the trial Tony would get his wish.

Three days later Tony was struggling. The strain was in his voice; usually so quiet and measured, it was wavering ever so slightly on the other end of the phone: 'I'm all right, I'm okay. I think I went well.' It was not convincing.

It was 7 pm and he'd just arrived home after a day in the witness box during which, in the words of journalists and police who had watched proceedings, he'd been 'smashed'. What they meant was that Tony had faced a tough cross-examination by Gordon Wood's defence counsel, Winston Terracini, SC.

Neither the prosecution team nor the police minding Tony saw the intensity of the coming attack. They believed that even Terracini, renowned as he was for such attacks in defence of his client, would refrain or at least be restrained with a 72-year-old man who was explaining not only the last weeks, days and hours of his beloved daughter but the death of his wife, Andrea.

Not so. Terracini launched into a tirade of accusation, labelling Tony's evidence as 'irrational ravings', and being a 'fantasist' and spreading 'malicious and spiteful allegations' about people he did not know. The questions ranged from the state of his memory to religion and why he and his family did not attend the funerals of either his wife or his daughter. He was accused of spreading lies and contributing to the mental breakdown of Adam Leigh, even asked if he was aware of Andrew Blanchette's movements on the day of Caroline's death.

The worst though was the intensity of the examination into Andrea's death. Terracini quoted slabs of a statement Tony had made to police in the weeks after her suicide in which he laid bare her long depression.

The day before she disappeared, Andrea had demanded that he transfer ownership of the family home into her name. He'd fobbed her off by saying it couldn't be done on Easter Saturday: 'Think about it over the weekend and we can do something about it on Tuesday,' he told her as he left for work, promising to be back quickly so they could talk.

He could hear her reply as he shut the door: 'That will be too late. It's got to be today.'

When he got back she had left, telling Caroline she had gone shopping and would be back in three hours. The display of keys and bank statements said she was angry. When she didn't return as promised he feared the worst.

It was a personal matter, he had decided after her death, and was not necessary to investigate given the clear nature of the way she'd killed herself. But now his words—humane as they appeared at the time—were being cast back as weapons and reasons why his daughter might have committed suicide.

'You're trying to put it on an incident that then led to these dreadful events rather than the fact that she had a very long history of psychiatric disorder, aren't you?' Terracini put to him at one stage.

'No, that's not correct. All her psychiatric problems were as a result of the breast implants,' he protested.

'In the same way you're trying to minimise your daughter's problems with depression as well, aren't you?'

'No.'

'You're even trying to minimise that she tried to take her own life, aren't you?'

'No.'

'But she did try to take her own life, didn't she?'

'No, it was just a cry for help.'

It would continue the next morning, first over his dealings with Andrea's doctor and then his own grief immediately after Caroline's death. Terracini quoted selectively from his letter to Inspector Kennedy written in January 1996 while trying to encourage police to re-investigate the death as a homicide. He read it out loud to the jury to make it sound like a poison-pen letter rather than a desperate plea for help from a grieving man. Rumours of homosexual liaisons between Rivkin and Wood became outright accusations. And there were questions about his friendship with Paul Jacob, as if suggesting it coloured his statement.

'You were quite happy to introduce other people's names and suggest that they had something to do with your daughter's death, and you had nothing to go on . . . Quite happy to defame?'

Tony denied it, of course, but the questions kept coming at him; sharp, staccato needles; phrase by phrase, word by word. Did he really believe Rene Rivkin was involved? Was he seriously suggesting that Wood's mother, Brenda, was covering for her son? He was under siege for doing what any father would do in the same circumstances—ask questions and seek answers.

Terracini was reading again—'"If, for some reason Caroline wanted to end her life, she would have most certainly, without a shadow of doubt, chosen the same method her mother had used". Did you write that?'

'That's correct . . . she would have, yes.'

'How on earth could you possibly know that?'

'Because she certainly would not have jumped over a cliff.'

'But how would you know that if she wanted, if she wanted to kill herself, she would do it in exactly the same way as your wife? How on earth could you possibly know that?'

'That's what I wrote and I believe even to this day . . .'

'Sir, it's a classic, I suggest to you, example of your irrational ravings.'

Then it was his suggestion that Gordon Wood had been a secret investor in Offset Alpine and had money stashed in untraceable overseas bank accounts. It was a suggestion he later realised was wrong but Terracini saw it as indicative of something else.

'You're just making it up,' he scoffed. 'You're a fantasist.'

There were times Tony fought back, once stopping Terracini in his tracks when he called Rivkin a media nymphomaniac.

'A what?' Terracini exclaimed.

'A media nymphomaniac, by his own admission,' Tony repeated before launching into his own tirade about Rivkin's sudden dismissal of his chauffeur within weeks of the launch of the Wyver investigation. 'If Rene Rivkin had believed that Gordon was innocent of any wrongdoing, I don't believe they would have parted company. I don't believe Rene would have publicly dissociated himself from Gordon if he believed he was innocent of any wrongdoing.'

'What about his own involvement?' Terracini had challenged. 'Apparently you have said on a number of occasions you thought that the man Rivkin himself was involved in your daughter's death.'

Tony didn't hesitate: 'I believed there was a strong suspicion at the time and I also believed that after the fact, he must have known exactly what happened.'

Terracini kept coming back to why Tony didn't attend the funerals of his wife or Caroline, trying to suggest his reason was that he was embarrassed by Andrea's suicide and an initial belief that Caroline had done the same. Tony's protests sounded feeble until Mark Tedeschi got up to re-examine after Terracini's tirade was finally over early on his fourth day in the box: 'Would you explain to the court why you didn't attend your wife's funeral and why you didn't attend Caroline's funeral?'

'I don't attend funerals of any description. It's just a personal feeling that I have. Personally, I think they're a waste of time and I'm nice to people when they're alive. I see too many hypocritical people at funerals.'

'Did you speak to your children about that?'

'I said, "If you want to attend, the extended family were attending the funeral", and I said, "I'm too upset, I would be better off at home just grieving" and they said, "Well, we will stay home with you, Dad".'

'What about Caroline's funeral?'

'It was the same. It was the same. Caroline's was a bit worse for me. I don't think I would be here today if I had attended her funeral.'

As he stepped down from the witness box Tony glanced at Terracini, whose head was bowed. The defence lawyer had surprised and beaten him on the first day, and they had tussled for two more. His credibility was at stake here, as well as that of the case. Outside Tedeschi and the others would assure him he had held his own on the stand. Tony felt battered but he had left with his dignity intact. The ground rules for the battle ahead had been set.

43

A POLICEMAN'S LOT

The weather couldn't decide what it wanted to do; hot and sticky one day, windy and cold the next. Paul Jacob wouldn't have cared except that he was stuck outside the courtroom most days. It might have been funny if it wasn't so ridiculous; a senior officer sitting on a bloody bench managing witnesses. He had no choice really; it was his case and after a decade he wanted to see it through. The court staff, sticklers for the rules as they were, would not even allow him to put his equipment inside the doorway when it threatened to rain, as it did on most spring days in Sydney.

Neither was he allowed to watch proceedings inside the court, which only added to the frustration. As a witness he couldn't be privy to the testimony of others until he had taken the stand himself, and that wouldn't happen until near the end of the Crown's case when the officer in charge of the investigation traditionally gave evidence.

There was another reason—his credibility. Jacob had been publicly humiliated the previous December when the Police Integrity Commission, which investigated police misconduct and corruption, released a scathing report on his handling of the case of missing Bathurst woman Janine Vaughan. The report had called for Jacob to be sacked, accusing him of misconduct for failing to thoroughly investigate whether other police had deliberately left out information which implicated a former detective, Sergeant

Brad Hosemans. The report had caused uproar inside the police force where Jacob was regarded as honest and one of the state's finest detectives. No-one had taken action against him but he'd been forced to wear the ignominy and worry about how it might affect the Gordon Wood trial. He expected to be targeted by Winston Terracini when he eventually took the stand.

It angered him more than anything else. His team—Mossy, Quiggy and the little analyst Bianca Comina—should be respected, not targeted. The homicide squad had been decimated after the Wood Royal Commission in 1996 and those left had to shoulder the burden of a squad with not enough manpower or experience to handle the constant influx of cases. He'd had to put aside the Irondale investigation for a year while he sorted out the mess in Bathurst. And what did he get in return? A kick in the arse. They'd worked hard for ten years to get this case to court which, in itself, was an amazing achievement, as he kept telling Tony. A conviction would be a bonus, although he was quietly confident.

But things were turning in his favour. In the weeks leading up to the trial, he'd received word that the force's professional standards command had re-investigated and disagreed with PIC's findings. It was unofficial but he was in the clear, only he would have to wait until the decision was formalised, hopefully before he could give evidence.

They would cut it fine. The letter arrived on 13 October, three days before he would take the stand:

> The Professional Standards Command created Strikeforce Ogilvy and conducted a re-examination . . . which drew different conclusions, on the available evidence, from the Police Integrity Commission. I wish to advise that on October 13, 2008 the Professional Standards Command agreed there should be no adverse finding made against you. This matter is now closed.

It almost made sitting outside the court worthwhile. The first few weeks of the trial had largely consisted of his police colleagues recounting the night they spent on the cliff top at Watsons Bay searching for Caroline Byrne and winching her shattered body from the rocks as Wood watched, all the time aware of where she was and how she got there. Jacob wished he'd been there on the night but no-one had thought to call in homicide. The assumption was suicide. In hindsight it was dumb and that's why they were all here thirteen years later. There were half a dozen coppers who would give evidence during September, all of them with the same story. It was dark and cold, visibility was nonexistent and they were all acting on information provided by Gordon Wood, who insisted not only that his girlfriend had jumped but he knew where she was.

Constable Tracey Smit was among those who had had their suspicions but did not voice them. She was standing near him when the rescue squad had arrived and began to search. Mark Tedeschi asked her if Wood had said anything as the rescue squad was searching the cliff face and base with torches.

'Yes, he kept saying words to the effect of, "I know she's down there".'

'And are you able to say anything about the manner in which it was said?'

'There was a confidence that what he was saying was true.'

'And why do you particularly remember it?'

'I had a feeling . . . I thought it was suspicious.'

Lawrence Daley was a constable stationed at Waverley. As rescue squad members were setting up their equipment he heard Wood say: 'I can't believe she's done it.'

'By that stage, had anybody been detected or seen at the base of the cliffs?' asked Tedeschi.

'No, they hadn't.'

Paul Griffiths was a young a constable on duty when Wood and Tony and Peter Byrne reported Caroline missing. He read from his statement: 'The accused came to the station and said words to the effect of, "I'm pretty sure my girlfriend has jumped off The Gap". I said words to the effect, "What makes you think that?" The accused said, "I'm pretty sure I know where she is" and I said, "How do you know that?" The accused said, words to the effect, “She’s been depressed lately” and the accused also said something in relation to finding her vehicle.’

The evidence of Allan Gale, the station sergeant at Rose Bay, would be one of the few transcripts requested by the jury as they deliberated a few months later, prompted by Tedeschi’s questioning of Gale’s exchange with Wood as Caroline’s body was being winched up the cliff face.

‘When you had been informed that a body had been located, did you see the accused?’

‘I did. He was just on the cliff edge.’

‘Would you tell the Court what he said?’

‘He just said, that I recall, “That’s her. I want to see her”.’

‘What did you reply?’

‘I informed him that he wouldn’t be able to see her at that time.’

‘When the police rescue squad directed their light onto the body, did you have a look at where their light was pointing?’

‘I did. I could see the silhouette of the body.’

‘Was there any way that he could have seen the body at the base of the cliff?’

‘No, it was not possible.’

‘Would you explain why?’

‘Because we were well back from the cliff’s edge, well back from the safety fence, and the cliff’s edge jutted out, so even the rescue squad was required to climb halfway down the cliff to be able to see the body with their torch.’

Constable Lisa Camwell was one of those who climbed down to help retrieve the body but only after an hour or more of carefully searching the cliff face with her team leader, Sergeant Mark Powderly, using a powerful Mitrolux light.

‘Can you recall the accused saying something in particular?’ Tedeschi asked.

‘Yes. “There she is, there. There she is”.’

‘Now, at that time, had you seen anything?’

‘No.’

Powderly also heard comments from a man standing behind him as he shone and re-shone the light on a white-coloured object that he thought might have been a leg. 'That's her. That's the clothes she was wearing', was what he could recall the man saying.

'Could you see any clothes at all?' Tedeschi asked.

'The only clothing that I could see was where I believe there was a leg that you could see was a cream area and then what appeared to be a black area.'

Unlike his colleagues, who came and went fairly quickly, Powderly spent the best part of two days in the witness box, most of the time in a tense stand-off with Winston Terracini who was determined to exploit the mistakes made by police in establishing exactly where Caroline Byrne's body landed.

He was an important witness for the prosecution because he was so emphatic about where she had landed. Coupled with the evidence of Professor Rod Cross that would come later, it concluded that Caroline Byrne could not have leaped to her death and, therefore, must have been murdered. Terracini had to cast as much doubt as possible and was aided by the blunder of police in marking the wrong landing point on maps and videos during the early years of the investigation.

Just as during the committal hearing a year earlier, Powderly was adamant that although embarrassing, the error made initially during the 1996 police video re-enactment was simply that—a mistake. He had not noticed his offsider, Constable Camwell, pointing to a crevice at the bottom of The Gap while he faced and spoke to a video operator, describing it as the 'exact location' of the body. Neither had he noticed the mistake during the coronial inquiry two years later because the video had only been made to bolster a media-relations exercise designed to encourage witnesses to come forward once it became a homicide investigation. For her part, Constable Camwell said she had only known vaguely where Caroline Byrne had landed because, unlike Powderly, she had spent most of the time at the top of the cliff while her boss spent almost an hour with the body and avoiding the surging ocean washing across the rocks. Terracini returned several times to the subject, accusing Powderly of conspiring with Paul Jacob to paper over their faulty investigation and concocting the story. But Powderly, stoic in the witness box, would have none of it.

Mark Tedeschi's re-examination produced another surprise. When asked about his attitude when viewing the video during the coronial inquiry Powderly suddenly changed his story.

'When I saw it in the Coroner's Court and I saw [Constable Camwell] indicating with her hands, yeah, I realised I had made a mistake then. But I had not been asked at that point to pinpoint the correct hole by anybody. It was being referred to as a location at the Pyramid Rock.'

Tedeschi was taken aback. Had he heard correctly? 'Now, I just want to get this abundantly clear: when you saw the video in the Coroner's Court, did you realise then, when you saw the video, that the incorrect spot had been indicated?'

'Yes.'

'Did you tell anybody?'

'No.'

'Did you do anything about it?'

'No.'

'Did you think that it was of any consequence at that time?'

'Not at that time.'

'When was the first time that you realised that there was some consequence to the video having incorrectly indicated the finding of the body?'

'January 6, 2004.'

Winston Terracini pounced: 'Who have you told that you knew about it at the coronial?'

'Nobody.'

'You just vouched, saved it all this time?'

'Yes.'

'That's nonsense, isn't it?'

'No.'

'Did you misunderstand the questions that I was asking you in cross-examination?'

'Probably.'

'Probably? That's convenient. You are trying to create the image, aren't you, just the friendly old cop, and you're a liar, aren't you?'

'I refute that.' Powderly stood and banged his chair in frustration as he left the dock.

44

HORSE HEAD

Paul Quigg had been assigned to pick up Tony Byrne each day and drive him to court. The cops wanted Tony sitting where the jury could see him. They appeared to acknowledge the father of the victim, or at least check that he was there, each time the fifteen walked into the room and took their seats. By contrast, none looked at Gordon Wood.

They were, by and large, an inscrutable group of people. As the trial moved through September and into October it would become a game among attending media to pick up clues and give nicknames to these anonymous judges. They appeared an accurate representation of society; roughly half men and half women and a range of ages from several in their early to mid-twenties to a couple perhaps in their sixties. There was the 'Mosman Housewife' always assiduously writing notes as did 'Galahad', a rangy fop-haired man gauged to be an engineering student. 'Horse Head' seemed another with an academic background whose nods and head-shaking to evidence accentuated his large, angular head. The 'Butcher' was forever folding his arms and grimacing while 'Skunk Head', named because of her multi-coloured hair, always sat at the back alongside a young man who looked fresh out of high school. Speculation mounted about a romantic attachment between the pair as the trial wore on. What struck the media and those at the bar table was the collective attentiveness of the jurors. At least four were taking notes at any time and often all of them at once. It would emerge later that they each had tasks during any period of evidence, as if working as a team.

There were no sick days during the whole trial; none of them were ever late and only one ever nodded off. 'The Sleeper' was actually prone to micro-sleeps rather than boredom. If Tony watched closely he could see that her eyes would close momentarily before she woke a few seconds later to make notes. She usually sat next to 'Wilma', a woman judged to be in her late thirties who often wore pearls and reminded the media of Wilma Flintstone. The foreman, who always sat at the front closest to the judge, was the most difficult to read although he, like the others, couldn't help smiling at Winston Terracini's cutting asides and sense of humour. It was a mark of the barrister's character, highlighted more so by the unflappable exterior of his opponent. The response of jury members to Terracini would lead to some false assumptions by those watching.

Tony refused to stay in the court when Terracini was on his feet for any lengthy period. He either stayed home for the day, dwelled a few hours longer before leaving or simply walked outside the courtroom and sat alone in the police room.

The cross-examination had rocked him. Tony felt as if he had held his own, particularly after the first day, but the shock of being challenged as crazy and a liar made it impossible to sit in the court while Terracini cross-examined other witnesses. Instead he would hear the evidence in chief and then leave. 'I only want to hear the good bits,' he insisted to those who noticed his absence. 'I can't stand the sound of Winston's voice, and I don't have a voice in there. He can say what he likes.'

Paul Jacob wanted Tony to sit in and listen to others being quizzed. 'You're not the only one Tony,' he tried to explain. 'Lots of them are getting a hard time in there; that's part of the process. It's tough but the defence has every right and Terracini is very good at it. It's not only Caroline's death but Gordon Wood's life which is at stake.'

Tony knew the argument, and didn't disagree, but after all this time he knew how to protect himself, and listening to Wood's lawyer attempt to tear down the credibility of the case, and all Caroline's friends and workmates, was not part of it. They had appeared as a procession through much of September. Caroline's closest friends like Natalie McCamley and Narelle Cook, and workmates like Tali Blumenfeld, Kylie Watson, Geraldine Howarth and Tania Zaetta. The girls from June Dally's came, and June herself and her daughters. The modelling agency boss Gordon Donald gave evidence as did some of the office staff.

It was beautiful, Tony thought, sitting contentedly in the gallery as they all spoke of their friend—his daughter—and her impact on their lives. Somehow, amid the sadness, anger and frustration, there was a blessing.

They talked about the young woman he knew including Caroline's dreams and fears and the relationship with Gordon Wood. Critically, they would also shed light on his reaction to her death and the versions he told in the days afterwards. Terracini leaped on anything his client was alleged to have said, particularly about seeing his girlfriend's body before it had been winched to the cliff top.

Natalie McCamley, now a married Natalie Butler, faced Terracini's wrath when she recalled a detailed conversation in which Wood claimed to have seen Caroline's shoes.

'Look, you're twisting it because you do not like Gordon Wood,' he snapped at one stage as he questioned the manner in which she had reported the conversations.

'That's not true,' she replied defensively.

'How old are you, by the way?'

'Thirty-seven.'

'No, so it can't be youth, or anything like that, that confused you about the importance of the occasion.'

He questioned her integrity again while reading out one of her statements, sentence by sentence. In one section, she had quoted Wood as saying 'When the police came later, I told them that they were looking in the wrong spot; she was where I'd seen her earlier.'

Terracini bristled: 'He never said that to you, did he?'

'Yes.'

'And: "I told them to look there and they found her." He never said that to you either, did he?'

'Yes.'

'"They were looking in the wrong area. It was taking so long to find her". He didn't say that at all?'

'That's what I believe that he said and I was told that story. I'm not making this up.'

'You know very well what you're trying to do, and it is trying to poison the minds of the jury because of your dislike for Gordon Wood. You want to put the spin on it, don't you?'

'No.'

Narelle Cook was another who copped his vehemence. Terracini did not challenge much of the evidence of Caroline's friends. His questions were more about the accuracy of their memories, the exact words and phrases which were purportedly used by Gordon Wood, and the interpretation people placed on them, particularly if, like Narelle, they didn't like him.

He ridiculed her complaints about Wood playing practical jokes on her during a weekend in the Blue Mountains, including: 'Do you remember telling the coroner about this breakfast that he cooked for you that you didn't like, that he put too much sugar in your coffee?'

'He actually filled my coffee cup a third full of sugar,' she protested.

'And you thought this was very serious, did you?'

'It was unpleasant at the time.'

'That he cooked you breakfast—"But there was too much oil underneath my breakfast with sausages, bacon and eggs"—that was something that you thought important enough to tell the coroner?'

'He actually made six of us breakfast and he poured the fat from the frying pan onto my plate and then put the food on top, but he didn't do that to anybody else.'

Tania Zaetta was just another promising model and hopeful actress when she met Caroline Byrne in 1992. Now, sixteen years later, she was a Bollywood queen as she strode through the gathered ranks of cameramen and photographers, chic in black and silver and bemused behind large sunglasses, to give evidence about the last days of her friend.

'The best way to describe Caroline would be to compare her in some ways to Charlotte from *Sex and the City*,' she declared within moments of taking the stand. 'Caroline was a gorgeous girl, both in her appearance and also in her personality. She was very prim and proper, not in any type of a stuck-up-type manner, but just in her lady style. That's the only way to describe her—an absolute lady. In some respects a little guarded, I would say. We would often make jokes that we couldn't get Caroline to lose her temper or swear or do anything wrong. She was just perfect.'

The relationship with Gordon Wood appeared genuine but she did query the number of calls Caroline would get from him during the day. At first it seemed sweet to have someone so doting 'who would call so frequently to see how she is, where she is, what she is doing'. But then it became something more, overbearing if anything: 'I thought it was probably a little bit too much. You know, what is there to talk about later on if you've checked in pretty much every hour or two with each other?'

She was nice and polite to everyone but the evidence of 81-year-old June Marie Clifford, aka June Dally-Watkins, dripped with poison for those defending Gordon Wood. The elderly doyenne of deportment preferred to talk about the last days of Caroline Byrne from memory rather than the notes she jotted down in the weeks after her employee's death, so fresh were the memories even after thirteen years. Her earnest sweetness would undoubtedly have an impact.

She recalled the last day she had seen the young woman recently appointed full-time as a student counsellor and Saturday manager. It was in the office about 5 pm on Saturday 3 June and

Caroline was sipping camomile tea to counter her flu as they planned a trip together down to Bowral in the Southern Highlands to visit the up-market girls' boarding school, Frensham, where they would make a presentation. Caroline had left a report on June's desk, describing her reaction to the first week in the new job. She had written that she very happy and enthusiastic and looking forward to their future together. She was also thrilled about the recent return from overseas of her boyfriend.

'Did you discuss with her the various aspects of her life, like her relationship, her housing, her family life?' Mark Tedeschi asked.

June nodded. 'On that day she was very excited, because she and Gordon had moved into a new apartment and she was talking about the furniture, and about how wonderful it would be with Gordon back, and the furniture and getting her apartment ready.'

'And was there anything that she said to you on that day that would indicate to you that she was depressed?'

'No, not even slightly.'

Like others in the days after Caroline's sudden death, she was told by Gordon Wood that Caroline had been hit by a car. When June finally challenged him about the account he confessed that she had died at The Gap and then blamed depression and hatred for the new job.

'I explained that she had only worked for us full-time for that one week, and we had a report left on her desk for us at the end of that week, and it said how happy she was, and how she was looking forward to her future with us. And he hesitated for a while, and he said, "Oh well, she was lying. She didn't mean that".'

'During the time that you had known Caroline, did you know her as a person who lied?'

'Never.'

June then recounted the day she and Kylie Watson had been to the Bad Dog Café at Watsons Bay and spoken to Craig Martin and Lance Melbourne about the beautiful young woman they had seen on 7 June. She was with two men, one of whom was tall and slim and wearing a brown jacket. A week or so later she had attended the second of two commemorative services held for Caroline. This was at McKell Park, organised by Gordon Donald and Gordon Wood.

'As you waited in your car, did you see someone?' Tedeschi inquired, anticipating an affirmative answer.

'Yes, I saw someone walk out of the park gates,' she replied daintily. 'It was Gordon.'

'Okay. And did you notice what he was dressed in at the time?'

'Yes. A brown jacket.'

'Did you notice anything about Gordon Wood's appearance and what the two men had told you in the café?'

'Yes . . . I was really shocked because it was an exact description of the two men from the restaurant. I picked up my camera and took a photograph . . .' A few days later she showed the photograph to the two men.

'Do you recall now if they said anything to you?'

'They considered that that was the person they'd seen.'

The clash with Winston Terracini lasted more than a day, descending at times into clashes which forced Justice Barr to intervene, particularly when June appeared to misunderstand questions. 'Listen,' he snapped one time before apologising. At one stage, a frustrated Terracini even accused her of being 'silly'. At the end of it all, however, she left the witness box with a grace that embossed her persona.

'Miss Clifford, we can let you go now,' said Justice Barr.

'I can go?' she asked, surprised and perhaps a little disappointed it was all over.

'And you are excused,' the judge added with a smile.

'Thank you so much, everybody. Okay. I'll pack up all my papers. And there's your pen. Thank you very much, everybody,' she waved to the bench, the bar table, the jury box and the public gallery as she swept from the courtroom with all eyes upon her.

* * *

Mark Tedeschi gave little away in or out of the courtroom. His delivery was unflustered, carefully modulated in comparison to his opponent's excited and demanding demeanour. Both were regarded in legal circles as effective given that one was passionately defending a man he believed was innocent and the other quietly compiling a case to put away a man he regarded as guilty.

There was a strategy to Tedeschi's format although for many observers, including the media, it was difficult to see some of the points being made. He couldn't turn to the jury after eliciting a nugget of information and tell them, 'Look at this; this is important.' He might pause for a second, as if stressing its importance, or repeat a question to get the answer again, but his technique was more about compiling information that would then be fitted into the jigsaw he would complete in his closing address.

By contrast Terracini was bouncy, holding court with journalists during breaks where he had no hesitation in critiquing his opponent's case. He had declared confidence within weeks of the opening, dismissing the Crown case as fragmented. Tedeschi was puzzled by the confidence so early into a long case. 'It's going as well as I expected,' he would respond to reporters eager to explore the byplay.

The question which begged an answer was if Terracini was going to put Wood on the stand to testify when the defence began its case. Tedeschi hoped so, as did the media but Terracini was undecided. 'I don't know yet,' he pondered. 'Only if the Crown case is strong enough.'

45

A TONGUE DRIPPING WITH LIES

Timing is an essential skill for a barrister, much like a polished entertainer. The pitch and delivery has to be just right to convince and enthral the audience, in this case a jury. Mark Tedeschi was normally a courtroom master but on the afternoon of 1 October—the 26th day of the trial—his skill deserted him with devastating effect.

The appearance of Andrew Blanchette was the most anticipated moment in the trial to date. Ever since the cross-examination of Tony Byrne, Winston Terracini had taken every opportunity to flag his intention to grill Caroline's long-time boyfriend when he appeared on the stand. Although the allegation was yet to be put, it was clear that Blanchette was being touted as an alternative killer of his childhood sweetheart.

For almost two hours Tedeschi carefully took the hulking former police officer through his sad tale of a schoolyard relationship gone sour as the pair grew into adulthood and found the world and its opportunities. He had known her intimately for years; her good bits, her foibles, even her scars. Critically, he gave evidence of his observations about her athletic ability. She was fit and a good swimmer at high school but when it came to ball sports she was hopelessly uncoordinated—and she couldn't jump: 'We used to call her a credit card jumper [because] you could barely slip a credit card under her feet. She couldn't get off the ground.'

Blanchette wept as he spoke of Caroline, how they had maintained contact after breaking up just before Christmas in 1992; frequent telephone calls, occasional meetings, flirting and even sex on two occasions. Why he revealed these indiscretions on Caroline's part was a mystery to those who watched. Thankfully, on the advice of Paul Jacob, Tony had stayed away.

It was approaching 4 pm when Tedeschi wound up. In hindsight he would wish he had stalled for another few minutes.

Justice Barr looked at the clock attached to the public gallery railing above Gordon Wood's head. 'I see that it's after 10 to 4. Do you wish to commence this afternoon, Mr Terracini?'

The terrier was on his feet in a flash, barely containing his anticipation at the verbal scrap which lay ahead. 'I can commence, your Honour, yes.'

It took five questions to light the fire. Terracini was aiming squarely at Blanchette's alibi for the night of Caroline's death. He had spent the night at the home of two sisters in Rose Bay, a suburb barely five minutes' drive from Watsons Bay. Blanchette was friends with the older sister but, despite a seven-year age difference, would have a physical relationship with the younger. When it began was critical, as Terracini honed in.

'What school did she go to?'

'She was at Kincoppal.'

Confirmation of the prestigious girl's school was the green light. 'She was a boarder. And you used to wait for her, whilst a police officer, when she would get out from boarding school and have sex with her, didn't you?'

Blanchette knew the attack was coming but bit anyway. 'That's absolute rubbish.'

Mark Tedeschi was back on his feet, objecting to no avail. Terracini sensed blood: 'How old was she?' he demanded.

'Seventeen; seventeen-and-a-half.'

'Did you know that she was a schoolgirl when you were having sex with her?'

'I don't think I did when she was at school.'

'You're not crying now, are you?' he sneered.

Tedeschi tried to object again. Justice Barr ignored the plea.

'Are you?' Terracini demanded again.

Blanchette was stone-faced. 'No, I'm not.'

The next eight minutes were a preview of the two days ahead—Blanchette locked in the witness box, at the mercy of a defence counsel intent on breaking not only the man in front of him but the entire prosecution case.

Where did he sleep, with whom and why did he get up during the night? How did he get in and out of the property? Was he still there when the girl left to return to school at 7 am the next day? Did he leave the house during the night?

Then the teaser for the accusation which lay ahead: 'How far is it from The Gap from Rose Bay, Mr Blanchette?'

'I couldn't tell you.'

Terracini was playing at the edges. 'What did you weigh around about June 1995?'

'105 kilos, I'd say.'

'You were immensely strong, weren't you?'

'Absolutely.'

Finally, almost reluctantly, Terracini looked past his client to the clock. 'All right. Is that a suitable time?'

Court was adjourned for the day. In a few minutes he had dismantled Mark Tedeschi's careful management of a problem witness. Instead of the jury mulling over a distraught ex-boyfriend still grappling with her death, they would be thinking about a large, powerful man allegedly sleeping with a schoolgirl barely five minutes' drive from where his old sweetheart was thrown off a cliff.

The drama began even before the jury was brought into the courtroom the next morning. The media, in its fervour for the events of the night before, had illegally published the name of Andrew Blanchette's schoolgirl friend, earning an admonishment and warning from the judge. Mark Tedeschi was also on his feet, complaining that Gordon Wood had accosted and threatened Blanchette the previous afternoon as he walked into the courtroom to begin his evidence. 'You'll get yours one day, you'll get yours,' Wood allegedly hissed as the pair crossed paths. Terracini denied the accusation 'as a lie' on his client's behalf.

It merely set the scene for the spectacle about to unfold which began almost immediately as Blanchette revealed that the alibi for his whereabouts during the afternoon of 7 June was wrong. He had not been at the gym as he'd previously stated, but attending a police rugby league game and attending after-match drinks at a pub, the name of which he could not immediately recall. The revelation had come to him in the early hours of the morning.

'At approximately what time did it become very clear to you last night, Mr Blanchette?' The sarcasm dripped from Terracini's lips.

'1.13 am.'

'Because, what, you were worried about something, were you?'

'No, not worried at all.'

'Most people aren't awake at quarter past 1 in the morning, Mr Blanchette, thinking about where they were thirteen-and-a-half years ago?'

The argument proceeded back and forth as Blanchette was challenged to prove his new story. Records would exist showing his roster, he claimed. There was a standing game every Wednesday during the winter. He had played police rugby ever since joining the force. At the time he was playing for the Newtown side but may have been on the sideline because he was recuperating from a broken leg. He couldn't remember where or who they played.

Terracini switched from subject to subject. His job was to unsettle and undermine, badger and confuse as he sought to discredit the prosecution's witnesses. By reputation he was good at it. To those watching the blood sport, he was brilliant. He wanted to know why Blanchette had told Tony Byrne and others that Gordon Wood was a homosexual and having an affair with Rene Rivkin.

'You had no reliable information whatsoever, did you?'

'No, I didn't.'

'And you wanted to defame him so that the young girl, Caroline Byrne, would ditch him and go back to you, didn't you?'

'He does enough to defame himself.'

'You tell lies, don't you?'

'No, I don't.'

'You tried to poison the mind of that girl and her family because of your jealousy and obsession with Caroline.'

'Never had that at all. That's completely incorrect.'

'You went around to everybody that you knew that knew Wood, telling them that, not only that he was a faggot but that he was a poofter.'

With that the court rose. It would be four days before it sat again—enough time for another twist in the saga.

About 6.50 am on Friday, 3 October, Andrew Blanchette made a telephone call from a public phone box in Camden. He would later tell the court that he had used a pay phone because his mobile phone was charging while he went out for a cup of coffee with a mate. The problem was not making a phone call but who he called—his former schoolgirl lover, now a married mother, who was due to give evidence after he had finished.

'Hello?' She could hear the coins drop as she answered.

'Don't hang up.' Blanchette guessed she would recognise his voice and react badly.

He was right. 'What do you want?'

'I need to talk to you about what is going on. You are going to be put through the wringer by the defence. I'm sorry that you have been brought into this; this has nothing to do with you. You have to listen to what I am saying. The defence are going to be really hard on you. There is stuff that I know that they're going to say about you. You have no idea, and you need to know what they are going to say.'

The conversation went on for another few minutes. Blanchette wanted to meet but the woman refused: 'I won't be meeting you.

There is nothing to discuss. I have made a statement. Everything I have said has been the truth. I've nothing more to say to you.'

Blanchette backed off. 'Okay. Nobody needs to know about this phone call. It didn't happen.' With that he hung up.

The woman immediately called Irondale police and reported the call. The police called Mark Tedeschi who was obliged to inform the defence. By Tuesday 7 October, the end of a long weekend in Sydney, news had filtered into the media ranks that there was a new Blanchette bombshell.

The jury would not know immediately of the incident. Instead, Terracini went back to Blanchette's alibi during the afternoon. He could now recall the name of the pub—the Duke of Edinburgh on Enmore Road—but the rest remained a haze.

Terracini was circling and now moved in for the kill: 'You didn't stay in bed with [her] all night, did you?'

'No, I didn't, sir.'

'You left and were out of her bedroom for a number of hours that night, weren't you?'

'No. That's not correct. I was backwards and forwards.'

'Did you leave the premises that night?'

'Definitely not.'

'Are you sure you haven't got something to do with the death of Caroline Byrne?'

'You're clutching at straws now, aren't you? That is not correct.'

'We will wait and see, Mr Blanchette. Are you sure you didn't have anything to do with her death?'

'As I said, it is absolutely ridiculous.'

It was time for the next attack. 'You know as a former police officer, when you're told not to speak to witnesses whilst you are under cross-examination that that has to be strictly adhered to, correct?'

Blanchette could only agree: 'That's correct.'

Tedeschi was on his feet but his objections were waved away. Terracini fired another rocket: 'And you know very well, again, because of your experience as a former police officer, to suggest that a witness should forget or alter any of the statements that they had made to the police is also grossly improper, isn't it?'

'They should tell the truth.'

'To suggest to a witness, by implication, that they should not tell the truth is a crime, isn't it?'

'I haven't done that.'

'Haven't you?'

'No.'

Terracini launched into details of the illicit phone call as Tedeschi sank into his chair. As if details of Blanchette's romantic dalliance with a schoolgirl wasn't bad enough, now this. He just hoped the jury would see it for what it was—a sideshow.

Blanchette insisted the telephone call was not about changing the woman's evidence but warning her about the media. He was planning a civil suit and wanted her to do the same.

Terracini scoffed at the proposal. 'So you just wanted to protect her, Mr Blanchette. And you feel that you have been victimised, do you?'

'I think I have been inappropriately portrayed in the media to the point I had to seek medical assistance on the weekend.'

'Oh, we are not going to do this cry-baby business, are we?'

'I don't need to cry to tell you the facts.'

'You were sobbing transparently, sobbing. You put on a performance to try and ingratiate yourself with the jury, didn't you?'

'Caroline's one of my dearest friends and I will never ever stop until I find out what happened to her.'

'Sir, your tongue is dripping with lies.'

'No, it's not. I am telling you factually.'

'You are not grinning anymore at the jury?'

The accusations, disguised as questions, were raining like hammer blows: 'You realise how serious it is, don't you?'

'It is serious if only you discuss the offence.'

'You were desperate to try and have her change her evidence, weren't you?'

'There is no way on God's earth she would ever change her evidence.'

'And you were obsessed with Caroline Byrne as well, weren't you?'

'That's not correct at all.'

'Because you're a very jealous and obsessive man, aren't you?'

'That's completely incorrect.'

Finally, after almost three days in the stand, Andrew Blanchette stepped down. The prosecution case, it appeared, was shattered. Tedeschi looked devastated.

46

DEAR BRETTY

It took a bit of fiddling but eventually Basquali fizzed into view as technology, albeit it black and white with a less than perfect audio, had come to a Victorian courtroom in Darlinghurst.

The New York-based photographer had been one of Gordon Wood's most vocal supporters although he hadn't seen or even spoken to his mate in at least a year. Still, he had no doubts about his innocence.

Mark Tedeschi took the man christened Brett Cochrane, before creativity and a famous lawsuit intervened, through his friendship with Wood and the events leading up to Caroline's death. Wood was a sensitive person who was on the way up with Rene Rivkin, assessing deals on behalf of his boss and taking a cut of the profits. 'No-one could get to Rene without going through Gordon first,' he told police. It mattered little that Gordie had exaggerated his importance. It didn't make him a liar. Mates did that sort of thing.

Just after midday on 7 June Basquali met Wood for lunch with another friend, Nick Samartis. As usual, the meeting had been arranged on the spur of the moment via mobile phone. 'Random', he called it, as their lives generally were in those days. Sometimes they met three times a week and at other times not for several weeks. There were a dozen cafés and restaurants, particularly along Victoria Road, where they would sit and talk, depending on what they felt like or just getting a table, preferably outside where they could watch the passing parade.

Wood arrived about fifteen minutes later than the other two. He ordered lunch, even though he later told police he intended to go home and lunch with his girlfriend, but then took a phone call and announced he had to leave to get 'his boss', his lunch forgotten. Phone records would show that at 1.18 pm Wood telephoned Basquali from his mobile. The prosecution would say he was already at Watsons Bay with Caroline Byrne and another man.

Like many others, Basquali was initially told by Wood that his girlfriend had been killed by a car. The story had changed two days later when he and another friend, Peter Cameron, met at North Bondi with Wood who suggested they drive up to The Gap. Basquali took photographs as Wood and Cameron walked along the fence line, talking. He couldn't hear the words but realised that Caroline had died here and not under the wheels of a car. He kept snapping away, as he had done all his life. Why? asked Tedeschi.

'I wanted to record the moment and record the story on a piece of artwork . . . It was composed in such a way that there was a lot of space in the top of the frame to read the sky to write on the print what had happened that day.'

Basquali left Sydney a few months later. He went to live in Cuba for a year during which time he and Wood stayed in touch by letter, a handful of which he had given to police during the investigation. Tedeschi was particularly interested in a missive written by Wood on 16 May 1996, a few weeks before the first anniversary of Caroline's death.

Dear Bretty, it began before complaining about Rene Rivkin's refusal to finalise an investment in a business Wood had started after leaving the businessman's employment. Rivkin was now refusing even to return phone calls:

> That's okay, I suppose, and quite frankly I don't care if I never speak to or have anything to do with him again,

> particularly after his strange behaviour which displayed a complete lack of backbone or character. But I would like to know the reasons for the switch. Just some understanding. I suppose after covering for him and having to do his dirty work for so long, it should come as no surprise that he wouldn't face me. Maybe it has something to do with the police investigation and he's scared to be associated with me. I'm glad it's over, except I still haven't seen the money promised to me from the Offset Alpine deal. I'm waiting to see if I get any money out of the sale of my apartment . . . I trusted him. What an idiot.

Peter Cameron had bought 5000 shares in Offset Alpine in January 1993 at the suggestion of Gordon Wood, and sold at a profit seven months later. He, like Basquali, would also recall the morning on the cliff top with Gordon, as well as what his friend told him about the events on that night and leading up to Caroline's death. In one statement to police he recounted what Wood said.

'He got the torch, he shone it around, he showed it around. He told us that he saw her ankle from the spot that he was, that he could see her shoe, her ankle skin and some portion of the lower leg of the trouser.'

Tedeschi stopped him. 'You said that with the torch . . . he shone it around . . . from the spot that he was. Now, by that, do you mean the spot where he was on the night when he was looking for her, or the spot that he was when he was talking to you?'

'I meant the spot he was on the night he was there.'

Cameron would also recount how Wood told him of Caroline's battle with depression and use of medication. According to Cameron's notes of the conversation, Caroline had been treated for a period of time and had been on medication.

'Gordon told me that in the week of her death there was a cancelled or "no show" appointment. He told me that she was in a quandary, whether she ever needed, wanted or ought to continue the therapy. I can't remember the exact conversation. The quandary was whether she believed that she didn't need, want or ought continue with her therapy.'

On the day of her death, Wood told his mate that he returned to the unit during the afternoon and spoke to Caroline, asking her if she wanted a tablet before finding two missing from the bathroom cabinet.

'I know that Gordy didn't confront her over the missing two tablets, so he gave her one. Nothing more that I know, except that it became clear to me, from what Gordy said post-death, that medication was a part of their lives.'

There was a problem with Wood's story that would emerge in the weeks after Cameron's testimony. Caroline could not have taken drugs that day because there was no sign of anything in her bloodstream. There were remnants of the sleep-disorder drug Rohypnol found in her urine but even an expert called by the defence concluded the pill would have been taken at least four days before her death. The scene described by Wood to Cameron, and others, simply could not have happened.

Like that of advertising legend John Singleton a week earlier, the appearance of former Labor MP Graham Richardson was in danger of becoming a media sideshow rather than the serious evidentiary impact on the trial.

Singleton spent ten minutes in the stand to discount the possibility that he was driving his rare green Bentley through Watsons Bay on the afternoon of 7 June, giving credence to the sighting of such a car as being likely to have been the one owned by Rene Rivkin and therefore driven by Gordon Wood around the time the prosecution insisted he was seen with Caroline Byrne and another man. Instead, the papers ran a photo of him wheeling a pram from the courthouse belonging to another celebrity witness, Caroline's GP Dr Cindy Pan.

Richardson was also giving evidence about not being in a green Bentley on the same afternoon. Wood had always maintained that he had picked up Richardson from the Alife Restaurant in

East Sydney, where he had been lunching with Rivkin, and driven him into the city. But Richardson's diary, confirmed by other witnesses, showed he was lunching that day at the San Francisco Grill in the Hilton Hotel.

Silver-topped and florid-faced, Richardson's evidence quickly turned into an entertaining glimpse into the world of Rivkin. The pair lunched most weeks, often because of an impromptu phone call by Rivkin, never for long but always at a quality restaurant usually in the eastern suburbs. He had permanent tables at several places so he could smoke cigars in peace. And he was always delivered by car.

'Rene basically didn't walk anywhere. More than ten metres from the door and he'd get a car,' Richardson quipped, adding, 'There were no Holdens.'

Wood's counsel, Winston Terracini, joined in the fun. 'Rivkin was a man who if he had the urge to exercise, would sit down and wait until it passed.'

'Yes, definitely,' replied Richardson with a smile.

47

'IT MATCHED GARY'

Michael Jaggard owned the Alife restaurant in Stanley Street where Rene Rivkin ate lunch the day Caroline Byrne died. For a time he lived with a girlfriend in the same apartment building as Rivkin kept his flat, The Sanctuary. He knew the businessman as a regular customer as well as his chauffeur, Gordon Wood, and minders like George Freris and Gary Redding.

The restaurant kitchen was designed so he could look out on his customers while he worked, to keep a check on things. Around 3 pm on 7 June 1995, he was cooking on an open grill when he noticed Rivkin gesturing wildly. He stopped what he was doing and watched, mainly because it was so unusual to see the man upset. He never ate alone and enjoyed the bonhomie of a meal as much as the food.

As he relived the scene thirteen years later under questioning from Mark Tedeschi, Jaggard clearly recalled the man to whom Rivkin was directing his ire—it was Gordon Wood, who had earlier dropped his boss to lunch, probably around 1 pm. Gary Redding stood behind Wood, just out of the conversation. The kitchen fans above his head made it impossible to hear what was being said.

'The discussion looked a little bit heated,' he told Tedeschi.

'It was heated?'

'It appeared a little bit heated and they quickly left.'

'How long did this heated conversation between the accused and Rene Rivkin take?'

'Oh, it wouldn't be long—a minute—then they walked out. That was it.'

In the months that followed Jaggard had several confrontations because of Rivkin's lunch that day which had been booked over the phone by Wood and, according to Rivkin's credit card statement, had cost $103.

The first problem was the arrival one day during the lunch rush of a couple of cops who wanted to know if Rivkin had been there and could they get a copy of his bill and payment. They annoyed Jaggard because rather than being discreet, they chose to arrive in the middle of lunch and act loudly enough to get the attention of his customers. It made him feel like a criminal, he told Paul Jacob a decade later when, after being found by the *Sydney Morning Herald*, Jaggard agreed to cooperate with police.

There were four other incidents, three of them with Gordon Wood outside Jaggard's restaurant. Wood was red-faced and angry when he first confronted the businessman, as Jaggard recalled when asked what the chauffeur said to him.

'He was trying to tell me not to say that I saw him that day he dropped Rene off,' he said.

'Would you tell the court as best you can recollect what he actually said to you?'

'It was in that kind of context: "Don't tell anybody that you saw me at your restaurant that day" or kind of else, you know.'

'In a single word how did it affect you?'

'Fearful.'

Wood accosted him again a few days later and said much the same thing, then a third time during which he mentioned a share deal in the United Kingdom.

'What did he actually say?'

'Basically, "I'll offer you shares to shut up".'

A few days after the last confrontation with Wood, Jaggard found himself in the lift of his building with George Freris and

Gary Redding. It was an uncomfortable fit for the three men and clearly not by chance.

'I took a breath to say something, it was a very stuffy situation in a lift, and George said "Just be quiet".'

Jaggard looked at the two men and knew instinctively what they meant. Caroline Byrne. He said nothing and they offered no explanation before getting out of the lift.

Winston Terracini did his best to dismiss Jaggard's evidence, challenging his account and ability to recall conversations when he couldn't recall the name or address of the apartment building or the exact car Rivkin was dropped off in that day.

'See, sir, what I am suggesting to you is that you are very confused about this time span and these conversations, aren't you?'

'It is a long time ago. Timing is difficult, but I remember the instances.'

Terracini tried again. 'Yes. But what I am suggesting to you is that . . . it would be almost impossible to remember precise details of conversations on a precise day so long in the past without any independent reference to records or times, and things like that.'

'Timing I agree with,' Jaggard nodded. 'But I know what happened.'

George Freris had already given evidence before Michael Jaggard gave his dramatic account but was recalled to the stand to answer the claim.

Under questioning from Tedeschi he readily agreed to having had a conversation with Jaggard, although not in a lift with Gary Redding and not about keeping his mouth shut.

'I think he was suggesting that he may have some information that he should go to the police with . . . I said to him, "If you have something substantial to say, then say it, but if you don't . . . then don't say it".'

Winston Terracini went over the same ground, confirming Jaggard's account that there had been a conversation between the pair. But rather than a dark threat, Freris insisted he was being friendly.

'Whatever the conversation was about, it definitely was not about you telling him to keep his mouth shut about anything to do with Gordon Wood having been or having not been at the restaurant?' Terracini proffered.

Freris laughed. 'That would be a little hypocritical, because I was already talking to the police about what I knew.'

Indeed he had been, as he detailed in his first stint in the witness box when he revealed his surprise at discovering that Gordon Wood had borrowed his car—a red pick-up truck kept below The Sanctuary nine city blocks from Wood's flat—on the night of his girlfriend's disappearance.

Unlike at the carpark across the road from Macleay Street where Rivkin kept a number of cars including the green Bentley Wood often drove, he was able to take Freris's truck without any security checks or records. Freris drove it almost every day. Wood had a set of keys but only drove it when he had to make a delivery for the Rivkin family.

When Freris went down to use the truck on the morning of 8 June, he noticed it had been moved. He was fastidious about parking the vehicle straight when he left it outside the lift. Not only was it crooked but the footbrake was on, something he never did.

Tedeschi asked: 'Can you think of any reason why [Gordon] would have needed to use the red pick-up truck the previous night?'

'No.'

'Would he normally have driven it at night?'

'Never. Not that I know of.'

'On all the previous occasions, had you been told beforehand that somebody else was going to use that truck?'

'Yes.'

Tedeschi changed tack. 'What were the vehicles that you most commonly saw the accused driving?'

'Probably the green Bentley. There was a blue Rolls Royce Corniche convertible, and also a maroony, crimson-coloured Bentley convertible.'

'Where were those three vehicles kept?'

'Most often in the carpark near Gordon's place.'

In fact there were two carparks between Freris's flat and the Macleay Street flat where Gordon Wood insisted he woke just before midnight to find the love of his life missing. There were four available bays in a carpark at Ward Avenue 100 metres or so from his front door where the Vitara was always parked and another in Forbes Street, off William Street down towards East Sydney. Both housed three or four vehicles. If he was telling the truth about what happened that night then Wood ignored the first two, both of which had security, and ran to Crown Street where he would have assumed the red ute was not being used. He had not bothered to phone Freris and ask if it was there.

The next day, a few hours after Caroline's body was recovered, Wood turned up at the Ward Street carpark and asked manager Warwick White if he could provide a computer printout for the movements of the Vitara for the previous 24 hours. He needed it for the coroner, he told White, who complied. When police tried to obtain the records some years later they were no longer available.

George Freris admitted that he and Wood had never got on well. As an example, he told the court of the occasion when Wood took him aside and told him: 'I wish you would drop dead.'

Why, asked Tedeschi.

'I think I was just in an enviable position. I was probably better friends with Rivkin than Gordon was.'

In terms of friendship, Freris counted Gary Redding as his closest friend in the group. But that didn't prevent him from dobbing in his mate when asked about the identity of the second man seen by Melbourne and Martin at Watsons Bay.

'Now, do you recall the police giving you a description of a man with black hair?'

'Yes.'

'Was this the description that they gave you: of a man about 5'7", Spanish appearance, black leather pants, black vest, black leather jacket and boots, slim with black hair?'

'Sounds like the description they asked me about.'

'And did they ask you if you knew anybody in the Rivkin group who matched that description?'

'Yes.'

'Would you tell the court who did it match?'

'I said, in my opinion, it matched Gary Redding.'

The appearance in the witness box of Gary Redding provided some problems for Mark Tedeschi. Justice Barr had refused to allow him to lead evidence about Redding being the second man at Watsons Bay during the afternoon of Caroline's death because Melbourne and Martin had identified the man as Adam Leigh.

The prosecution had realised subsequently that it almost certainly wasn't Leigh. The man had no real connections with Gordon Wood other than a few casual meetings and he had been back at the modelling agency around 7 pm that night sending faxes around the same time they believed Wood and another man had Caroline cornered at Watsons Bay. Besides, he was a tall man, around the same height as Wood, rather than the short, dark squat man seen by the two restaurateurs.

Redding would, of course, deny being there, as he would being at the gym when Caroline was called a 'fucking idiot' by Wood and being at Alife with Wood at 3 pm when Rivkin became upset, let alone being in a lift with Freris when Michael Jaggard was warned to keep quiet.

Tedeschi asked anyway.

'I cannot recall that absolutely at all,' Redding protested. 'I can't recall it. I really can't.'

Tedeschi continued: 'On that day, Wednesday, 7 June 1995, were you with the accused and Caroline Byrne at Watsons Bay?'

'No.'

And lastly: 'At any time during that day or that night, were you at Watsons Bay with the accused and Caroline Byrne?'

'No. Absolutely not.'

Winston Terracini took Redding back to a lengthy interview he gave police in 2004 when they tracked him down to his mother's house in Kent just outside London. He was asked 830 questions over several hours.

Towards the end—question 752—Redding was asked if there was anything he wanted to add to what had been said already.

'If I could help you or shed light on Caroline's death in any way, shape or form,' he began before trying to explain that no-one really understood him. 'You don't know who I am. You see me all tattoos and stuff. I live my life quite pure, you know. I live my life like that. I'm a wild cat, but I do not believe in hurting other people in any shape or form.'

The cop chipped in: 'Just to clarify for the tape, we're talking about Gordon Wood.'

'That's right, yeah, Gordon Wood,' Redding continued. 'I never had nothing to do with him. I've just been so shocked, and I don't know if astounded is the word, but gobsmacked at the amount of attention that's been directed at me. It's been ridiculous.'

48

SATISFIED IN EVERY WAY

Peter Byrne occasionally came to court to keep his father company. Having given evidence, unlike Robert and Deanna, he was free to hear other witnesses but it was the conclusion that interested the Byrne children more than the detail. There would be more than 50 days of evidence of which Tony would sit through all but a handful, mostly alone.

He listened in amazement to the evidence of Angelo Georgiou who told the court he had been reluctant to become involved and had only come forward after being contacted by the *Sydney Morning Herald*. Winston Terracini questioned the accuracy of his memory but Georgiou had stood firm about Caroline's concerns over her safety and Gordon Wood's proposals to invest in Offset Alpine.

Craig Martin and Lance Melbourne gave their descriptions of watching Caroline and Wood with the second man at Watsons Bay during the afternoon. Tony had heard it during the coronial inquest in 1998 but had not been allowed to listen at the committal because he would be a trial witness. He knew the details but it was somehow comforting to hear it again, unchanged in all this time. There was some argy-bargy with Terracini over whether the restaurant had even been open to the public at the time but it was irrelevant in the sense that the men were there on the day and had stopped whatever they were doing to watch his daughter laughing for probably the last time in her life. It was difficult to control his emotions at times, particularly when both men pointed to Gordon Wood in the dock as the man they had seen with Caroline. He hadn't heard the evidence of Sandra Munro before, the wife of Melbourne who said she'd noticed the white Vitara parked in the laneway around lunchtime. It was important evidence, Paul Jacob told him later, because it supported the sighting of Caroline by the two men and debunked Wood's claim that she was home in bed, drowsy on drugs.

Munro told Tedeschi: 'It would have been around lunchtime. I went from the café over to the restaurant. It was parked there. I didn't take too much notice, being the middle of the day. Again, that night when we left, when we closed the restaurant, we were quite surprised to see it, because there were very rarely any cars in the back lane. It was still there. And then again the next morning when we arrived, it was still there.'

She, like the two men, had also seen a green Bentley just like the one Wood drove for Rivkin, going to and from Watsons Bay that afternoon. None of them saw the driver properly, other than a blondish man, and Terracini questioned what they had seen because they got the number of doors wrong on the car. Tony thought they were credible and hoped the jury would too. Why would they lie, he kept asking himself of all the witnesses. None had a motive and although specific details may be wrong, the essence of what they had seen had not been questioned.

He listened to the artist John Doherty and the fishermen Norman Wano and Mick Brunetta. He knew their accounts but hadn't heard them first-hand. Doherty, like Basquali, gave evidence via video from his home in Ireland. The identification of Caroline and Wood outside his studio that night wasn't as conclusive as Tony had hoped but it was pretty clear, even without seeing their faces, that it was the same group of people seen earlier by Melbourne and Martin.

Doherty's answers were clipped when asked by Tedeschi how the man he saw compared to the man he watched on the *Witness* interview three years later.

'He had a similar stature,' Doherty responded.

'What do you say about the height?'

'To the best of my ability, it looks similar.'

'What do you say about the build?'

'Yes, he was slim.'

'What do you say about the build of the man that you saw?'

'I said he was the same slim build.'

'What do you say about the head shape?'

'The hair was similar.'

'What do you say about the head shape?'

'It was similar.'

The *Witness* interview itself was a cut-up version of what went to air, questions and answers removed from the final version seen by the jury because of successful arguments by the defence accepted by Justice Barr. The Crown was dismayed when Justice Barr ruled that the powerful ending, when Wood asked the interviewer Paul Barry 'So, do you think I did it?' had to be edited out. Still, Tony thought Wood looked bad when challenged, his answers almost daring anyone to catch him rather than being genuine explanations or showing concern about Caroline.

It was among many things not put before the jury for various legal or tactical reasons. Tony didn't understand some of the arguments but the defence was determined, as he would have expected, to limit any damaging evidence about Wood and his behaviour. Apart from the dissected *Witness* interview, there was the evidence of Redding's girlfriend about his violence, the physical similarity between Redding and the second man seen at Watsons Bay in the afternoon of Caroline's death and the evening beneath Doherty's window, the evidence of the morgue attendant about Wood asking to see Caroline's 'tits', Wood's stripping of Caroline's bank accounts in the days after her death and attempting to have her gym membership transferred into his name. Then there was the photographer, Jamie Fawcett, who says he was told by Wood that the Offset Alpine fire was set up and who benefited from it. And most damaging, he reckoned, was Kylie Watson's account of Wood sleazing onto her just weeks after the death of Caroline, the woman he supposedly loved like no other. It was far worse than Blanchette's apparent desires for the schoolgirl.

He wished the guy would take the stand but Terracini had all but ruled it out to the media. The only chance the jury were going to get to hear Wood defend himself apart from this interview would be audio tapes of interviews with police and the recording of the phone message he left Carel Clifford the night before Caroline went missing. There was silence around the court when it was played, the sound and message from the past hanging eerily, considering what was about to happen.

The evidence of Christine McVeigh bothered him. Tony was aware of it from media reports during the committal but to hear the woman from City Gym talk about his daughter being stood over by Gordon Wood and Gary Redding and called a 'fucking idiot' was distressing.

'It was almost like reprimanding, in an aggressive manner; like attacking her for doing something stupid,' she told Tedeschi.

'What did Gordon appear to be doing? What did he look like?'

'Angry, confrontational, very, very close to Caroline; almost too close for comfort. He seemed to be dominating the situation completely.'

Glenda Williams was working that night. She didn't see the confrontation because she was busy with a membership application, but remembered being told about the argument by McVeigh, and that 'Gordon was being a bit rough on her'. She also saw Caroline Byrne run out of the gym, crying. The corroboration by Williams made Redding's later denials seem hollow.

The evidence of Joseph Grech shocked Tony because it showed how much the man who professed to want to be his son-in-law had planned to isolate Caroline from her family and friends. Grech was not only Wood's GP but a friend who mixed with him socially, mainly because the surgery was on the same street as Joe's Café and even the doctor hung around the café. He sometimes ate with Wood, who bragged about his sexual prowess.

'He would often speak of that relationship in . . . magical terms, as if it was a relationship of such quality that others could not possibly imagine what it was like to know that kind of love,' he told Tedeschi.

'Did he speak about whether or not he was able to satisfy Caroline?'

'On a few occasions Gordon would have boasted of his prowess in his ability to satisfy her.'

'Physically, mentally or both?'

'Oh, in every way.'

But Grech drew the line when the chauffeur phoned him on 6 June to ask for a medical certificate for his girlfriend. Phone records showed Wood called around 6 pm, a few hours before he left the message for Carel Clifford. It appeared to contradict his story that he only found out about Caroline's visit to Cindy Pan after she got home that night.

Grech recalled that Wood said Caroline was unwell and then said they wanted to go to the Blue Mountains to spend time together. 'I insisted at the time that a medical certificate could only be given if Caroline was to actually be seen. So, one was not given.'

Grech also gave an insight into Wood's health and worries. He saw him 30 times over a four-year period. On five occasions in 1994 Wood was prescribed the drug Normison to counter insomnia. It is a drug similar to Valium or Serapax and a milder version of the Rohypnol he said had been taken by Caroline on the day she died.

Gordon Wood had attempted to persuade Caroline to see his GP but she had refused, according to Jamie Fawcett, the controversial paparazzi photographer who had spent time with Wood after he left Sydney in 1998.

Fawcett recounted a conversation he'd had with Wood around the swimming pool at a Florida motel during which he'd tried to steer towards encouraging Wood to talk about his girlfriend's death. Much of the conversation, which included details of Wood's theories about the Offset Alpine fire, would not be heard by the jury but Mark Tedeschi was allowed to question Fawcett about Caroline's growing anxieties in the days before her death.

She pined after him while he was overseas with Rene Rivkin, Wood told Fawcett, which turned to anxiety when he returned and was ordered to front up for the ASC investigation.

'Did he say whether or not Caroline was concerned about the summons for him to appear at the ASC?' Tedeschi asked.

'I think she had been concerned, yes.'

'Could you tell us what he said about the ASC inquiry?'

'Mr Wood said to me that he had explained to Caroline that he wasn't able to say terribly much about what had gone on, and that worried her.'

'Now, in relation to the last 24 hours of her life what did he tell you?'

Fawcett read from his police statement: 'He did tell me that in the last 24 hours, Caroline was under extreme pressure, and he had spoken to Dr Joe Grech and asked him about Caroline. Wood said he had approached Grech about Caroline's depression and had asked Caroline to see Grech. Wood said Caroline would not see Grech as she did not like him and instead she went to see another doctor.'

Cindy Pan was Caroline's preferred GP, who would later count Joseph Grech as a colleague. She could still recall the clothes and demeanour of Caroline Byrne as she sat in front of the doctor the day before she died—dark blue jeans and a shirt with a woollen sleeveless dark blue, maroon and white-patterned vest finished with dark blue shoes and socks the same pattern as the vest. 'I can picture her perfectly sitting there with her legs crossed,' she told Mark Tedeschi. 'Very composed, calm and serene; a very lovely person to deal with. Very easy to talk to, respectful, and grateful for what I did for her. She accepted the referrals very graciously and thanked me. And she said she would go on the Wednesday, and again, she struck me as a very conscientious person. She wanted to follow up getting the referral for the dermatologist who she had already seen. She was a very ordered sort of person. That's my memory of her.'

Dr Pan also recalled two mornings later when Gordon Wood and Caroline's brother, Peter, appeared at her door to announce that her patient was dead. Gordon was on edge and agitated as she met the pair at the front counter and they followed her down the corridor to her consulting room. 'He was asking me how this could have happened. He was very alert and my recollection is that they didn't sit down.'

Mark Tedeschi interrupted: 'Did he behave in a particular manner?'

'Well, yes . . . he was sort of energised and alert, and clearly wanted to know what I thought about this. I remember I was trying to express my sympathy and condolences, because I know how it had affected me. I think I may have asked him if he needed some counselling . . . and he didn't want that. It was sort of like he was trying to solve a puzzle, and I would have liked to help more, but I was, myself, at a loss to explain how this could have happened.'

'What about Peter Byrne?'

'He was more in the background . . . he was more sort of flat. I don't recall him asking me anything, whereas I do recall Gordon asking me sort of the same thing more than once.'

And how did her death affect Dr Pan, Tedeschi inquired.

'I went and talked to Dr Sippe about it because I was so shocked and upset. And I couldn't understand it.'

49

AVERAGE TESTIMONY

Rod Cross, honorary associate professor of Physics at Sydney University, had learned a lot in the sixteen months since the committal hearing. He'd produced yet another report refining his already emphatic opinion that Caroline Byrne could not have leaped to her death. There were now seven reports written over four years. And he'd been preparing himself for the expected courtroom showdown with Winston Terracini, accepting the galling necessity to break his arguments down to digestible chunks for the layman.

Although he had one of Australia's foremost experts giving evidence, Tedeschi also wanted to establish the simplicity of the calculations involved. It had to be simple enough for the jury to understand if they were to accept it. The scenario boiled down to two measurements: Caroline Byrne fell 30 metres in just over two seconds and ended up head-first in a rock fissure exactly 11.8 metres out from the cliff face. How did she get there?

'Professor, having determined what the horizontal distance was and what the vertical distance was, was it very easy for you to work out what the launch speed must have been for someone going over the cliff to end up where Caroline's body was found at Pyramid Rock?'

'Yes, it was.'

'Is it rocket science or is it university-level science or high-school-level science?'

'I would expect a good student at physics at high school to be able to determine those numbers.'

The answer was a speed of 4.5 metres per second if the person landed feet first in the hole. He calculated that to land head-first required an extra 0.3 metres per second to account for the natural braking impact of someone planting their foot and rotating in a diving motion. All the experts to follow, prosecution and defence, would largely agree with these measurements and the scientific principle that a diving motion had to begin at the moment the person left the ledge.

So could Caroline Byrne have killed herself?

The short answer was no. Cross had not only tested the running ability of eleven female police cadets but was given access to data on tests given to 174 cadets which he compared to an Australia-wide study on 1000 teenage girls. The results, even though done over slightly different distances, were virtually the same. Of the cadets he tested, six were of above-average ability and only one of them, a former champion hurler and state netballer, could run at the required speed. Even then she could not dive with sufficient speed. On the available evidence Caroline Byrne, while aerobically fit from gym classes, was a leggy model with flat feet and far from an elite athlete.

'What conclusion did you come to about what level of fitness would be required to launch oneself at 4.5 metres per second and end up head-first at the base of Pyramid Rock?' asked Tedeschi.

'I concluded that it would only be possible for a person of elite or Olympic standard to do such a thing.'

'What do you mean by a person of elite athletic ability?'

'A female who could run a 100-metre race in ten or eleven seconds . . . you would only find one in a thousand females would have elite athletic abilities.'

Having ruled out suicide, and a brace of alternatives such as tripping, slipping, running or being pushed, Tedeschi took his star witness through the experiments he carried out to test his theories and come up with the 'spear throw', as he'd named it to describe the arc through the air that Caroline would have travelled. Tony stayed to listen and see the videos the professor had taken of his experiments. He watched as male cop after male cop threw female cop after female cop into a swimming pool, replicating how Caroline may have died. It seemed surreal more than anything, probably because of the sounds of summer in the background; laughter and light rather than screams and the dark on a windy cliff top.

What about the throw? asked Tedeschi. Most people might think the greatest speed would be achieved if two people were involved, each holding one of the arms and legs and swinging like a pendulum before letting go after a one, two, three, heave.

That, in fact, was a low-speed throw, Cross said as he launched into an explanation. It was difficult to exert any force on an object at arms-length. Much more force could be exerted if you got your shoulder and entire weight behind it and pushed. Like a shot-putter.

The spear throw—for want of a better term—was exactly that. A right-handed thrower would use the left hand in the chest area to support the front of the body, as a guide. The right hand was placed in the crotch area. The thrower then runs a few quick paces and pushes as hard as possible, using all the larger muscles in the chest, back and arms, along with the legs, to launch the body as far as possible. Gordon Wood, a tall man who was 31 years old at the time and could bench-press 100 kilograms, was physically capable of using the spear throw to launch his 57-kilogram girlfriend into the hole at Pyramid Rock. Tony winced at the thought.

It was difficult at times to hear from the back of the room, given the Victorian acoustics. Tony strained to follow the arguments which he knew were critical. Despite all the evidence from friends about how unlikely it was that Caroline would have killed herself or the strange behaviour of Gordon Wood afterwards, it was this man, Rod Cross, who would make or break the case. He had explained why he was so certain of the launch point at the northern rock ledge. There was an area to the south where someone could have got a run-up of 20 metres but the ground was uneven and ended uphill which made the leap even more difficult.

And the hole at Pyramid Rock was the only one of the two holes—called Hole A and Hole B—in which Caroline could have landed, given her injuries. Hole B, which had been incorrectly identified by Constable Camwell in the 1996 video, was not even wide enough to fit her shoulders.

'Correct me if I am wrong, professor, but what you're saying is this: that either from the northern rock platform or the southern rock platform at any point, it is not possible for a female of average athletic ability or less to have done a running dive to end up in either the correct location at Pyramid Rock or the incorrect location?'

'That's what I'm saying, yes.'

'And, as opposed to that, it would be possible for a strong male, able to bench-press 100 kilograms, to have thrown a 57-kilogram female into the correct location at Pyramid Rock from the northern rock platform or into the incorrect location from the southern rock platform?'

'Yes.'

Winston Terracini wasn't impressed with Cross's qualifications. Being an expert on bouncing balls and lawn bowls did not equate to giving opinions on bodies falling from cliffs, he ventured, particularly when he had two experts for the defence who would disagree with some of his conclusions.

'Well, in essence, you just say they've got it wrong; is that right?' he challenged.

Cross stood his ground. 'No. A lot of what they have written is correct, but some specific criticisms of my report are incorrect.'

'Well, you've seen what they've said, and in general terms they say it could be done; that is, a person can jump and land in the position that the deceased found herself. Correct?'

'They are saying . . . that it may be possible.'

'Well, we all can't be right, can we?'

'No, we can't. I'm saying that I am right and some of their assumptions and data can't possibly be correct.'

And so the combat would continue. Terracini disputed with him about running speeds and the abilities of Olympic champions Carl Lewis and Florence Griffith-Joyner. Terracini questioned the conclusions drawn from surveys and his own testing, angles of take-off and the effect of rigor mortis on throwing a body. He even wanted to debate the work of Sir Isaac Newton and whether a person simply running off a cliff could twist in mid-air and perform a dive.

'What studies have you been involved in to determine the rotational effect of the human body when they fall from considerable heights?' he challenged at one stage.

'I don't think anybody in the world has,' retorted Cross.

There were heated exchanges over Cross's experiments and his results. The professor reckoned Terracini did not understand physics and the barrister chided the academic for obfuscating. This exchange was typical:

'How many if any of your volunteers achieved the distance in this spear-throwing technique?'

'Nobody threw the female volunteer 11.8 metres.'

'No-one at all?'

'No, they threw the volunteer about two metres in a swimming pool, they didn't throw them off a cliff.'

'Sir, we are not asking you about a cliff, just distance. How many of the people that you tested got anywhere near the distance? It's pretty simple.'

'11.8 metres is halfway across the swimming pool. Nobody got anywhere near that distance.'

'Right. Did you ask them to throw as far as they could?'

'No, I didn't.'

'What did you ask them?'

'To throw as fast as they could.'

No-one was quibbling about the credentials of Dr Marcus Pandy. Not only was he chairman of mechanical and biomedical engineering at the University of Melbourne but he specialised in research on how people walk and run and had done work on gravity and human movement for the United States Air Force and NASA space programs. Neither were there any doubts about his testing equipment or the accuracy of his results, even though he conceded it was done quickly for the court case.

The question mark over his testimony centred on his choice of two test subjects. One was a post-graduate student of his and the other a student of a colleague's. Both were given two tasks—to run as fast as possible over the four metres and then to run and perform a jump. After a couple of practice runs, they were each tested four times.

It was their results that raised eyebrows. One was able to run almost as fast as the best of Rod Cross's eleven police cadets, herself a former champion hurdler, who tested at 4.8 metres per second. The second ran much quicker at 5.28, not far below the speeds run by Griffith-Joyner and easily enough to have dived into the hole at Pyramid Rock.

Winston Terracini knew his witness would be questioned about the ability of his subjects, given that he had described them as 'average' in his written report. The slower one had been a competitive runner in her teens but apart from a couple of social games of netball each week only went on occasional bike rides and walks. The faster woman had come from New Zealand where she had played for the national handball side as a teenager and was also a gymnast, as well as playing state volleyball for eight years before doing a cruciate ligament in her knee.

'This 5.28 metres per second that she achieved over four metres, does that have some significance, in terms of its speed? Is it incredibly fast, or what?' Terracini asked.

'Well, I don't believe it is,' his witness replied.

'No?' Terracini checked.

'I have talked with, you know, other people who are knowledgeable as well about how fast people can run, and they weren't struck at all by the magnitudes of these speeds.'

Mark Tedeschi didn't agree. Had he compared the results with a larger group of females of a similar age? No, conceded Pandy.

Tedeschi was going to press home his point. Pandy's measurements might be accurate but this unnamed woman's atheltic ability was not a fair comparison to that of Caroline Byrne.

'Your second subject represented the nation of New Zealand in representative sports?'

'Yes.'

'She was such a good athlete that she represented her nation in competitive sport, correct?'

'Yes. It was handball.'

'You know that she represented the national handball team of New Zealand when she was at high school?'

'That's right.'

'She was such a good athlete, such a good national handballer, that she represented her national team while she was still at high school, correct?'

'That's right.'

'She played competitive volleyball in a state team and a national league team for seven to eight years?'

'That's right.'

'So, at some stage of her life she has been an elite sportswoman?'

'Yes.'

The next day the jury asked if there was a video available of Pandy's tests, like the one Rod Cross had done. The reply was negative but a series of slides could be put together.

Would that help? Justice Barr asked.

No, replied the foreman.

50

BETWEEN FACT AND FICTION

When Paul Jacob finally took the stand he began by explaining the many and serious mistakes made by police on the case. It was a lengthy and untidy legacy and appeared to observers like Tony to be a strange tactic, but Jacob always believed that one of the strongest points of the case was his determination to find the right answers, even if it took time and involved error.

The first and most serious blunder had been the assumption of suicide made by uniformed officers that meant no crime scene unit officers were called in, who would have examined and photographed the scene and collected evidence. Likewise there was no police officer at the post-mortem which would have been the case if they were investigating a suspicious death. Even the pathologist was relatively junior.

He had taken the case in 1998, in effect the fourth investigation taking into account the coronial inquiry which had returned an open finding. Although he was given an investigative path, he and his team were forced to begin again. The size and availability of his team waxed and waned over the years—as Tony knew so well—but it managed to conduct hundreds of interviews and source thousands of documents from all over the world. Jacob was proud of their work and achievement to get the case so far.

But there were more mistakes. The position of the body, for example, was more an oversight than anything else but nonetheless unfortunate. Luckily, like other aspects of the case, it was rectified and the correct conclusions drawn.

And there was one last twist as they prepared for trial. When arresting Wood at his home in London in 2006, police seized a laptop computer on which they found a draft manuscript for a book—an autobiography written by Wood titled *The Gap between fact and fiction.* When printed out it came to 140-odd pages in which Wood, unsurprisingly, maintained his innocence and insistence that Caroline had committed suicide. But he also provided an alternative theory, pointing the finger at his romantic predecessor Andrew Blanchette over allegations that he had been stalking his ex-girlfriend. Why hadn't police looked at him? It was the first time Blanchette had been raised by anyone and looked to Jacob like a desperate move from a guilty man. Still, it had to be investigated. Blanchette was asked to account for his movements on the night and the sordid tale of his links to the schoolgirl emerged. Although there was no evidence of any involvement, it was clear Wood's defence team would make hay of the issue during the trial.

So Winston Terracini had and would attempt again as he spent more than a day quizzing and critiquing Jacob's investigation techniques and decisions. He queried the method of identification by Melbourne and Martin, the pursuit of Adam Leigh, the treatment of his client and Gary Redding, and if he pursued allegations that Rene Rivkin was involved in homosexual affairs.

Predictably, the cross-examination was dominated by questions over Andrew Blanchette and why he hadn't been considered a suspect. He intimated that Jacob had ignored evidence contained in notes and statements from several witnesses, particularly about the incident outside June Dally's when Blanchette argued loudly with Caroline in the street, drawing attention to the ruckus because he was dressed in police uniform. There was also a suggestion in some notes taken by a colleague of Caroline's that she had sought an Apprehended Violence Order against Blanchette.

Jacob confidently batted away the criticism before Mark Tedeschi re-examined with pointed questions. Jacob faced the jury with each single-word answer.

'In any of his interviews has the accused suggested that Blanchette might be a suspect for the murder of Caroline Byrne?'

'No.'

'Has anybody else ever suggested to you that Blanchette should be considered a suspect for the death of Caroline Byrne?'

'No.'

'Did you at any time consider that Blanchette should have been a suspect for the death of Caroline Byrne?'

'No.'

'Has the accused at any time, during any of his interviews or any of his contacts with the police, suggested that the death of Caroline Byrne was anything other than suicide?'

'No.'

As Jacob left the stand many in the public gallery wondered if Terracini had overplayed his hand on Blanchette.

Tony couldn't really understand the specifics of the arguments being waged between the pathologists paraded by the prosecution and defence. He didn't really want to know because it meant listening to the details of the multitude of injuries to Caroline when she landed at Pyramid Rock.

The overall sense of her death was bad enough without listening to them discuss the way her head was split open as it hit the rock, her ribs being crushed inside the hole, and the likely or possible reasons for other scrapes, breaks and bruises. It was all a bit theoretical, like the Adelaide suicide specialist who argued for the defence that Caroline was a high risk of suicide because her mother had killed herself before Mark Tedeschi got him to agree that 95 per cent of such people do not kill themselves.

Tedeschi had two expert witnesses: the man who did the autopsy on Caroline, Dr Simon Hillery, and the head of emergency services at St Vincent's Hospital, Dr Giordian Fulde. The defence had countered with Dr John Hilton, who was chief pathologist at the morgue when Caroline died and the current head, Dr John Duflou who had been Hilton's deputy and oversaw Caroline's autopsy. It seemed a very crowded room poring over Caroline's remains. Tony steeled himself.

Hillery had not qualified as a pathologist at the time which, as Tedeschi pointed out, showed that her death was immediately treated as suicide. It was not that his work was sub-standard but that more detail would have been sought if it had been deemed suspicious and it would have been conducted by one of his superiors. Hillery, like the men who would follow, could only state the obvious categorically: that she died from plunging 30 metres. Exactly how she landed was almost impossible to tell but it appeared it was head-first and he could not exclude the possibility some injuries were caused in self-defence.

Dr Fulde had been down to the site and scrambled around among the rocks where Caroline landed. He ventured the theory that the big number of rib fractures on all sides happened when she became wedged in the fissure.

He explained his logic. 'Put very simply, if one gets hit by a car or a rock or anything from one side, one gets injuries on that side and that absorbs the force of the injury, and the damage is done on that side. So, to have the numerous rib fractures on both sides is a result of a compression, virtually simultaneously.' He used his hands to show the body being wedged in a hole.

He also pointed to the fracture of the fifth vertebrae of the spine, between the shoulder blades, as being unusual and again indicating that the top half of the body had been trapped so the lower half swung violently and snapped the spine.

Hilton had a different view. Now retired, he had conducted almost 15000 post-mortems in his long career, the summary of which Winston Terracini took ten minutes to read out. The jury stopped taking notes after the first few titles.

He had also been to the base of The Gap and argued there were probably two impacts within milliseconds—head and chest—

and that Caroline had landed not head-first but on a 'horizontal slope' before sliding into the hole. Rigor mortis had been the cause of her becoming wedged so tightly that it took two police officers to remove her body. He added that there was no way of knowing for certain, from her injuries, if she ran, slipped, was pushed or thrown from the cliff.

Johan Duflou was less certain. 'I don't know how many impacts there were, I must say. There may have been one and there may have been more than one. The injuries are not inconsistent with having been caused by a single impact. Again, this is from my experience of doing numerous autopsies of people who have fallen from heights, and specifically fallen from The Gap, or it may have been the result of two impacts. There's nothing there specifically which indicates to me that it is one or more than one.'

He was more certain, however, that the body landed chest- rather than head-first and then became wedged. This was because there was no cervical spine fracturing. There was another reason, he told Terracini: 'Almost certainly if a person goes head-first down, there's the reflex of putting out of the hands. So I would expect to see hand injuries, plus fractures of the bones of the arms. And essentially, with the exception of one fracture, from memory, of the 5th metacarpal of the left hand and a fracture of the right upper humerus, there's no suggestion of falling on to an outstretched and/or outstretched hands.'

Mark Tedeschi saw something significant. 'If she fell head-first, haven't you said to Mr Terracini that most people will put their hands out and get massive injuries to their hands, wrists and lower forearms?'

'Yes, absolutely,' he replied.

'And she didn't have anything like that, did she?'

'Correct, no.'

'Is that consistent with her being unconscious at the time of falling?'

'Yes, it could be.'

Although the colossal injuries caused by the fall had covered any signs of a cliff-top struggle, it was the absence of injuries to her arms and hands which Mark Tedeschi believed showed why she was so easily cast over the cliff. Caroline had been knocked unconscious before she was thrown.

51

50 QUESTIONS

In most of his cases Tedeschi would sum up by taking the jury through the case in a chronological fashion, ending with what the prosecution would say was the logical and damning conclusion. In this case, however, he wanted to begin with the bottom line—the 'killer point'—of his case. How could Gordon Wood have claimed to so many people that his girlfriend was at the bottom of The Gap but he knew almost exactly where her body lay?

There were numerous places along the cliff top where she could have gone over and yet Wood had been adamant that police look at the northern-most point, the place where he had earlier claimed to have seen shoes with a weak torch. It was almost exactly where her body was found. The only rational explanation was that he was there when Caroline Byrne went over the cliff.

'It's not the only evidence—there's a lot of other evidence—but we submit that this is an irrefutable point. There is no other rational explanation other than the guilt of the accused.'

There was no disputing that Caroline Byrne's body was found at the base of the cliff and Tedeschi said if the jury worked back from that point then the prosecution's case made sense. She died between 11 and 11.30 pm which meant the scream heard by John Doherty and the fishermen must have been her scream. It was preceded by an argument involving two men and a woman, and those same voices had been heard and the people involved seen by Doherty at about 8 pm that night.

'It is inconceivable that there were three other people arguing for an hour at The Gap immediately prior to Caroline's death,' Tedeschi said. 'With all of the publicity that this case has generated over the years, don't you think that if there were three other people who were arguing, who had nothing to do with Caroline's death, that they would have come forward?

'In any event, we're talking about a freezing cold winter's night . . . so why on earth would three unrelated people be arguing . . . just by sheer coincidence in the same location where Caroline must have gone off the cliff to her death? In our submission, it is inconceivable that it had nothing to do with Caroline's death. The scream must have been hers. The argument must have been her and two males that she was with; and it must have been the same people that Mr Doherty saw outside his flat at about 8 pm.'

The jury was entitled to have questions, he acknowledged, the most obvious one being why Wood wanted to throw Caroline out as far as he could from the northern rock platform. Why not just throw her over the cliff at the easiest spot or roll her over? A number of jurors nodded in agreement at the question.

'Ladies and gentlemen,' he began, 'it was so dark that night that the accused couldn't see whether there were any rock ledges just below that northern rock platform. He wouldn't have wanted to stand right at the very edge of that rock for fear of going over himself, so he threw her a little bit back, maybe a fair distance back, from the very edge and with great force to make sure that she would go over the edge and land at the base of the rocks and die.' He watched as all fifteen jurors took notes.

And suicide? Just use their own common sense and observations made during their three visits to The Gap, he suggested. 'No athlete, not even an elite athlete, would have been able to run off that cliff at 4.5 metres per second in complete darkness and on uneven ground. It just defies rationality that anybody could have done that, because Caroline Byrne was not an elite athlete. She was not even an above-average athlete.'

Rod Cross had tested exhaustively, using average Australians, unlike the defence's use of elite athletes, and there was only one of his subjects who could possibly have got anywhere near getting into the hole at Pyramid Rock—and that was during the day on a flat surface into a swimming pool, not on a wintery night in a denim jacket where you couldn't see the hand in front of your face. 'Do you really think that Caroline Byrne in that condition would have been able to propel herself at such a fast speed to get head-first into the hole?'

Even her injuries suggested otherwise. The defence's own pathologist had acknowledged that the absence of serious injuries to her hands and arms was consistent with her being unconscious when she fell, arms trailing behind rather than in front, instinctively shielding herself. She had been bashed and knocked unconscious at the top of the cliff—the single, short scream told you that—before being hurled like a spear.

The throw itself made sense, he argued, as instinctive as picking up a child in a swimming pool and throwing them, rocket fashion, as high and far as they could to get the biggest splash. It made use of the big back and chest muscles, as well as the legs as they were planted to propel Caroline, as a shot-putter might.

And so he went on, a procession of detail garnered from witnesses and statements during the course of the trial that he could now place in context. This was a circumstantial case which did not mean it was weak. Quite the contrary—it was a thousand-piece puzzle with only three or four missing pieces. That made it strong.

There were the sightings of Wood and Caroline at Watsons Bay during the day. Just as importantly were the sightings around the same time of her car—'If the Suzuki Vitara was at Watsons Bay then Caroline was at Watsons Bay.' And if she was there then her boyfriend was lying.

Wood's alibi about driving Graham Richardson had been destroyed as had his claim to a number of people that Caroline had taken the drug Rohypnol. Even the defence's own experts had dismissed the notion that she had consumed any drugs or alcohol that day.

Then there was Wood's strange behaviour, like switching off his phone all night and not answering a boss who was notorious for tantrums. He created a medical excuse for Caroline not to go to work even before he learned of her visit to the GP. Then he told lies about how she died, even pretending to his mother and sister that Tony Byrne had phoned him to concoct the story. He didn't telephone Caroline's father when he supposedly woke up after falling asleep in his flat and realised she was missing, then pretended to have run nine city blocks to get a car when there were cars available in a carpark across the road from his flat. Why did he threaten Alife restaurant owner Michael Jaggard? The list went on.

When it was done he asked them to consider a list of 50 questions, 'the answers to which will assist you in deciding how you resolve this case'. To his surprise, the jurors wrote them all down.

1. How did the accused know exactly where Caroline's body was located before it was found by the police?
2. How did he know she was feet up before she was found by the police?
3. Why did Caroline tell Angelo Georgiou such terrible things about the deterioration of their relationship and the grave fears she held for her safety?
4. What was the argument in the gym about that was witnessed by Christine McVeigh and why was Gary Redding standing shoulder to shoulder with the accused?
5. Was the accused expecting massive bonuses from Rene Rivkin, and if so, when and after what deal had been done?
6. Why was it that the accused's employment with Rene Rivkin was under such a threat in about March 1995, and what was the plan that he devised to get around this?
7. If the accused had been advising people to buy Offset Alpine Printing company shares at a time when he knew that the price was going to massively increase, was this insider-trading

information? If so, had he disclosed such insider-trading information to Caroline and Tony Byrne and, indeed, to others?

8. If the ASC inquiry was important enough to cause Rene Rivkin to go on a three-week overseas trip to speak to bankers, was the accused under any pressure at being called before the inquiry on Tuesday, 6 June?
9. Was Caroline concerned about Rene Rivkin's intentions towards the accused? And did those concerns heighten during the overseas trip?
10. Why did the accused order his lunch with Basquali and Samartis at Ditto's if he was planning afterwards to go home and have lunch with Caroline?
11. Why is there no phone record of Rene Rivkin contacting the accused on his mobile phone on 7 June to ask him to drive him, other than a call at 11.38 am?
12. How did the accused get it so wrong about having driven Graham Richardson before and after lunch on 7 June when he spoke to his friends just three days later on the Saturday?
13. Is it just an amazing coincidence that Mr Martin and Mr Melbourne described two people at Watsons Bay around lunchtime who so closely fit the description of Caroline Byrne and the accused?
14. What was the Vitara doing at Watsons Bay at lunchtime?
15. What was it that apparently made Caroline so groggy at lunchtime on 7 June, as related by the accused? And why was there no trace of any drug or alcohol in her blood at the time of her death?
16. What was it that the accused reported to Rene Rivkin at the Alife restaurant, when he arrived with Gary Redding, at about 3 pm on the 7th that caused Rene Rivkin to become so agitated?
17. Why was it that the accused became so defensive about Mr Jaggard having seen him at the Alife restaurant at about 3 pm on 7 June, that he threatened Mr Jaggard and offered him a share deal in the UK?

18. Why did Caroline purchase some petrol and a Freddo frog and get $50 out of the bank between 3 and 4 pm on the 7th?
19. What was the Vitara doing at Watsons Bay at 4 to 5 pm on 7 June?
20. Did the argument at Watsons Bay that went for three and a half hours, leading up to the scream, involve Caroline Byrne?
21. Would Caroline have voluntarily gone over the fence onto the rock at the cliff line if she was having a severe argument with two men during which she had been sobbing?
22. Why would Caroline have only issued a very brief scream?
23. How would anybody, athletic or not, do a running dive from the top of The Gap in almost total darkness and on uneven ground into either hole A or hole B?
24. In the light of Professor Cross's testing, is there any other way of throwing someone into hole A other than a spear throw by a very strong man?
25. In 1995 was the accused a very strong man?
26. Why did the accused fall asleep for four and a half hours, as he says, when he got home?
27. Why didn't he hear his beeper going off?
28. Why was his mobile phone switched off and the voice mail diverted?
29. Why was Caroline's mobile phone switched off and the voice mail diverted?
30. Did the accused listen to the messages on the answering machine?
31. When he awoke, why did he get into a panic?
32. When he got into a panic, why didn't he try ringing Caroline's mobile?
33. When he got into a panic, why didn't he ring the Connaught?
34. Why didn't he look for Caroline in coffee shops at Kings Cross or in the city?
35. Why did the accused walk nine blocks to get the Ford pick-up truck from The Sanctuary?
36. Why didn't the accused go into the Connaught to see if Caroline or her car was there?

37. Was it sheer coincidence that the accused found the Vitara at Watsons Bay?
38. When he found her car at Watsons Bay, did he think she might be with Peter or one of her friends at the hotel, or one of the restaurants?
39. When he searched her car, did he find the note from Lateef and, if so, why didn't he become concerned that she might be with another man?
40. Why did he conduct such a brief search, and only to the north of the fishermen?
41. Why did he abandon the search in order to pick up Tony and Peter Byrne when they could just as easily have come to Watsons Bay themselves?
42. Why did he engage in a charade when he gave the wallet to Peter and Tony to look at?
43. Why did he engage in such a cursory search with Tony and Peter between the fishermen and the house?
44. If his mobile phone battery was really flat, why didn't he use a landline to call to see if Caroline had come back home? And why didn't he access his messages when he got the battery for the phone?
45. How did he know precisely what clothing Caroline was wearing?
46. Why were Caroline's keys found on her body but not her handbag, her wallet, her mobile phone, her watch, her referral and her recent receipts?
47. What made the accused think that Caroline had been at The Gap on the evening of Tuesday, 6 June?
48. Why had the accused tried to get a medical certificate from Dr Grech before Caroline came home on Tuesday, 6 June?
49. How did the accused know that Caroline had been laying a trail from Paddington to Vaucluse towards The Gap on the afternoon of 7 June?
50. Why did the accused never mention any of his concerns about Andrew Blanchette to the police?

* * *

Winston Terracini had a list of his own but they were reasons, rather than questions, of why Gordon Wood should be acquitted. His style, as usual, was in contrast to Tedeschi as he slashed his way through the Crown's case as if harvesting a wheat crop, his tool sharpened by wit and heaved with gusto rather than precision.

He scattered 'scientific nonsense' expressions like confetti in a parade, flinging handfuls to emphasise his point that merely repeating a statement didn't make it true: 'Like a red rag to a bull,' he stormed. 'Bulls are colourblind. It wouldn't matter whether the matador had a black one or a green one. And fish don't drink, by the way. They don't.'

He wasn't suggesting that Crown witnesses such as Craig Martin and Lance Melbourne were lying—'we weren't suggesting that they had come along and lied'—rather they were mistaken; their memories less than perfect—'there is a big difference between giving honest evidence and reliable and accurate evidence'.

Likewise, the evidence of Michael Jaggard should be discounted because he was an unreliable historian who couldn't remember details such as where he lived at the time or what type of car Rene Rivkin drove. 'It was nine years, approximately, after the event that he was first asked to turn his mind to the events that took place on 7 June 1995. How accurate do you think he was? Well, it is put to you it wasn't accurate at all. Perhaps it was doing the best he could, but he was very, very inaccurate.'

Then there were the police who kept blaming each other for failed investigations, eventually compiling what the Crown claimed were 'mountains and mountains' of evidence against his client. 'I tell you what, it must have been a pretty slow-growing mountain because it took until 2006 to get around to charging him. You need to focus on these matters, members of the jury. It was spectacularly good, wasn't it? Cast iron in 1998, '99, 2000, 2001, and time just goes on. Well, it can't have been that good.'

And Wood was always cooperative. 'He is interviewed repeatedly; thousands and thousands of questions. He didn't have to answer one, but he did. Is there any evidence of any kind that at any time he tried to avoid being apprehended? Is there any evidence of any kind at any time that he sought to go to a place so he couldn't even be extradited or whatever? There isn't.'

Andrew Blanchette by contrast was despicable. 'You will remember the pathetic howling performance that he put on,' he growled. 'It was just frankly, it was disgusting. Really, he put it on. You know he put it on. You know he lied to you. What was the purpose of that namby-pamby performance? I mean, it was pathetic.

'The Crown says you can't rely on anything Blanchette says unless it's corroborated by somebody else. What was he doing in the morgue looking at the body?

'If you think that he's a reasonable possibility of having something to do with the death of Caroline Byrne then you have to acquit the accused.'

The free-wheeling display leaped from subject to subject and back again, with promises to point the jury to the necessary passages which, in some cases, never eventuated. He challenged the Crown's claim that the relationship between Caroline Byrne and Gordon Wood was in trouble, even quoting a letter written by Caroline to Gordon for his birthday in December 1994 in which she referred to him as 'my God, my king'.

The overwhelming evidence was of a happy relationship with a clear intention, at some stage, to marry. Yes, he may have called her four or five times a day but who was to say this was excessive. Likewise, there may have been an argument in the gym witnessed by Christine McVeigh during which Wood swore at Caroline and made her cry but it was not abnormal in itself for partners to argue and raise their voices.

'If you take the language out of it . . . the conversation is simply: "Caroline, don't be an idiot." Now, it depends what emphasis you put on it, of course, but . . . there is no threat of violence.'

By contrast, the Crown and the Byrne family had tried to minimise the death of Caroline's mother as well as her own suicide attempt in 1991.

'One can readily understand family members trying perhaps to put a gloss on that death, perhaps trying to, in their own mind, suggest it was caused by other reasons rather than abject depression. The aspect of the breast implants is simply an afterthought.'

Likewise, he said, 'The attempt to minimise the attempted suicide by the deceased and clothe it or cloak it in terms like "a cry for help" and that "she didn't really mean to do it", can I ask you this, members of the jury, rhetorically: What did she want to do, other than try to kill herself?

'If you can't be satisfied as to the suicide, then you cannot convict the accused. It's the Crown that has to do that; they have to be able to exclude it.'

He defended his experts and denounced Rod Cross, raised a series of identification errors by witnesses including the length of Gordon Wood's hair, the colour of the tights Caroline was wearing, whether Rene Rivkin's Bentley had two or four doors. At the end he produced his list to counter Mark Tedeschi. There were twelve points:

1. The identification of Wood at The Gap during the afternoon by Lance Melbourne and Craig Martin was unreliable.
2. The people John Doherty saw arguing later that night were not the same as the ones Mr Martin and Mr Melbourne claim to have seen.
3. There was no credible motive.
4. There was no reliable evidence of a definite break-up in the relationship.
5. Caroline Byrne was a 'high risk' of suicide.
6. Defence witnesses had demonstrated that Caroline could have landed in hole A without being thrown.
7. The 'inexplicable conduct' of former boyfriend Andrew Blanchette.
8. There was evidence that Wood and his girlfriend had a loving relationship.
9. Because of the time taken to have material aired, there was an inherent unreliability of an enormous number of witnesses.
10. The forensic evidence did not support the Crown's case.

11. Before he could be convicted on circumstantial evidence, the jury would have to be satisfied that the 'only rational and reasonable explanation is consistent with the evidence that he is guilty'.
12. The delay in charging Wood had affected the reliability and accuracy of the memories of those involved.

'That's not his fault,' he ended.

52

'WE CAN DO THIS'

Thursday, 13 November 2008, 1 pm: The jury is finally out after twelve weeks and 104 witnesses minus three of their original fifteen, all men, who would not take part in the final decision. They had left the room, dejected, after the ballot. One member of the final twelve—seven women and five men—would later tell *Sydney Morning Herald* journalist Kate McClymont that it wouldn't have made any difference to the result which jurors went. Ultimately, the verdict would be delivered unanimously and the three had privately agreed.

It was hard for Tony to know what to do now. Should he leave the court complex? Could it be over in an hour or a day or a week? The jury had been unreadable and attentive to the last, their questions indicating they still had an open mind.

There had been a third visit to The Gap, this time during the day as opposed to the night visit in October when one of Jacob's officers heard a couple of jurors exclaim: 'It's so dark. I can't see a thing.' Tony survived on these snippets and what they might mean, like the day they asked about the location of the so-called 'Halley's Comet Hole'.

At the time Tony struggled to recall its significance but then he remembered; it was the spot Gordon Wood had seen the comet as a university student, he had mentioned as they searched for

Caroline. She knew about the spot and might be there, he said. But he never looked.

Maybe the jury was asking why he never looked. Justice Barr couldn't help them because no-one knew where it was, other than south of the *Dunbar* anchor and out of the search area. No-one but Wood, of course, who hung his head and said nothing.

His silence had weighed heavily in the room, as did the decision that he would not take the stand. The judge had told the jury that it could not be part of their consideration. Wood didn't have to defend himself. It was up to the Crown to prove he murdered Caroline. Still, they'd have to be inhuman not to question why he didn't answer his critics. There were so many questions left unanswered.

Why, if he loved her so much, did he kill Caroline? The answer, according to Mark Tedeschi, was that Gordon Wood loved himself more.

Contrary to the perception, their relationship was actually unravelling, Tedeschi had told the jury. Gordon Wood had become very abusive and threatening because of problems with Rene Rivkin and the fallout from Offset Alpine. They were under scrutiny. Rivkin's own future was threatened and would, eventually, come apart at the seams. Caroline was scared and didn't know how to get out of the relationship cleanly. Things were going from bad to worse.

Tedeschi had summed it up. 'From his point of view, Gordon Wood stood to lose everything: love, employment, money, future fortune, self-esteem, the facade of prestige that he had built up with others. His whole life was about to unravel. Caroline must have intimated to him that she wanted out; and it must have been obvious to him that this time it was going to be forever.

'He decided to make one last desperate attempt to woo her back into their relationship, and that's why he made arrangements for her not to be at work on 7 June 1995. When he failed to convince her to stay in their relationship, he killed Caroline rather than losing her and losing everything else in his life.'

Robert and Deanna had given evidence at the end of the Crown case. Tony was proud of them. They had spoken beautifully about their sister. Robert had gone first. He seemed a little surprised when asked by Tedeschi to describe Caroline, then he wiped away a few tears. 'She was a wonderful all-round person. She was somebody that you could confide in, always supportive, a very happy, lovely and outgoing person. You couldn't meet Caroline and not be impressed by her. She just had these, I suppose you would say, old-world qualities.'

Deanna was remarkably composed on the stand. She spoke quietly and deliberately about her older sister. 'She was very mature. I felt that she was more than two-and-a-half years older than me at times. She was very sociable and friendly. She had a lot of friends and they all adored her. You know, she was a very supportive sister and daughter to my father, yeah.'

'Yeah'. The word seemed to sum up how difficult it was to voice emotions—a segue to move on. The family had been through so much and come so far. This moment had not seemed possible and yet the justice system had worked. Tony would get a decision and then life would begin again.

Monday, 17 November, 4.15 pm: The jury had been out three days. They looked angry and divided tonight as they filed back into the room at 4 pm to be dismissed for the day. It was a bad sign for the prosecution who needed unity to get a conviction.

The Butcher sat at the front with his arms crossed as did Skunk Head at the back, her hair now plain brown in deference to the serious decision facing them. Were they angry at each other or were they isolated in their opinion from the majority? Had Skunk Head really shoved Wilma as they left the court or was it the other way around? And what about the other juror who smiled across at Terracini as if to say, 'It's all under control mate. We'll get you an acquittal.'

It was all supposition, of course, but what else could those watching and waiting do but look for any sign when the jury walked into the courtroom and sat down. The rest of the time they were outside on the bitumen, which accentuated the muggy heat, afraid to leave even for a coffee in case the jury returned in their absence. The wait was torturous. The only one who appeared comfortable was Gordon Wood, whose future depended on the result.

His demeanour had barely changed throughout the trial, staring vacantly at the witness giving testimony if he was content or head bowed scribbling furiously if uncomfortable at a piece of evidence. As the throng melted and worried, he leaned casually from the window of the defence's room opposite the court and handed out licorice allsorts to members of the media. The police watched, furious. Others watched in bewilderment.

An acquittal, surely not? Tony hadn't seriously considered it before. He'd convinced himself that a hung jury was the worst outcome. He loved Quiggy's enthusiasm when he picked him up in the morning, never doubting he'd be convicted. Had they convinced themselves blindly?

And what if it was a hung jury? That would mean another trial. Where once Tony would have cherished the idea, he now simply didn't have the physical and psychological strength.

Maybe that was the best outcome, or the best he could hope for—a hung jury where he could accept the decision and claim a moral victory. They'd been a good jury. Nobody could complain that justice hasn't been served. If they acquitted it didn't mean he was innocent; just that the prosecution hadn't been able to prove beyond reasonable doubt that he killed Caroline.

Thursday, 20 November, 8 pm: The night air had yet to take the sting out of the day's heat. The tone in Paul Jacob's voice was light, almost joyous as he answered the phone at Kincumber, sated after a meal with his family and now relaxing out the back with at least his tenth cigarette of the day. But he was smoking in contentment and anticipation rather than his previous apprehension.

As the court broke up that afternoon—the seventh day of deliberation—the mood had changed. The jury had clearly moved to an end-point and Jacob was confident. 'I think we're there. I think we're there,' he repeated before recounting the heart-stopping moment a few hours before when the jury, via the bailiff, had asked for an extra five minutes. The request sparked a panicked expectation among those in the court, only to have it dashed at 4 pm when the jury foreman simply asked for them to be allowed to go home. Justice Barr, at the suggestion of Terracini, had reminded them they could ask questions if they wanted. The offer was greeted with silence.

What did it all mean?

'They're united,' offered Jacob. 'I think they've made their decision and they're happy with it. I think they're going to convict.' He seemed emphatic.

'One of our boys saw them coming out afterwards. They walked off down the street laughing and talking. They wouldn't do that if they were going to acquit. I reckon they've gone home to sleep on it then come back tomorrow, have a coffee and a chat and give their decision.'

Mark Tedeschi agreed with Jacob; quietly confident, he told the journos who bothered to ask. But Winston Terracini reckoned something different. There were a few who were holding out against the others. The majority wanted to acquit, he told anyone who would listen. Only one of them would be right.

Jacob was worried about Tony, who had stayed away from the court for three days. He wanted to steer clear of the Wood women, as he called them. 'It's one thing for Terracini to have a go at me defending Wood but it's another for these women to say I made phone calls when I didn't. I don't want to be near them or even see them,' Tony said later.

It was a rare flash of anger in a man who appeared unnaturally patient. And he was beginning to appreciate his own physical and psychological limits.

'We've decided, as a family, that we don't want to be in the court. We'll stay in the police room and someone can come and tell us when it happens. It doesn't matter if we miss it, and I couldn't stand watching those women if he gets off. An acquittal would be hard enough without having to watch the celebrations,' Tony told Jacob.

Jacob wasn't convinced. 'I'll call him. If he doesn't want to be there then fair enough. But he'll regret it if they convict. It will be something he will always wish he'd been there to see.'

Jacob was right. The next day, the jury had made a decision and was going to deliver quickly. He'd also convinced Tony to be in court. He, Robert, Peter and Deanna were sitting in the front row when, at 10.17 am, the jury filed into the court for the last time. A few glanced his way as they took their seats although none would have noticed that Wood's mother and sisters were not in the room.

Only the twelve men and women knew the drama that had unfolded in the jury room a few moments before. The foreman had asked each in turn what they had decided. The decision was unanimous but weighed heavily on them. Three had begun crying.

'We can do this,' the foreman said as he led the twelve into the courtroom.

Justice Barr, who had begun the trial in August by telling the jury that he was the judge of the law and they 'of the facts', turned as the foreman stood with his arms clasped in front.

'Have you reached a verdict?' he asked.

'We have, your Honour,' he replied as his colleagues nodded in silent assent.

Justice Barr's associate took over the formalities: 'Is the accused Gordon Eric Wood guilty or not guilty of the murder of Caroline Therese Byrne?'

'Guilty.'

A single word produced a collective gasp around the room, not because of the result they would say, but that it was finally over. Tony Byrne dabbed a tear from his eye with a handkerchief, leaned past Deanna and shook Paul Jacob's hand. Brenda Wood, barely inside the door in time to hear the verdict, sobbed uncontrollably in the arms of her daughters. At the bar table Winston Terracini looked stunned. Mark Tedeschi smiled.

Above them in the dock Gordon Wood was still, his bravado from the day before gone in a moment, dinner reservations at Woolloomooloo now abandoned. He would say later that he couldn't bear to turn and face his mother. Instead, face flushed, he took a polystyrene cup of water and gulped down the contents before court officers led him to the cells below. Judgment was cast.

Outside in the throng of well-wishers and the herd of media that swelled as news of the verdict swept the city, Tony tried to compose himself and his thoughts. A few days earlier he had decided on the words he would say, no matter the result. They were on a note in his pocket which he now struggled to read:

> I am not the first parent, nor the last sadly, who will go through the nightmare of losing a child and despairing for answers. I didn't think I could survive Caroline's loss but I did. What I haven't been able to come to terms with is why and how. They are answers a parent needs to hear. That is why I kept going. Now I can move on. I have been told there are many lessons from the death of Caroline. If that is true then she did not die in vain, and that is a blessing. Justice is a strange word. Until you have sought it you can never understand what it means and why it is so important.

ACKNOWLEDGEMENTS

The Killing of Caroline Byrne is not just about the horrific death of a young woman, the various police investigations, and subsequent trial and ultimate conviction of Gordon Wood.

It is the journey of a parent—a father in this case although it could just have easily been a mother—to find an answer to the death of his daughter. Such a death is difficult enough for a parent to face without there being doubt or mystery which means they cannot hope to close the door.

Tony Byrne's thirteen-year journey almost never began and almost ended many times. It survived because of his patient insistence, the continued excitement of the media and the persistence of a small group of police officers led by Detective Inspector Paul Jacob. It asked questions not only of the case but of our system of justice; the assumptions made on the spur of the moment, the battle between priorities of an under-manned police force, the expectations of the public and the judicial process itself.

It was the first case with a fifteen-person jury and set new parameters in evidence, such as the use of physics by Associate Professor Rod Cross to show it would have been impossible for Caroline to have cast herself from the top of The Gap on 7 June 1995.

When I met Tony in 2004, the idea that police would be able to put together a case strong enough to charge Gordon Wood seemed unlikely. Too much time had passed and too many mistakes made. Suspicion was one thing, proof beyond a reasonable doubt entirely another. During our many conversations, Tony's expectations moved from merely the comfort of the opinion of a senior detective, to the hope of a statement by the coroner, the excitement of an arrest, the satisfaction of a committal, the roller-coaster of a trial and finally the justification of a verdict. Throughout it all he maintained a quiet dignity. This was never about revenge but the truth.

I'd like to thank Tony for trusting me enough to write about the most vulnerable parts of his life, especially to accept that in order to tell the story credibly it would have to include the good and the difficult.

I thank my family for their support and also acknowledge the fine work by many journalistic colleagues both within the Fairfax organisation and in rival media companies such as News Limited. I was a relative late-comer to the story which had already been followed for seven or eight years by others.

I would also make mention of Paul Jacob and his team. As I witnessed, a police investigation is something which evolves with evidence. Mistakes can be made along the way but what mattered, as he told me, was that they eventually arrived at the right answer.